# THE HOWLING
## *of the*
# COYOTES

# THE HOWLING
## ⌣of the⌣
# COYOTES

*Reconstruction Efforts to Divide Texas*

·

BY ERNEST WALLACE

Texas A&M University Press
*College Station and London*

Library of Congress Cataloging in Publication Data

Wallace, Ernest.
  The howling of the coyotes.

  Bibliography: p.
  Includes index.
  1. Reconstruction—Texas. 2. Texas—Politics and govern-
ment—1865-1950. I. Title.
F391.W33        976.4'06        79-7405
ISBN 0-89096-083-6

*Manufactured in the United States of America*
FIRST EDITION

*For Ernesteen and Eddie*

.

# CONTENTS

·

# LIST OF ILLUSTRATIONS

.

# PREFACE

.

In 1953, while researching another topic in the Rare Book Room of the Library of Congress, I examined a copy of a pamphlet entitled *Constitution of the State of West Texas*. The thirty-five-page, paper-bound document revealed no author, no publication data, nor any other explanatory information. Subsequently, six other copies have been located, including one afterward destroyed by a fire. Four copies are in public libraries (Bancroft Library, Texas State Library, Texas Tech University Library, and the University of Texas at Austin Library), one copy belongs to a private collector of Texana, and one copy is for sale (spring, 1979) by a book dealer. There may be, of course, additional copies.

Because of its vast area (until 1850 larger than the present area of the original thirteen states plus Maine and West Virginia), many proposals have been made to divide Texas into two or more states and to dispose of a portion of its public domain. The most fanatical, the most emotional, and the nearest to becoming a reality—but possibly the least documented—effort occurred in 1868–1869 when the radicals in the Texas Reconstruction Convention drafted a Constitution of the State of West Texas and did their utmost to secure its approval in lieu of a constitution for Texas. Since western Texas was largely unsettled, the opponents of division derisively referred to the proposed state as the State of Coyote and to the efforts of its zealous advocates as the howling of the Coyotes.

After twenty-five years of intermittent research to fill this void in the history of Texas, I had more than adequate materials for an absorbing, book-length story that would reveal new and significant insights into the history of the Reconstruction era, primarily in Texas but also in the national capital. Not all available sources have been examined (no book likely has that distinction), but most have been—more than enough to attain reliability. To assure balance and fairness, newspapers used included those that supported all three political factions (radical Republican, moderate Republican, and Democratic), but the *Daily Austin Republican* was cited most for several reasons. It was the organ that stood midway between the editorial voices of the radicals and the conservatives; it printed most of the debates pertaining to the division issue; and, largely because of its location, its information generally was more accurate, current, and complete than that of any other newspaper. Since the information in official journals is normally limited to motions, roll calls, committee reports, and votes, newspapers or other sources, which contained the debates and valuable comments, have been used rather frequently as supplemental documentation.

In the preparation of this book, I have, like every author, become deeply indebted to many people. Miss Betty Bell, a teacher of Texas history in the Lubbock public schools and for many years my able grader and highly competent research and editorial assistant, missed her 1978 summer vacation to aid in its completion. The roots of the story run deeply into dissertations and theses written under my supervision by Ronald N. Gray, the late Betty J. Sandlin, and the late John C. McGraw. To these three, whose labors contributed both substance and insight, I shall always be grateful. The staff in the Southwest Collection at Texas Tech University, without exception, were always courteous and helpful beyond their professional duties. Had it not been for a grant-in-aid by Mr. and Mrs. William D. O'Brien, Lubbock philanthropists, the book might never have been completed. Funds from the grant provided Miss Bell some compensation for her invaluable service, assisted Mr. Gray with the research on his dissertation, and paid for the typing of this manuscript. Thanks go to the Friends of the University Library of Texas Tech University for permission to use in chapter 1 material that appeared in slightly different form as "Texas: Efforts to Divide and to Reduce," *Ex Libris* 9 (September, 1977): 1–20. And finally, to my wife, Ellen, who graciously and understandingly spent many evenings alone while the manuscript was being written, I add still another sincere "thank you."

# THE HOWLING
## *of the*
# COYOTES

# ⌒1⌒

## EFFORTS TO DIVIDE AND TO REDUCE,
## 1844–1866

.

Every sane, intelligent, practical, and economic reason is in favor of division of the State, . . . but nature is not established upon a practical, common sense basis. 'Remember the Alamo'; 'Remember Goliad'; recall the glorious history of Texas and the inborn pride of our native sons. These forestall the possibility of division of this great State." Thus wrote a secretary of the Chamber of Commerce of a west Texas city in the early 1920s.[1] The immense area of the state, the wide variations in its climate, the diversity of its topography, soils, and flora, and the differences in national origins and economic interests of its people have provided, it would seem, more than adequate cause for division or reduction were it not for the unifying historic bonds.

On December 19, 1836, the First Congress of the Republic of Texas defined her boundary to be from the mouth of the Sabine River west along the Gulf of Mexico three leagues from land to the mouth of the Rio Grande, thence up that stream to its source, thence due north to the forty-second parallel, and thence along the boundary line as defined in the 1819 Adams–de Onís Treaty between the United States and Spain to the place of beginning. The Republic of Texas laid claim to an area that encompassed 379,054 square miles, more than 12 percent of the present area of the entire United States. It could have been divided into 312 states, each the size of Rhode Island. Even after the cession in 1850 of 104,687.5 square miles of its territory to the United States, Texas could be divided into 32 states, each the size of the State of Massachusetts. Orange and El Paso are closer to the Atlantic and Pacific oceans, respectively, than they are to each other; Texarkana is nearer Chicago than it is to El Paso; and Brownsville is

[1] Quoted in W. J. McConnell, *Social Cleavages in Texas*, pp. 191–192.

more than one hundred miles closer to Mexico City than it is to Texline, at the top of the Panhandle.[2]

Texas extends from a region of tropical palms northward almost eight hundred miles into the winter wheat belt and from the watered timber belt of the Old South across the Great Plains to the front range of the western mountains. It could be divided into at least seven states, each a relatively natural geographic unit: the Gulf Coastal and Rio Grande Plain, delineated on the west by the Balcones Escarpment; the Eastern Timber Belt, lying north of the Gulf Coastal Plain and adjacent to Louisiana and Arkansas; the Central Prairies, lying between the Eastern Timber Belt and the Western Cross Timbers and between the Colorado and Red rivers; the Rolling Plains, lying north of the Colorado River and between the eastern line of the Western Cross Timbers and the High Plains; the Edwards Plateau, bounded by the Balcones Escarpment, the Colorado River, and the Pecos River; the High Plains, extending northward from the Pecos River to the top of the Texas Panhandle and westward from the Caprock, an abrupt geologic uplift, to New Mexico; and the Trans-Pecos Mountain Region. The people of eastern Texas have less in common with the folk of west Texas than with those of the states to their east; similarly, the Texas Panhandle is more akin to Kansas than to the Gulf coastal region. A majority of the settlers of eastern Texas were transplanted Southerners, white and black; a majority of the settlers of western Texas until after the Civil War were Germans and Northerners who opposed slavery. Confronted with such regional diversity and unwieldy size, politicians and malcontents attempted on numerous occasions to promote their own interests or to remedy some unsatisfactory situation by dividing Texas into two or more states or by selling some of its territory to the United States.

In their first national election, on the first Monday in September, 1836, the Texans, with only ninety-three opposing, voted in favor of requiring the newly elected president to negotiate for annexation to the United States. President Sam Houston, in accordance with the popular mandate, duly presented the offer, but for political reasons both the executive and legislative branches of the United States government reacted unfavorably. Consequently, in 1839, after he became president of Texas, Mirabeau B. Lamar formally withdrew the offer

2 Texas, *Laws of the Republic of Texas*, 1:133–134; Thomas L. Miller, *The Public Lands of Texas, 1519–1970*, pp. xi, 61, and 63.

and began to lay the foundation for an independent nation whose western borders eventually would be the Pacific Ocean. His initial step —to extend Texas' control over the settlements in New Mexico as far as the Rio Grande—was a failure, but his negotiations with European nations were more successful. By 1843, in the midst of Houston's second term as president of Texas, Britain's trade with Texas, particularly in cotton, and her interest in promoting abolition, both adverse to the South's basic economic system, had aroused the fears of John Calhoun and other Southern leaders. To them, the solution to the problem was the annexation of Texas.

Fate played into their hands. President John Tyler, a Virginian and a former Democrat who had been elected vice-president on a Whig ticket with William Henry Harrison, was out of harmony with the Whigs and fearful of the growing British interest in North America. In October, 1843, he officially proposed to Isaac Van Zandt, the Texas minister in Washington, the annexation of Texas to the United States.[3] In February, 1844, Secretary of State A. P. Upshur, who had been hesitant to accept the conditions demanded by President Sam Houston, was killed by an explosion on a ship. He was succeeded a few days later by John C. Calhoun, who was anxious to secure the annexation of Texas and to thwart the British designs in America. Calhoun agreed to Houston's terms and on April 12, 1844, signed a treaty with Van Zandt whereby Texas would be annexed to the United States as a territory.[4]

Confronted with a Senate rejection of his treaty but backed by a voter mandate in the November elections, Tyler in December, 1844, asked Congress to annex Texas by a joint resolution. Opposition to the request came largely from those opposed to the extension of slavery. Several prominent leaders wanted Texas divided into two states or territories, one slave and one free. Early in the debate, on December 11, Senator Thomas H. Benton of Missouri proposed division. The Senate-rejected treaty, he declared, had been drawn not merely to obtain Texas but to bring that country in as a territory with the intent of later dividing it into several slave states. To prevent such a possi-

[3] Letter from A. P. Upshur, Secretary of State, to Isaac Van Zandt, October 16, 1843, in U.S. Congress, Senate, *Proceedings of the Senate and Documents Relative to Texas. Message from the President of the United States*, 28 Cong., 2 sess., 1844, Senate Doc. No. 341, p. 37.
[4] Message from President John Tyler to U.S. Senate, April 22, 1844, ibid., pp. 5–13; *Niles' Weekly Register*, 66:230–233.

bility, he introduced a bill providing for a reduction in the size of Texas at the time of annexation. The proposed State of Texas was to be no larger than the largest existing state in the Union; the remainder of the area, to be called the Southwest Territory, was to be held and disposed of by the United States. When the Committee on Foreign Relations, to which the bill was referred, reported unfavorably, Benton on February 5, 1845, recalled his bill and introduced another. The only major difference was the deletion of the provision that the assent of Mexico to such annexation was necessary. The new bill was never reported out of committee.[5]

On January 10, during the House debate on annexation, Congressman John P. Hale, a Democrat from New Hampshire, proposed an amendment. This amendment required that, after the question of boundary between the United States and Mexico had been settled and before she was admitted to the Union either as a state or as a territory, Texas should be divided as nearly as possible into two equal parts, with no slavery in the western portion. The proposed division line was to begin on the Gulf of Mexico midway between the limits of Texas and extend "in a northwesterly direction to the extreme boundary thereof." Hale's proposal reflected the attitude and desire of a majority of Northerners, but it provided for fewer states and for greater restriction of slavery than the South was willing to concede and therefore failed to receive the two-thirds majority necessary for adoption.[6]

An article in the Joint Resolution for the Annexation of Texas, signed by President Tyler on March 1, 1845, provided a legitimate basis for the future efforts to divide the state. It permitted Texas to create as many as four additional states out of its territory, with slavery prohibited only in the state or states formed out of the territory north of 36°30′. In the House, where a change of twelve votes would have defeated the measure, most of the opponents wanted a more equitable division of free and slave states.[7]

[5] U.S. Congress, *Congressional Globe*, 28 Cong., 2 sess., December 16, 1844, p. 19, and February 6, 1845, pp. 244–248.
[6] Ibid., January 10, 1845, p. 121; J. H. Smith, *The Annexation of Texas*, p. 330.
[7] U.S., *Statutes at Large*, 5:797–798; Congress, *Congressional Globe*, 28 Cong., 2 sess., January 23 and January 28, 1845, pp. 180–184, 193–194; *Washington Globe*, February 28, 1845. The final vote in the House was 120 to 98.

When the Texas convention assembled on July 4 to consider the United States' annexation proposal, a few delegates, to gain greater representation in the national government, wanted to provide for the establishment of one or more additional states. However, Chairman Thomas J. Rusk, in his opening directive, apparently dampened their enthusiasm for the cause. Rusk told the members that "our duties here, although important, are plain and easy of performance. The formation of a State Constitution is the only act to be performed. . . . We have one great object in view; and that is to enter the great American confederacy with becoming dignity and self respect. Let us then lay aside all minor considerations, and avoid all subjects calculated to divide us in opinion." The convention acted with amazing speed; on its first day, without debate and with only one dissenting vote, it accepted the United States' offer and then turned to the task of drafting a state constitution.[8]

The question of division, however, was soon raised. On July 10 James S. Mayfield of Fayette County, a former secretary of state who had moved the adoption of the ordinance accepting the annexation offer, asked for the appointment of a committee to report on the expediency of vesting the legislature with the power to cede to the United States the public domain of Texas in return for the assumption of the public debt of the state and for an ample provision for educational purposes. The resolution was accepted but received no further consideration.[9]

When it appeared that the Mayfield resolution was doomed, Richard Bache of Galveston, the only delegate to vote against annexation, proposed a constitutional provision that would authorize the legislature to erect as many as four new states out of the territory of Texas whenever there was "sufficient population." The resolution was never considered on the floor of the convention.[10] Apparently the delegates regarded its adoption as superfluous since the terms of annexation, which granted Texas this right, were appended as an ordinance to the constitution. The delegates overwhelmingly agreed with Chairman Rusk that the only objective of the convention was to incorporate Texas into the American union.

---

[8] Wm. F. Weeks, reporter, *Debates in the Texas Convention, 1845*, pp. 7, 11, 12.

[9] Ibid., pp. 19, 29. The vote was 30 to 25.

[10] Ibid., pp. 469, 529.

For a short time after annexation, the problems of establishing a state government, fighting a war with Mexico, and defending the frontier against Comanche war parties made division seem of little importance, perhaps even undesirable. By 1847, however, the South had become alarmed over Congressman David Wilmot's proposal to prohibit slavery in any territory acquired from Mexico. Although it was defeated, the proposal regenerated the sectional power struggle. The erection of new states out of Texas would maintain, for a time at least, the balance in the Senate on the side of the South. The effort to achieve this goal was led by Isaac Van Zandt, who, as minister from the Republic of Texas to Washington during the two years preceding annexation, had actively worked to get into the resolution the provision that made possible the division of Texas. Anxious to convert permission into reality, Van Zandt announced for the office of governor with division as the major plank in his platform. During his canvass of the state he promised, if elected, to take advantage of the increased political power in Washington. He argued that a single state government could not possibly function efficiently over such an immense area while it had inadequate public communication facilities and a sparse population with a wide variety of interests. Although he would have settled gladly for less, he generally advocated the creation of three additional states out of Texas.[11] He died, however, during the campaign.

After Van Zandt's death, the question of division did not excite public attention again until the national crisis in 1850. One aspect of that crisis involved whether Texas or the United States had jurisdiction over New Mexico east of the Rio Grande. Texas had not been able to extend her jurisdiction over Santa Fe. Nonetheless, in March, 1848, after the Treaty of Guadalupe Hidalgo had provided for the cession of New Mexico to the United States, the state legislature created the County of Santa Fe and the Eleventh Judicial District to include the area of New Mexico east of the Rio Grande.[12] The United

---

[11] O. M. Roberts, "The Political, Legislative, and Judicial History of Texas, 1845–1895," in *A Comprehensive History of Texas, 1685–1897*, ed. Dudley G. Wooten, 2:24–25.

[12] Texas, *Journals of the Senate of the State of Texas* (hereafter cited as *Texas Senate Journal*), 2 Leg., 1847–1848, pp. 519, 520; Texas, *Journals of the House of Representatives of the State of Texas* (hereafter cited as *Texas House Journal*), 2 Leg., 1847–1848, pp. 901–903, 990, 1022; H. P. N. Gammel, comp., *The Laws of Texas, 1822–1897*, 3:95–96, 218–219.

States military commander in New Mexico, however, prevented the organization of the Texas government there. Governor George T. Wood protested the action of the United States officials and, when President Zachary Taylor responded unfavorably, sent a bellicose message to the legislature on November 6, 1849, asking that all the resources of the state be placed at his disposal to maintain the right of Texas to her statutory limits. Both the voters and the press over the state supported the action of the governor. In fact, before they learned of Wood's strong message, the voters elected as governor Peter H. Bell, who had taken a more belligerent stand than Wood during the campaign.[13] The *State Gazette* called for the use of force, if necessary, to extend the jurisdiction of Texas over the disputed territory: "Rather than surrender to the usurpation of the General Government one inch of our blood-bought territory, let every human habitation in Santa Fe be leveled to the earth, and we [*sic*], if the necessity of the case requires it, be buried beneath its ruins."[14]

Both Governor Bell and Congress, however, recognized the seriousness of the situation and took steps to resolve the problem without resorting to armed force. Bell, after prevailing upon the legislature to create four counties rather than one out of the disputed region, sent Robert S. Neighbors to organize governments in each, and Congress set to work to devise an acceptable compromise. Neighbors succeeded in organizing El Paso County, but elsewhere the military commander again blocked the efforts of the Texans. The first compromise proposal in Congress was made on January 16, 1850, by Senator Benton. Benton proposed that Texas sell all her territory lying north of the Red River and west of the 102nd meridian to the United States for $15 million. He further suggested that the remainder of the state be divided by a line formed by the Colorado River from its mouth to its intersection with the 98th meridian and thence north along that meridian to the Red River. The area west of the line was to become a state as soon as its population reached 100,000. Although Benton spoke for almost an hour in defense of his proposal, his oratory was not convincing. The bill, after some delay, was referred to the Committee on the Judiciary, where it was allowed to die.[15]

[13] Ernest Wallace, *Texas in Turmoil, 1849–1876*, p. 34.
[14] *State Gazette* (Austin), December 5, 1849.
[15] *Texas House Journal*, 3 Leg., extra sess., 1850, pp. 6–18; *Congressional Globe*, 31 Cong., 1 sess., January 16, 1850, pp. 165–166; U.S. Congress, Sen-

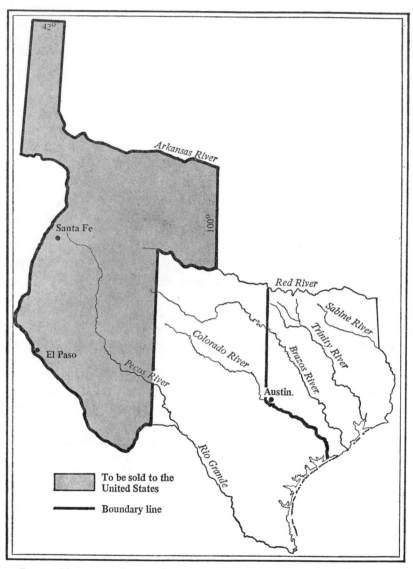

1. Benton Plan, 1850. Senator Thomas Hart Benton proposed this compromise to the controversy over the New Mexico jurisdiction.

On the same day that Benton introduced his bill, Senator Henry S. Foote of Mississippi introduced a bill to organize the region east of the Brazos River and south of the "northern boundary line of the state of Texas as laid down in the act of the Republic of Texas" into the State of Jacinto. The area between the Brazos River and the Rio Grande would constitute the new State of Texas. After heated discussion indicated that it was unacceptable to northern antislavery people, the bill was referred on January 22 to the Committee on Territories, where it too was allowed to die.[16]

A third proposal, made on February 28 by Senator John Bell of Tennessee, provided for the division of Texas into three states—with the Trinity and the Colorado rivers as the dividing boundaries—and the cession of all territory north of the 34th parallel to the United States. This proposal, like the previous, was never reported out of the Committee on Territories.[17] None of the three proposals was taken seriously by the Senate or by the Texans.

A joint effort by both houses of Congress to find an acceptable compromise, though seriously undertaken, was likewise futile. On April 19, 1850, Congress created a Committee of Thirteen, with Henry Clay as chairman, and charged it with the responsibility of proposing a solution of all five of the inflammable sectional issues then facing the Congress, including the Texas boundary dispute. Clay's committee, as a part of its Omnibus Bill, proposed in May that Texas relinquish her claim to all territory north and west of a line intersecting the Rio Grande twenty miles above El Paso and the Red River at the 100th meridian, an estimated 79,957,120 acres. In return for this concession, the United States would assume Texas' public debt.[18] President Taylor, however, opposed the compromise, and Clay could not get sufficient votes to enact the bill.

Just when it appeared that no acceptable solution to the crisis could be found, President Taylor died, and Millard Fillmore, his successor, though making it emphatically clear that he would use the military

---

ate, *Journal* (hereafter cited as *Senate Journal*), 31 Cong., 1 sess., 1849–1850, p. 87.

[16] *Congressional Globe*, 31 Cong., 1 sess., January 16, 1850, pp. 166–171, 213; *Senate Journal*, 31 Cong., 1 sess., 1849–1850, pp. 87, 99–100.

[17] *Congressional Globe*, 31 Cong., 1 sess., February 28, 1850, pp. 436–439; *Senate Journal*, 31 Cong., 1 sess., 1849–1850, pp. 184–185.

[18] *Congressional Globe*, 31 Cong., 1 sess., May 8, 1850, pp. 780, 945–947; *Senate Journal*, 31 Cong., 1 sess., 1849–1850, pp. 301, 327.

against any Texas Rangers sent to New Mexico, wanted a compromise. As a result, Congress in separate bills enacted into law the various compromise measures. The Texas boundary dispute was settled by a bill introduced by Senator James A. Pearce of Maryland. The Pearce Bill, which passed the Senate by a vote of 30 to 20 and was enacted on September 9, had the support of moderates north and south as well as the entire Texas delegation in Congress. It provided that Texas was to renounce all claims to the territory lying north of latitude 36°30′ between the 100th and 103rd meridians and north of the 32nd parallel between the 103rd meridian and the Rio Grande in return for $10 million.[19]

When news of the Pearce Act reached Texas, the press ended its bombastic denunciation of the United States' aggression and called for the acceptance of the measure. According to editor Charles DeMorse of the Clarksville *Northern Standard*, the "offer of five times the worth of the territory it [Texas] will relinquish" was a "sensible reason" to "sacrifice principle." At a special election the voters, concluding that a "better bargain" could not be made, favored the proposition by a two to one majority. The legislature in special session then accepted it, and on November 25, 1850, Governor Peter H. Bell signed the act of acceptance.[20] Although the Pearce Act had reduced the territory claimed by Texas by approximately one-third, the arguments for division had been made no less sound.

The next movement for division, the first by the Texas legislature, occurred in 1852. Bitter sectionalism on an east-west basis, with the Brazos River as the line of demarcation, had been a major characteristic of Texas politics since the early years of the Republic. Hoping to put an end to this continual animosity (or possibly to improve his own chances for political gain), Representative James W. Flanagan of Rusk County, on February 16, 1852, introduced a resolution calling for the division of Texas into two states, subject to approval by a majority of the electorate. Following the generally recognized distinction between the sections, Flanagan proposed that the common boundary of the two states be the Brazos River from its mouth to its inter-

---

[19] *Congressional Globe*, 31 Cong., 1 sess., August 5 and August 9, 1850, pp. 1520–1521, 1554–1556; U.S., *Statutes at Large*, 9:446–447.

[20] *Northern Standard* (Clarksville, Texas), September 28, October 5, and October 8, 1850; *Texas House Journal*, 3 Leg., extra sess., 1850, pp. 51, 54; Gammel, *The Laws of Texas*, 3:832–833.

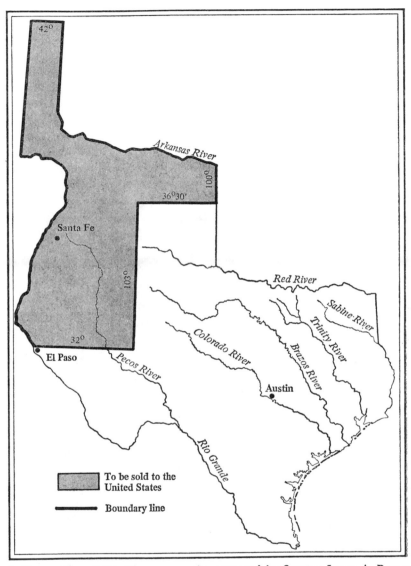

2. Pearce Plan, 1850. The compromise proposed by Senator James A. Pearce to resolve the issue of Texas' jurisdiction over New Mexico produced the current boundaries of the Lone Star State.

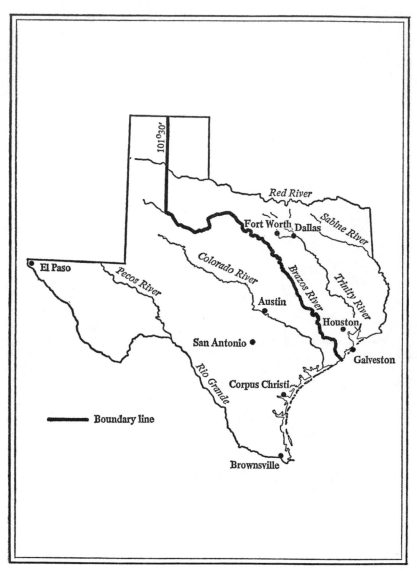

3. Flanagan Division Plan, 1852. Representative James W. Flanagan of Rusk County proposed the first division measure to originate in Texas.

section with longitude 101°30′ and thence due north to the border of the state (latitude 36°30′). The House immediately rejected the proposal by a vote of 33 to 15. Significantly, a majority of those who voted for the proposal lived east of the Brazos River. Although the opposition to division was not as strong as the vote indicated (some opponents favored division along other lines), the majority of Texans apparently were more united by bonds of historical heritage than divided by sectional differences. The *State Gazette* voiced the popular objection by means of questions: "Who will be willing to give up the name of Texas?" "Which State will give up the emblem of the single star?" "Who will give up [Senators] Houston and Rusk?" "Who will give up the bloodstained walls of the Alamo?"[21]

The last movement to divide Texas before the Civil War was by a group of abolitionists outside the state, and very few Texans ever had any inkling of it. By 1857 the New England Emigrant Aid Company of Boston, convinced that it had enlisted, subsidized, and armed enough emigrants to assure the admission of Kansas as a free state, began looking for other territory to conquer. A German reformer from San Antonio and Frederick Law Olmsted, the famous landscape architect who had helped raise money to arm the free-staters in Kansas and who had been impressed, almost beyond words, with the Texas Germans' opposition to slavery, influenced the company to begin preparations to repeat its Kansas role in southwest Texas. Olmsted, however, soon decided against the project, and the New England Emigrant Aid Company was unable to generate enough interest in New England, Germany, England, or southwest Texas to get the project off the ground.[22]

No further attempt to create a new state or to alienate any territory occurred until Reconstruction. By that time the bonds of unity had been considerably weakened, and the process of reconstruction had provided the proponents of division with a propitious opportunity. In keeping with President Andrew Johnson's reconstruction program, Provisional Governor A. J. Hamilton, who had opposed secession and afterward had gone to the North, issued a proclamation on November

[21] *Texas House Journal*, 4 Leg., 1851–1852, p. 867; W. C. Holden, *Alkali Trails*, p. 105; *State Gazette*, October 30, 1852.

[22] Frederick L. Olmsted, *A Journey through Texas*; Phillip R. Rutherford, "The New England Emigrant Aid Company, Frederick Law Olmsted, and Texas Colonization" (Phillip R. Rutherford, Gorham, Maine).

15, 1865, calling for an election to be held on January 8, 1866. Voters would name delegates to a constitutional convention to convene in Austin on February 7 for the purpose of amending or revising the Constitution of the State of Texas.[23] Before the convention assembled, the newspapers of the state mentioned the possibility of boundary changes. Some of the conservative papers reported rumors of a bill before Congress to establish a "territory of Texas [evidently the extreme western area] in which to colonize ALL the Negroes." The *Houston Telegraph* declared that the project would cost $100 million but sarcastically expressed its delight because "this little sum would help us out greatly in paying our taxes" and the Comanches and Apaches would "completely eliminate the Negro problem."[24]

With very few exceptions, the voters selected delegates who had had considerable experience for the task before them. The *Cincinnati Commercial* commented that the delegates "displayed talents highly creditable to Texas or any other State," and Ben C. Truman, a reporter for the *New York Times*, wrote that no other Confederate state "has had in Convention such a strong body of Simon-pure Union men" or as many of "outstanding ability."[25] The majority were conservative; a strong moderate minority, including within their number both Unionists and former Confederates, wielded the balance of power; and a small group of radical Republicans, predominantly from southwestern Texas, was active but impotent. Of sixty-seven members whose attitude toward secession in 1861 is known, thirty-seven had favored it and thirty had opposed.[26] Although it might appear unlikely that such an experienced and conservative-moderate delegation would consider seriously any wild or unusual schemes, it did become involved with the question of division.

During the debate on the legislative article, German-born Edward Degener from San Antonio, a strong Unionist throughout the Civil War and the leading advocate for the enfranchisement of all adult males who were "able to read and write . . . *understandingly*," introduced one such ordinance. That ordinance authorized the legislature to sell to the United States the public domain west of a line extending

[23] Texas, Executive Records, Register Book 281, Archives, Texas State Library, Austin, pp. 124–128.

[24] *Dallas Herald*, February 3 (from *Houston Telegraph*, n.d.), 1866.

[25] *Cincinnati Commercial*, March 11, 1866; *New York Times*, February 14, 1866.

[26] Wallace, *Texas in Turmoil*, pp. 169–172.

4. Degener Sale Proposal, 1866. Edward Degener's 1866 division proposal was reintroduced by A. J. Evans in 1868.

from the mouth of the Pecos River to "a point on the Red River, near the north boundary of its most northern county [in 1866, Hardeman County]," and to set aside the proceeds from the sale as a school fund. This proposal was referred to the Committee on Public Lands.[27]

Irked by Degener's suffrage proposal and hoping to turn the resolution to sell a part of the public domain to his political advantage, O. M. Roberts, who had been chairman of the Secession Convention in 1861, on March 5 countered with a resolution that provided for the establishment of a territory for the segregation of Negroes. "The permanent preservation of the white race being the paramount object of the people of Texas," Roberts stated, "the legislature shall have power to pass all laws . . . necessary and proper to secure their [Negroes'] ultimate removal or colonization, as to give place to an unmixed white race, should it in the future be found expedient and practical."[28] Although Roberts' racial view may have been held by a majority of the delegates from eastern Texas, his resolution aroused little interest because it was obviously impractical, the western delegates opposed it, and some delegates, both western and eastern, were more interested in dividing Texas into two or more states. The Germans, who had settled on the southwestern frontier and had opposed slavery and secession, were especially anxious to obtain separate statehood. Some eastern delegates favored division to enhance their personal political opportunities, to prevent, they hoped, the "africanization" of their area, and to shed the responsibility and expenses of defending the frontier against hostile Indians and of subsidizing the development of the immense western region.

The initial motion for division was by James W. Flanagan, who was no less anxious than in 1852 to erect a State of East Texas. Flanagan's resolution called for the organization of a new state out of the area east of the Trinity River and the western line of Dallas, Collin, and Grayson counties and for the apportionment to that state of a proper share of the public domain, school fund, and public debt. After excluding Dallas County and providing for the approval by a majority of voters in the proposed new state, the convention on March 16 passed the proposal on the first reading.[29]

[27] Texas, *Journal of the Texas State Convention*, 1866, pp. 81–91 (hereafter cited as *Texas Convention Journal*, 1866).
[28] Ibid., p. 119.
[29] Ibid., pp. 135–136, 188.

The convention then accepted on first reading other ordinances that called for the sale of a portion of the public domain or for the establishment of a new state. One was Degener's proposal that authorized the legislature to sell to the United States all territory west of the 101st meridian and all that north of the Red River, the price to be determined by the legislature. Two other proposals were reported the following day by A. B. Norton, chairman of the Committee on Condition of the State, who had opposed secession, and who was editor of the *Intelligencer*. He had also, incidentally, for twenty-two years kept his vow never to shave until Henry Clay should be elected president of the United States. Norton's first proposal, designed with the intent to raise revenue for badly needed internal improvements, empowered the legislature to sell to the United States all that portion of the state lying west of a line extending from the mouth of the Pecos River through Fort Lancaster to the intersection of the Red River and the 102nd meridian. His second proposal empowered the legislature to erect a new state or states and to adjust proportionately the school fund and the public domain.[30]

The convention never gave further consideration to the proposal either for the erection of a new state east of the Trinity River or for the sale of a part of the public domain. It waited until Saturday, March 31, its next-to-the-last day, to take up the ordinance providing for the organization of a new state or states. Opponents of the measure put up a strong but unsuccessful fight. After they had lost motions to adjourn until Monday and for a call of the house, James M. Norris, representing Burleson, Coryell, Palo Pinto, and Coleman counties, offered a poorly prepared substitute designed to prevent division. The convention then adjourned until Monday morning.[31] The opponents now felt confident of victory. Even should the Norris substitute fail, there was not sufficient time before final adjournment for the original question to reach final passage without suspension of the rules, and they believed they had enough votes to block that possibility. But they underestimated the determination and ruthlessness of some of the divisionists.

When time arrived on Monday for consideration of the Norris substitute, E. J. Davis of Webb County, who had opposed secession and

---

[30] Ibid., pp. 193, 202.
[31] Ibid., pp. 354–355.

afterward had served in the Union Army, moved the previous question, and the convention ordered the ordinance to be engrossed. Aided by the violation of parliamentary rules by presiding officer W. M. Taylor of Houston County, who strongly wanted division, the proponents then suspended the rules and passed the ordinance by a vote of 31 to 17. The opponents, led by J. K. Bumpass of Collin County, protested that the rules of the convention, which required a vote of four-fifths of the members for suspension, had been violated and that a quorum had not been present when the final vote was taken. Nevertheless, the action of the convention held.[32]

An analysis of the vote reveals no clear-cut east-west alignment of the delegates. If an arbitrary east-west boundary is set along the Brazos River from the Gulf to Waco and thence on a line northward along the western limits of Dallas, Collin, and Grayson counties, nineteen of the delegates voting for the ordinance were from east Texas and twelve were from west Texas.[33] Of the seventeen opposing votes, nine were cast by delegates representing west Texas. Significantly, most delegates from northwest Texas, including the sparsely settled frontier being harassed at the time by the Comanche Indians, opposed division, while most of those from southwest Texas, including the German- and Mexican-American-populated areas, voted for the ordinance.[34] Although it cannot be regarded as a definitive reflection of prevailing sentiment, the vote surprisingly shows that the east Texas delegates were more interested in division than those from west Texas. Although nearly evenly divided on the issue, more west Texas delegates, by one, voted against than for the ordinance. Furthermore, both Flanagan and Norton, who introduced the proposals for division, were from east Texas.

The passage of the ordinance practically assured a debate on the question of division in the next session of the legislature. During the interval, the proponents endeavored to gain support for their cause.

[32] Ibid., pp. 357, 358–359. The *Texas Convention Journal*, 1866, contains eighty-nine signatures, including that of Chairman J. W. Throckmorton. The ordinance, Ordinance No. 13, may be found in Texas, *The Constitution as Amended*, pp. 45–46.

[33] In the few instances where a delegate's district lay astride the above-designated line, the vote has been tabulated in the predominant area.

[34] For a roll call vote on the division ordinance, see *Texas Convention Journal*, 1866, p. 357.

In his message to the Eleventh Legislature, which convened on August 6, 1866, Governor James W. Throckmorton recommended the sale of the Panhandle (the area north of the Prairie Dog or Main Fork of the Red River) to the United States for an Indian Territory. In response to the governor's suggestion, the House Committee on Public Lands, on September 6, reported a bill for the sale of not only the territory north of the Red River but also all that lying south of the Red River and west of the 101st meridian. In support of the bill, the report explained that, if the country was ever settled, it would have no common interest with east Texas as it would be "purely a mining and grazing country." Since the cost for the development and defense of the settlements of this large area would be beyond her means, the report continued, Texas should sell it, even at a low figure, and place the proceeds in the permanent school fund.[35]

A minority report was then read by J. F. Barrett of Wise County, where the population had dropped from 3,160 in 1860 to 1,440 in 1870, primarily because of Indian raids. Barrett favored the sale of the territory north of the Red River, but he was unwilling to sacrifice the whole western domain even though he lived "where almost daily raids" by the Indians occurred. By selling the other portion, "an area greater by 500,000 acres than the state of Georgia," he argued, Texas would lose control of any transcontinental railroad built across the state and also would lose the income from millions of head of livestock that soon would be grazing in the area. When on October 5 the House called up both reports for debate, the minority report was adopted and then tabled by a vote of 51 to 23.[36]

Hoping to subvert further effort to sell a portion of the state or to organize a new state, D. C. Barmore of Burnet County in west Texas on October 20 introduced a resolution to bar further consideration of any bill or resolution having as "its object the dismemberment or division" of the state. A motion to table lost by a vote of 29 to 44, but four days later, when N. M. Burford of Dallas County offered a substitute motion—"that it is inexpedient to divide the State of Texas at this session of the Legislature"—the House by a vote of 42 to 28 postponed further consideration of the question until the last day of

[35] *Texas House Journal*, 11 Leg., 1866, pp. 231–232.
[36] Ibid., pp. 242–243, 507.

the session. Then, on that date, it adjourned without reference to the subject.[37] The proponents of division or of the sale of a portion of the public domain simply did not have enough votes to maneuver a debate on the subject.

The Senate, on the other hand, completely ignored the governor's recommendation. On August 24, accepting a resolution by Senator W. M. Neyland of Jasper County, it directed its Committee on State Affairs to "inquire into the propriety of dividing the State." Then, on October 2, almost two months into the legislative session, it sent to the same committee a bill, introduced by Senator R. H. Guinn of Cherokee County, that provided for the establishment of a new state within the territorial limits of Texas. On October 17 Chairman J. W. Stell of Gonzales reported that a majority of the committee were of the opinion that "it would be impolitic, unwise, and even dangerous" to divide the state.[38]

Two days later, Neyland and W. G. W. Jowers of Anderson County offered a minority report. Senators Jowers and Neyland, both of far eastern Texas, claimed that division was "being agitated" by the people of their area and that the sectional diversity of the state was being ignored by the legislature. The interests of the sections were antagonistic to the extent that no major enterprise could be carried out, as illustrated by the failure to locate the state university. For years, they claimed, the public had been hopefully anticipating division. Therefore, the question of division should be submitted to the electorate, separate from all other political issues. The common boundary of the two states, if the proposal was approved by a majority of the voters, would be the Brazos River from the Gulf to the southeast corner of Young County and thence the west line of Jack and Clay counties. East Texas, Jowers and Neyland calculated, would get less than one-fourth the territory but would have about one-half the wealth and population. Such a division, in their opinion, would result in a unity of interest within the respective states.[39]

The Senate on the next day began consideration of both reports. After considerable parliamentary maneuvering, largely by Guinn and Neyland, it adopted on October 29 the majority report (against divi-

[37] Ibid., pp. 652, 687–688.
[38] *Texas Senate Journal*, 11 Leg., 1866, pp. 259, 59, 299, 390.
[39] Ibid., pp. 425–426.

sion) by a vote of 16 to 10. Of the ten senators voting for division (against the report), only one resided in the western area; eight represented districts adjacent to or near the Louisiana-Arkansas border.[40] The east Texas senators were divided almost equally on the issue; the western senators, on the other hand, almost solidly were opposed to division. Thus, the movement in 1866, largely by east Texans, to divide Texas into two or more states and to sell a portion of its public domain had been thwarted by west Texans. It is conceivable that the question never again would have received serious consideration had it not been for the victory of the radicals in Congress.

The divisionists, however, refused to concede defeat and appealed to Congress. On December 6, 1866, Degener wrote that the large German and Unionist population would form a separate state at "a mere Congressional suggestion."[41] A few days later George W. Brackenridge, J. A. Paschal, Edward Degener, George W. Paschal, and twelve others addressed to Congress a "Memorial in Behalf of the Citizens of Western Texas," asking for the division of Texas into two states, the common boundary to be either the divide between the Colorado and Brazos rivers or the Brazos River.[42] The "Memorial" was referred to the Committee on Reconstruction. After hearing the arguments of E. J. Davis, L. D. Evans, and others and after gathering considerable relevant information, the committee concluded that the erection of a new state would not only serve to reward the people of western Texas, particularly the Germans who had generally opposed secession and remained staunch Unionists throughout the war, but would also provide increased political support for the radical cause. To inaugurate the measure, Thaddeus Stevens, on December 3, 1867, introduced in the House a resolution directing the Committee on Reconstruction "to inquire into the expediency of dividing the *territory* [italics added] known as the State of Texas into two or more states to be admitted into the Union when duly qualified." Representative Charles A. Eldridge of Wisconsin, a radical Republican, blocked the

[40] Ibid., pp. 459–484.
[41] Edward Degener to E. M. Pease, December 30, 1866, and January 21 and October 24, 1867, E. M. Pease Collection, Austin Public Library, Austin, Texas.
[42] Memorial by J. A. Paschal, *et al.*, to Congress, December 17, 1867, in U.S. Congress, House, *Memorial on Behalf of the Citizens of Western Texas,* 39 Cong., 2 sess., 1867, House Misc. Doc. No. 35, pp. 1–4.

proposal with his objection that "one Texas was enough to be held under despotic government."[43] Thus, Stevens had to wait until Congress had set aside the presidentially reconstructed state governments and a new Texas constitutional convention had convened.

[43] Ibid.; *Congressional Globe*, 40 Cong., 2 sess., December 3, 1867, p. 11; *San Antonio Express*, December 6, 1867.

## ⌒⟨2⟩⌒

## PRELUDE TO THE
## RECONSTRUCTION CONVENTION

·

The radicals in Congress watched the progress of reconstruction under President Andrew Johnson with rising resentment and hostility. To them, the president's plan was returning too rapidly the state governments of the late Confederacy to the former slaveholders. Since the constitutional provision of counting only three-fifths of the slaves for apportioning representation no longer held, the South would actually gain representation in the House of Representatives and in the electoral college. Thus, when it convened in December, 1865, Congress moved to set aside the president's program and to impose its own plan. It refused to seat the representatives from the former Confederate states, created a Joint Committee on Reconstruction to draft a new reconstruction policy, and struck at the "black codes" enacted in the South with a bill to extend the Freedmen's Bureau. Unable to override the president's veto of this bill, Congress successfully countered in April, 1866, with the Civil Rights Act, which forbade the states to discriminate against citizens on account of race and authorized the use of the military to secure enforcement. To circumvent any question of its constitutionality, the radicals next incorporated the principles of this act into the proposed Fourteenth Amendment to the Constitution and sent it to the states on June 3, 1866. Tennessee ratified the proposal and was readmitted to the Union by Congress. The other ten Southern states, because ratification meant the repudiation of the Lincoln-Johnson reconstruction governments, a complete social revolution, and an admission that secession had been treason, rejected the amendment, and ratification failed.[1]

In the congressional election that autumn, the voters expressed a preference for the radical viewpoint. Consequently, when Congress convened in December, the radicals, with a two-thirds majority in

[1] Ernest Wallace, *Texas in Turmoil, 1849–1876*, pp. 190–192.

25

each house, ignored what had been done by the president and the Southern states and enacted into law their own reconstruction program. The first Reconstruction Act, passed on March 2, 1867, over Johnson's veto, declared that the former Confederate states, except Tennessee, had no legal government—the existing governments were provisional only. The act divided the South into five military districts, with Louisiana and Texas constituting the Fifth. Each district was placed under the command of a major general whose duty it was to protect all persons and property, to suppress insurrection and disorders, and, at his discretion, to bring to trial before military tribunals all criminals and disturbers of the peace. To regain representation in Congress a state had to call a constitutional convention of delegates elected by voters who were eligible regardless of race or previous condition of servitude but ineligible if disfranchised as former rebels. These delegates then had to frame a constitution guaranteeing Negro suffrage; this constitution had to be ratified by a majority of qualified voters, both white and black, and had to be accepted by Congress; and the new state legislature had to ratify the Fourteenth Amendment.[2]

The act neither defined the procedure for calling a constitutional convention nor specified what oath was to be required of the voters. Thus, after the commanding generals had asked for more specific instructions, Congress on March 23 passed a supplementary Reconstruction Act. This act made it the duty of the commanding general of each district to appoint registration boards to register each otherwise eligible voter who could and would take a loyalty oath. The registrant had to swear that he had never held a legislative, executive, or judicial office in any state or taken an oath as an officer—legislative, executive, or judicial—of the United States, "and afterwards engaged in insurrection or rebellion against the United States, or given aid or comfort to the enemies thereof. . . ." Furthermore, upon the completion of the registration, the commanding general was to call for an election in which the qualified voters were to vote for or against a constitutional convention and to name delegates thereto, provided a majority of all registrants voted on the question and provided a majority of those voting favored a convention.[3]

On March 19, 1867, General Philip H. Sheridan was made commander of the Fifth Military District, and General Charles Griffin

[2] U.S., *Statutes at Large*, 14:428–429.
[3] Ibid., 15:2–3.

became commander of the subdistrict of Texas. Both men regarded all former Confederates as rebels and identified antiradicalism with disloyalty. Griffin was not pleased with the existing government. On March 28, he wrote Sheridan that no civil officer in Texas could be trusted and that Governor Throckmorton should be replaced by Judge Colbert Caldwell, a longtime resident of the state. Sheridan forwarded the letter to Washington with a request for specific authority to replace civilian officers.[4]

A major conflict between military and civilian authorities arose over the extent of exclusions intended in the prescribed voter-registration oath. Sheridan maintained that the clause "or given aid or comfort to the enemies thereof" applied not only to those who were unquestionably excluded. Instead, he directed his registrars to exclude all those who had ever held any position of public responsibility and afterward "given aid or comfort" to the Confederacy, including justices of the peace, court clerks, coroners, policemen, jurors, auctioneers, pilots, county recorders, notaries public, members of boards of health and school boards, city surveyors, school superintendents, public inspectors, and cemetery sextons.[5] When the United States attorney general ruled in support of Throckmorton's contention (that the law excluded only those who had taken an oath to support the Constitution of the United States and afterward supported the Confederacy), Sheridan, with General U. S. Grant's permission, ignored the opinion.[6]

---

[4] Letter from Charles Griffin to P. H. Sheridan, March 28, 1867, and telegram from P. H. Sheridan to U. S. Grant, April 2, 1867, in U.S. Congress, House, *Reconstruction. Letter from the Secretary of War*, 40 Cong., 1 sess., 1868, House Exec. Doc. No. 20, pp. 62–63. The first Reconstruction Act provided that any existing civilian government in the Southern states was provisional only and that the United States had the authority to abolish or modify the same at any time, but the law failed to place the responsibility on any specific officer or agency of the government.

[5] James W. Throckmorton, "Address to the People of Texas," *State Gazette* (Austin), August 10, 1867; memoranda from P. H. Sheridan to U. S. Grant, April 16, 1867, in House, *Reconstruction*, 40 Cong., 1 sess., 1868, House Exec. Doc. No. 20, pp. 80–91. A copy of "Memoranda of Disqualifications for the guidance of the boards of registration under the military bill passed March 2, 1867," from Throckmorton's address is quoted by Charles W. Ramsdell, *Reconstruction in Texas*, pp. 164–165.

[6] General order from Adjutant General to commanders of military districts, June 20, 1867, in U.S. Congress, House, *Interpretation of the Reconstruction Acts. Message from the President of the United States*, 40 Cong., 1 sess., 1868, House Exec. Doc. No. 34, pp. 5–8; telegram from U. S. Grant to P. H. Sheridan, June 28, 1867, in idem, *Reconstruction*, 40 Cong., 1 sess., 1868,

Encouraged by Sheridan's action, the radicals became increasingly aggressive. They organized a Republican party in Texas, condemned as disloyal all who opposed congressional reconstruction, and inaugurated a campaign to remove Governor Throckmorton from office. Because of the conflict between military and civilian officials, because of the failure of the first Reconstruction Act to clothe any specific person with authority to remove civilian officials, and because of the ambiguity of the oath in the second Reconstruction Act, Congress on July 19, 1867, enacted the third Reconstruction Act. This act invested the military commander of a district with power to suspend or to remove from office any civilian officer and to appoint his successor. It also clarified the oath required of all voter registrants.[7]

Eleven days later Sheridan removed Throckmorton from office on the grounds that he was an impediment to reconstruction[8] and named in his place Elisha Marshall (E. M.) Pease, a popular Democratic governor of Texas during the 1850s. Pease, after his defeat by Throckmorton in the 1866 gubernatorial election, had joined a group of Southern radicals in Washington to seek the overthrow of the presidentially reconstructed state governments. Pease and Griffin moved quickly to replace the conservative officeholders with "loyal" men who could and would take the oath as interpreted by Sheridan. On August 17, President Johnson sent Sheridan to command the Department of the Missouri and named as his successor General Winfield S. Hancock, a Democrat in sympathy with the policies of the president.

---

House Exec. Doc. No. 20, pp. 92–93; Wallace, *Texas in Turmoil*, pp. 194–195.

[7] U.S., *Statutes at Large*, 15:14–16. ". . . no person who has been a member of the legislature of any State, or who has held any executive or judicial office in any State, whether he has taken an oath or not, . . . and who has afterwards engaged in insurrection or rebellion against the United States, or given aid or comfort to the enemies thereof, is entitled to be registered or to vote; and the words 'executive or judicial office in any State' in said oath mentioned shall be construed to include all civil offices created by law for the administration of any general law of the State, or for the administration of justice." Under this act, some persons previously excluded by Sheridan became eligible to register, but exclusions were no longer limited to those who had taken an oath to support the Constitution of the United States.

[8] Special Order No. 105, Fifth Military District, quoted in *Dallas Herald*, August 8, 1867; report from P. H. Sheridan to U. S. Grant, November 21, 1867, in U.S. Congress, House, *Message of the President of the United States. Report of the Secretary of War*, 40 Cong., 2 sess., 1868, House Exec. Doc. No. 1, p. 380; James D. Richardson, ed., *A Compilation of the Messages and Papers of the Presidents, 1789–1897*, 6:556.

However, before Hancock assumed command on November 29, General J. J. Reynolds, who had become commander in Texas after Griffin's death on September 15, had already won the applause of the radical press for having swept out the "rebel" officials in more than sixty counties.[9]

Upon assuming command of the Fifth Military District, Hancock notified the civil administration to resume its normal functions and informed Governor Pease that he did not intend to use military tribunals until it was apparent that there were not enough citizens available who would enforce the law. "At this time the country is in a state of profound peace," Hancock wrote, and the existing state government "possesses all the powers necessary" to carry out the laws.[10]

Soon afterward, on December 18, Hancock ordered an election to be held at each county seat for five consecutive days, February 10 through February 14, 1868. The purpose would be to approve or reject a constitutional convention and, if the convention was approved by a majority of the registered voters, to name ninety delegates, one from each district used for the lower house of the legislature. At the same time, Hancock also ordered the registration boards to regard Sheridan's instructions to them as "null and of no effect," to revise the lists of voter registrants in adherence "to the laws and to the laws alone," and to use their own judgment in deciding cases of questionable voter eligibility. When the registration ended on January 31, almost 5,000 names—about 14 percent of the white and 27 percent of the black population—had been added to the lists of registered voters, bringing the total to 109,130 (59,633 whites and 49,497 blacks).[11]

[9] General Orders No. 77 and No. 81 by Andrew Johnson, August 17 and August 26, 1867, in House, *Message of the President of the United States*, 40 Cong., 2 sess., 1868, House Exec. Doc. No. 1, pp. 26, 27; *Austin Republican*, November 13, 1867; Wallace, *Texas in Turmoil*, p. 200; Richardson, *A Compilation of the Messages and Papers of the Presidents*, 6:557.

[10] Letter from W. S. Hancock to E. M. Pease, December 18, 1867, in U.S. Congress, House, *Message of the President of the United States*, 40 Cong., 3 sess., 1869, House Exec. Doc. No. 1, pp. 245–246.

[11] W. S. Hancock, "Special Order No. 213," December 18, 1867, ibid., pp. 215–218; *State Gazette*, December 20, 1867; report of Richard C. Buchanan (commander, Fifth Military District), April, 1868, in U.S. Congress, Senate, *Report on Registration of Voters by the General of the Army*, 40 Cong., 2 sess., 1868, Senate Doc. No. 53, p. 12; Ramsdell, *Reconstruction in Texas*, p. 196. General J. J. Reynolds on April 16, 1870, reported the total registration as 60,455 whites and 49,550 Negroes (Betty J. Sandlin, "The Texas Re-

After Hancock announced the dates for the election, the state buzzed with political activity. The conservatives were unable to unite solidly behind any specific strategy. The influential Throckmorton led a vigorous campaign in opposition. A constitutional convention, he maintained, had been held already and its constitution should govern. Furthermore, he was angry over the unfair manner in which the radicals had administered the registration of voters. With the extensive disfranchisement of responsible citizens, even after the revision Hancock had ordered, Throckmorton believed the state would have "a radical legislature to make the state laws, and a radical judiciary to expound them, and radical juries composed of the meanest of God's creatures, and negroes to enforce them, and radical members of Congress to aid in the subversion of the constitution." To defeat the convention, which required approval by a majority of all registrants, he advocated that eligible voters remain away from the polls. Some of the Democratic leaders, fearing that the radicals would win both the convention and its delegates if the conservatives did not vote, called a meeting in Houston on January 20 for the purpose of agreeing on a plan of action. There, the small group in attendance, representing only twenty counties, resolved that it was "opposed to the Africanization of the State" and recommended that all who were eligible should register and vote against the convention and for delegates who were opposed to Negro suffrage.[12]

The radicals were more aggressive. They were led by James P. Newcomb, who had recently returned to San Antonio and acquired a one-third interest in the *San Antonio Express*,[13] by James G. Tracy and his *Houston Union*, and by Morgan C. Hamilton and his *Austin Republican*. These influential men launched an aggressive campaign for the convention and for the election of radical delegates. They also developed a specific program, including the division of the state and *ab initio* (the doctrine that all statutes, ordinances, and all other legal actions by the state or its governmental subdivisions from the time of

---

construction Convention of 1868–1869" [Ph.D. diss., Texas Tech University, 1970], p. 27). Registration figures are also discussed in Ronald N. Gray, "Edmund J. Davis" (Ph.D. diss., Texas Tech University, 1976), p. 107.

[12] J. W. Throckmorton to Ashbel Smith, September 21, 1867, *State Gazette*, October 26, 1867; Claude Elliott, *Leathercoat*, pp. 182–186. The resolution is partially quoted on p. 186 of Elliott.

[13] Dale A. Somers, "James P. Newcomb: The Making of a Radical," *Southwestern Historical Quarterly* 72 (April, 1969): 463–465.

secession until the removal of Governor Throckmorton were null and void).

The radicals, as part of their campaign, held rallies throughout the state. For example, soon after Hancock called for the election, Judge Charles Colbert Caldwell, an associate justice of the Texas "Military" Supreme Court who resided near Jefferson, began holding rallies in favor of the convention and for his personal candidacy as a delegate. On December 30, 1867, a meeting he had called in the courthouse at Marshall was broken up by conservatives after he had spoken "briefly" and black Scipio McKee had led the Negroes in singing "Rally Round the Flag."[14] In January, the radicals held a successful rally in Marshall that lasted for several hours. A number of prominent leaders, including Caldwell, A. B. Norton, James W. Flanagan, and George W. Whitmore, spoke at that rally to a large group of Negroes and about forty to fifty whites.[15]

On the other side of the state, on January 22, Newcomb and Edward Degener addressed an estimated fifteen hundred white Unionists.[16] The radicals also had the active support of the Loyal Union Leagues, headed in Texas by George T. Ruby, a Northern-born mulatto who in 1866 had moved to Galveston to promote Negro education in Texas. The Loyal Union Leagues had been created to "educate and guide" politically the freedmen. By election time, largely due to Ruby's untiring energy, the Leagues had chapters in most of the communities where there were large numbers of freedmen. The Leagues wholeheartedly advocated a vote in favor of the convention and the election of radical delegates.[17] Indicative of League success was the number of white League leaders elected delegates to the convention.

Meanwhile, the divisionists, in addition to undertaking efforts with

---

[14] James Curtis Armstrong, "The History of Harrison County Texas, 1839–1880" (Master's thesis, University of Colorado, 1930), p. 192; Allen W. Trelease, *White Terror*, pp. 138–140; letter from C. C. Caldwell to E. M. Pease, January 2, 1868, in U.S. Congress, House, *Affairs in Texas: Letters from Governor Pease and Hon. C. Caldwell*, 40 Cong., 2 sess., 1868, House Misc. Doc. No. 57, pp. 2–6; report on the disturbances in Marshall, Texas, from W. H. Wood to Headquarters Fifth Military District, February 3, 1868, in House, *Message of the President of the United States*, 40 Cong., 3 sess., 1869, House Exec. Doc. No. 1, pp. 254–255.

[15] *Texas Republican* (Marshall), February 1, 1868.

[16] *San Antonio Express*, January 25, 1868.

[17] See correspondence, newspaper clippings, memoranda, and miscellaneous items in file number A 34/56, J. P. Newcomb Collection, Archives, Barker Texas History Center, University of Texas, Austin.

Congress, sought to link their cause with the forthcoming election and convention. Degener, who insisted that a pretense must be found to allow the western citizens to express their desire for division, endeavored to persuade Governor Pease to permit a plebiscite on division at the same time as the one on a constitutional convention. Even if the state as a whole rejected both propositions, he argued, a favorable vote in western Texas, which he considered certain, would give the military commander a good reason to call a convention composed of delegates from that area for the purpose of forming a new state out of western Texas.[18] Pease, however, preferred to sell a portion of the western territory and, consequently, took no action on Degener's proposal.

The election went off far more quietly than might have been expected. The plan of the Democrats to defeat the convention by not voting almost worked—but not quite. Of the 56,129 votes cast—1,583 more than required to approve the convention—44,689 (7,757 white and 36,932 Negro) favored and 11,440 (10,622 white and 818 Negro) opposed.[19]

Due to deaths and resignations during the course of the convention, a total of ninety-four, rather than ninety, delegates actually served at one time or another. The composition of the group was unusually cosmopolitan. Of sixty-six whose place of birth is shown on the census rolls, forty-three were born in the South, fifteen in the North, six in a foreign country, and two in Texas. At least twenty-three had resided in Texas for more than twenty years, while no fewer than thirteen had arrived in Texas after the Civil War. The seventy whose occupations are listed (seven had two or more) included twenty-one farmers and stockmen, eighteen lawyers, twelve merchants, seven newspapermen, four physicians, four ministers, four federal jobholders, two millers, two hotel operators, two carpenters, two educators, one blacksmith, one tanner, one surveyor, one watchmaker, one clerk, and one laborer. Of the total ninety-four, ten were Negroes, of

18 Edward Degener to E. M. Pease, December 30, 1866, January 21, and October 24, 1867, E. M. Pease Collection, Austin Public Library, Austin, Texas.

19 Wallace, *Texas in Turmoil*, pp. 200–201; Ramsdell, *Reconstruction in Texas*, p. 199; Texas, Secretary of State, "Election Returns," 1868, Archives, Texas State Library, Austin. Reynolds in his April 16, 1870, report gives the vote as 44,683 for and 11,441 against the convention (Sandlin, "The Texas Convention of 1868–1869," p. 35).

whom four, at least, could read and three could write. It is not possible to determine the exact number of carpetbaggers, that is, Northerners who had come South following the war, often for political or economic gain. Thirteen delegates are shown as having been in Texas for three years or less. Of this number, at least eight unquestionably were carpetbaggers, and some of the twenty-five whose length of residence in Texas is not known may have belonged in this group. The Negroes and the carpetbaggers together constituted a much smaller proportion of the total than in the reconstruction conventions in the other Southern states. Even so, they provided a sizable bloc on whom the radical leaders could depend. Two of the twenty-eight who rendered property to the census taker in 1870 reported in excess of $15,000, and four reported less than $200 each.[20]

Two prominent Republican editors early concluded that the convention was composed of "as good quality people as any public body that has ever assembled in Texas" and "the most able body of men that have ever met in Texas."[21] In fact, no more than one-third possessed any professional or advanced formal education. On the other hand, a relatively large number of the ninety-four had served in some civil or military capacity. In civil affairs four had been in the service of the Republic of Texas, thirteen in the service of the United States, and twenty-nine had held a county or local political office. At least twenty-seven were serving, or had served, in a judiciary capacity— three on the Texas Supreme Court, five as district and thirteen as county judges, and six as justices of the peace. Eight had had experience in a Texas constitutional convention (two in 1845 and six in 1866), and one had been in the German National Assembly at Frankfurt. At least twenty-six had been in military service—five under the Republic of Texas, one during the Mexican War, eleven or more for the Confederacy, and nine for the Union.[22]

[20] Sandlin, "The Texas Convention of 1868–1869," p. 38.

[21] *Daily Austin Republican*, June 16, 1868; *New York Daily Tribune* (dateline, Austin, June 12, 1868), June 27, 1868.

[22] The above analysis of the delegates is derived from U.S. Department of the Interior, Census Office, *Ninth Census of the United States: 1870* (Texas Population); Sandlin, "The Texas Convention of 1868–1869," pp. 36–41, 249–261; Walter P. Webb and H. B. Carroll, eds., *The Handbook of Texas*, vols. 1 and 2, and Eldon Stephen Branda, ed., *The Handbook of Texas*, vol. 3; Wallace, *Texas in Turmoil*, pp. 187, 201–202; Ramsdell, *Reconstruction in Texas*, p. 201; Trelease, *White Terror*, p. 140.

During the first session of the convention, twelve delegates were generally regarded as conservatives. Of this group, no more than ten, possibly only seven or eight, were Democrats.[23] Only two of the twelve, Lemuel Dale Evans and James T. Armstrong, had been politically prominent. Fifty-eight-year-old Evans, a native of Tennessee and a lawyer, had moved to Texas in 1843 and had represented Fannin County in the convention of 1845. After being defeated by Pease in his bid for governor in 1853, he was elected to Congress in 1855, presumably with the aid of the Know-Nothing voters. In 1857 he ran with the support of the Know-Nothing party for reelection as a Union Democrat but was defeated by John H. Reagan who campaigned as a states'-rights Democrat. Opposed to secession, Evans went north for the duration of the Civil War. After the war, he settled in Marshall but was elected to represent Titus County in the convention of 1868–1869 (this made him a "saddlebagger," or one who did not reside in the district he represented), in which he worked consistently and diligently for the creation of a State of East Texas. In fact, because of his failure to stand firm with the conservatives on division and several other matters, the *State Gazette* early in the convention "read" the judge out of the Democratic party. Afterward, from 1870 to 1873, he was a justice of the Texas Supreme Court.[24]

Sixty-two-year-old, Kentucky-born James T. Armstrong, a farmer, had arrived in Texas early in 1836 in time to serve in the Army of the Republic. Settling first in Jasper County and later in Jefferson County, Armstrong rose to political prominence as a county land commissioner, a representative in the Texas Congress, and a district attorney. While serving as a representative in Congress in 1844–1845, he helped to locate the capital at Austin, and, as a member of the convention of 1845, he signed the annexation ordinance. In 1851 he became a state senator, and with the reemergence of the Democrats in

[23] Ramsdell, *Reconstruction in Texas*, p. 200. The *Dallas Herald*, March 28, 1868, and the *Texas Almanac for 1869*, pp. 222–223, claimed that only seven were "conservatives" (Democrats). According to Throckmorton eight delegates were Democrats (*Dallas Herald*, August 11, 1869). George W. Paschal thought there were ten or twelve conservatives (*New York Daily Tribune*, June 27, 1868). The *Daily Austin Republican*, August 5, 1868, reported that there were seventy-eight Republicans and nine conservatives, without accounting for three. Delegate W. W. Mills, *Forty Years at El Paso 1858–1898*, p. 100, many years later wrote that there had been ten Democrats.

[24] Wallace, *Texas in Turmoil*, pp. 36, 59, 43–44, 201; *Handbook of Texas*, 1:576; *Daily Austin Republican*, July 10, 1868.

1873 he was elected a state representative.[25] Too weak to carry out their own program, the conservatives, regardless of party affiliation, aligned with the moderate Republicans.

By the time the convention met, the Republican delegates already were dividing into moderates and radicals, primarily over the issues of *ab initio*, the political status of the former Confederates, and the division of the state. The moderates adhered to the doctrine—followed by the convention of 1866, the Throckmorton administration, Governor Pease, and the Supreme Court—that all acts not in support of the war and not clearly unconstitutional were legal and binding. They wanted only a limited disfranchisement of former Confederates, advocated a practical and realistic view regarding property rights, and generally opposed the division of the state.[26] The radicals, on the other hand, maintained that all legislative and administrative acts of the Confederate states, including secession, were null and void, called for the strict application of the test oath, and wanted to divide the state.

Andrew Jackson (A. J.) Hamilton, the acknowledged leader of the moderates, had the support of a relatively large number of delegates. The most powerful and influential were Charles Colbert Caldwell and Livingston Lindsay, associate judges on the Texas Supreme Court, M. L. Armstrong, and William Wallace (W. W.) Mills. A. J. Hamilton (Jack or "Colossal Jack" to his friends and "Big Drunk" to his enemies) was the dominating personality of the convention and the leader of the fight against division of the state. He was born in Alabama in 1815, was admitted to the bar in 1841, moved in 1846 to La Grange, Texas, became attorney general of Texas in 1849, and from 1851 to 1853 served as a member of the Texas House of Representatives. Elected to Congress in 1859, he opposed secession and remained in Washington until after all other Southern representatives had left. He returned to Austin in 1861, but to escape an anti-Unionist mob he left the state, suffering severe hardship during his flight. In 1862, he was commissioned a brigadier general in the Union Army and returned to Texas in 1865 as provisional governor. On

[25] *Handbook of Texas*, 1:69; Sandlin, "The Texas Convention of 1868–1869," p. 249; *Daily Austin Republican*, August 5, 1868.
[26] John L. Waller, *Colossal Hamilton of Texas*, pp. 105–111; Texas, *Journal of the Reconstruction Convention*, 1868, 1 Sess. (hereafter cited as *Texas Convention Journal*, 1868).

December 10, 1867, he was appointed associate justice on the Texas "Military" Supreme Court, in which capacity his opinions, though comparatively few, were moderate and "noted for learning, dignity, and force." As a lawyer, according to his contemporaries, he had few if any peers in Texas, and his genial manner made him popular with all classes. While still a supreme court justice, Hamilton was elected to represent Travis County in the Reconstruction Convention.[27]

Colbert Caldwell, a native of Tennessee, had engaged in the Santa Fe trade between 1840 and 1845, had practiced law in Arkansas, and had served in the Arkansas legislature before moving to Navasota, Texas, in 1858. Later he moved to Jefferson, Texas, where, after the Civil War, he was regarded for a time as a radical and an advocate of Negro suffrage. In October, 1867, he was named associate justice of the Texas "Military" Supreme Court, on which he served until removed in February, 1870. In 1868 he was elected to represent Bowie, Davis (Cass), and Marion counties in the convention of 1868–1869. By then he was regarded as a moderate.[28]

Sixty-one-year-old, Virginia-born Livingston Lindsay had graduated from the University of Virginia and had practiced law and taught school in Kentucky before moving in 1860 to La Grange, Texas, where he again practiced law. Appointed in September, 1867, he was still an associate justice of the Texas "Military" Supreme Court at the time of the convention.[29]

Sixty-two-year-old M. L. Armstrong, a Lamar County farmer, election registrar, and close friend of A. J. Hamilton, had moved from Tennessee to Texas in 1852. He had served in the Texas House of Representatives (1859–1861), as a district clerk, and as a member of

[27] Waller, *Colossal Hamilton*, pp. 136, 7–20, 111–112; *Handbook of Texas*, 1:759–760; Elyse D. Andress, "The Gubernatorial Career of Andrew Jackson Hamilton" (Master's thesis, Texas Tech University, 1955); Sandlin, "The Texas Convention of 1868–1869," pp. 57–58; John C. McGraw, "The Texas Constitution of 1866" (Ph.D. diss., Texas Tech University, 1959); James R. Norvell, "The Reconstruction Courts of Texas, 1867–1873," *Southwestern Historical Quarterly* 62 (October, 1958): 143–148. The quote about Hamilton is from page 136 of Waller.
[28] *Handbook of Texas*, 2:134; Lucille B. Bullard, *Marion County, Texas, 1860–1870*, p. 94; Armstrong, "The History of Harrison County," pp. 192–194; Norvell, "The Reconstruction Courts of Texas," pp. 144–146.
[29] *Handbook of Texas*, 2:59; Sandlin, "The Texas Convention of 1868–1869," p. 249; Norvell, "The Reconstruction Courts of Texas," pp. 144–146.

the Constitutional Convention of 1866. In 1869 he became Lamar County clerk.[30]

W. W. Mills, a native of Indiana, had moved to El Paso, opposed secession, and served for a short time as a lieutenant in the Union Army. In 1862 he became collector of customs at El Paso, and, despite the controversy he created by allowing arms to cross the border to Benito Juarez, he still held the job at the time of the convention. In addition, Mills was active in business and had organized the Republican party in El Paso. In October, 1868, the Texas Supreme Court awarded him $50,000 in damages for false arrest and illegal confinement during the Civil War. At the time of the award, Mills was courting Mary Hamilton, the daughter of A. J. Hamilton, who wrote the opinion. The thirty-two-year-old Mills was aggressive, contentious, and a vehement speaker.[31]

Other moderate delegates included Judge Andrew Phelps McCormick, A. M. Bryant, Fred W. Sumner, and James W. Thomas. McCormick, a thirty-six-year-old native Texan, had graduated from Centre College in Kentucky. He had then practiced law in his home town of Brazoria, fought in the Confederate Army, served as chief justice of Brazoria County, and been a member of the Constitutional Convention of 1866. After the Reconstruction Convention he became a district judge, a Republican state senator, a United States attorney, and a federal district and circuit court judge. In the convention of 1868–1869, McCormick was the major architect of the plan for financing the public schools.[32] Bryant, a forty-nine-year-old farmer, had moved from Kentucky to Texas in the early 1850s, had served in the Confederate Army, and from 1865 to 1867 had been the Grayson County judge. Sumner, also of Grayson County, a native of Vermont and a watch repairman, had come to Texas prior to 1860. Thomas, who had come from Tennessee to Texas some eight or more years

[30] Sandlin, "The Texas Convention of 1868–1869," p. 249; Ramsdell, *Reconstruction in Texas*, p. 289.

[31] *Handbook of Texas*, 2:201; Waller, *Colossal Hamilton*, pp. 3–111; Mills, *Forty Years at El Paso*; *Texas Convention Journal*, 1868, 1 Sess.; *Daily Austin Republican*, July 16, August 3, and August 18, 1868.

[32] *Handbook of Texas*, 2:104; Sandlin, "The Texas Convention of 1868–1869," p. 256; Ramsdell, *Reconstruction in Texas*, p. 255; Texas, *Journal of the Reconstruction Convention*, 1868–1869, 2 Sess., pp. 417–422 (hereafter cited as *Texas Convention Journal*, 1868–1869).

earlier, was editor of the *McKinney Messenger*. As the registration supervisor of Collin County, he had disbarred lawyers on the basis of their professional oath.[33]

The majority of radical delegates were Texas Unionists, officeholders appointed by the military and federal authorities, carpetbaggers, Negroes, or Loyal Union League leaders. Of those identifiable, twenty, possibly more, had borne arms for the North, had left the state for the duration of the Civil War, or had opposed secession but remained quietly at home. Most prominent were Edmund Jackson (E. J.) Davis, Edward Degener, James W. Flanagan, and James Pearson Newcomb. Not counting voter registrars, of whom there were a large number, at least ten were congressional reconstruction office appointees. Of these the most active in the convention were Morgan Hamilton, state comptroller, and Nathan Patten and Robert K. Smith, federal tax collectors. A dozen or more of the radicals had moved to Texas after the Civil War; among the most prominent were George T. Ruby, R. K. Smith, and George Washington ("Dog") Smith. Ruby, as mentioned earlier, was a Galveston educator and president of the Grand Council of the (Loyal) Union Leagues of Texas. Dr. Robert K. Smith ("notorious" would more appropriately describe him than "prominent") had come from Pennsylvania to Galveston to be a federal tax collector. During the convention, he was indicted in connection with the mysterious disappearance of $5,000 in tax money. George Washington Smith was a New Yorker and a captain in the Union Army who came to Jefferson in Marion County immediately after the war to engage in business and, he said, for the purpose "of assisting the Negro in his efforts to escape the oppression of the rebels."[34] Of the ten Negroes only one, George T. Ruby, became an active and influential leader in the convention. These ten, nevertheless, wielded an influence out of proportion to their numbers and abilities, for they voted consistently and almost solidly with the radicals. Without their support, the radicals would have had no chance to win their fight in the convention for division. Other than Ruby, the Union Leaguers included William R. Fayle, a white Harris County judge and minister who hailed from England and served as the head

[33] Sandlin, "The Texas Convention of 1868–1869," pp. 259, 260, 24.
[34] Traylor Russell, *Carpetbaggers, Scalawags, and Others*, p. 52; Bullard, *Marion County*, pp. 92–95; Trelease, *White Terror*, p. 140.

of the Union League in Houston; Newcomb, who later replaced Ruby as the state leader; George W. Smith, who headed the organization at Jefferson; and George W. Whitmore, a white Smith County lawyer who was the vice-president of the Union Leagues of Texas.[35]

A relatively small but determined and uncompromising number provided the leadership for the radical program, which included the establishment of a new state or states out of Texas. The radical leadership devolved upon forty-one-year-old E. J. Davis, who in 1838 had come from Florida to Texas and who was the mastermind behind the move to establish a State of West Texas. Davis had served as a deputy customs collector at Laredo, practiced law at Laredo, Brownsville, and Corpus Christi, and served as judge of the lower Rio Grande district. During the Civil War he recruited a regiment of Texas cavalry for the Union and served as its colonel, ultimately attaining the rank of brigadier general. At the end of the war, he returned to Corpus Christi. In the Constitutional Convention of 1866 (as previously noted) he favored *ab initio*, unrestricted Negro suffrage, and disfranchisement of the former Confederates. According to Ben C. Truman, a Democrat correspondent for the Republican *New York Times*, Davis preferred that "negroes rather than secessionists should rule the country."[36] His own contemporaries characterized him as able, well known, and popular within his own party—a man of conviction and firm resolve. A recent historian, however, has concluded that Davis was determined to remake society according to the dictates of moral theory and was satisfied that he alone possessed truth and justice.[37]

As early as July, 1866, Davis had already conceived a plan whereby the radicals could control, if not all, at least a part of the state. "It

[35] The above analysis of the radicals is compiled from *Handbook of Texas*, vols. 1, 2, and 3; Sandlin, "The Texas Convention of 1868–1869," pp. 249–261; Ramsdell, *Reconstruction in Texas*, pp. 200–201, 206–207, 209, 230–231, 242, 244, 249, 257, 261; *Texas Convention Journal*, 1868–1869, 1 and 2 Sess.; Gray, "E. J. Davis"; Waller, *Colossal Hamilton*; Somers, "James P. Newcomb," pp. 463–469; Russell, *Carpetbaggers, Scalawags, and Others*, p. 52; Bullard, *Marion County*, pp. 92–100; Armstrong, "The History of Harrison County," pp. 192–202; Trelease, *White Terror*, pp. 138–141; Wallace, *Texas in Turmoil*, pp. 201–209. Additional sources include numerous manuscript collections (especially the Newcomb Collection), official records, articles, books, and extant files of Texas newspapers, 1865–1876.

[36] *New York Times*, March 11, 1866.

[37] Gray, "E. J. Davis," pp. 431–443, 112.

seems to me," he wrote to Pease, "that we should now move for division of the state, taking for boundary the Brazos up to a point about opposite Austin and thence North to Red River."[38]

Next to Davis, the radicals most eager to create a new western state were Edward Degener, Morgan C. Hamilton, and James P. Newcomb. Degener, probably the best-educated and most experienced delegate in the convention, had studied in both Germany and England and had served twice in the legislative assembly of Anhald-Dessay and in the first German National Assembly at Frankfurt in 1848. Migrating to Texas in 1858, he located at Sisterdale, where he engaged in farming. During the Civil War he was imprisoned by the Confederates for his ultra-Unionist stand. After his release, he engaged in the wholesale grocery business in San Antonio. As a delegate to the convention of 1866, as noted previously, he strongly advocated Negro suffrage and the creation of a new state out of western Texas.[39]

Fifty-nine-year-old Morgan Calvin Hamilton, a native of Alabama and the older brother of A. J. Hamilton, had lived in Austin since 1837. Twice he had served briefly as the secretary of war of the Republic of Texas. Although a strong Unionist, during the Civil War he had remained in Austin, where he engaged in business. Worth an estimated $1 million, he was apparently the wealthiest delegate in the convention. In 1867 he was appointed state comptroller, in which position he made an issue of *ab initio*. When General Hancock called for an election for delegates to a constitutional convention, he announced as a candidate from the Austin district. However, when his more popular brother, A. J., returned from a sojourn in Mississippi and announced his candidacy in opposition, Morgan withdrew from that race and was elected instead to represent Bastrop. Considered by

[38] E. J. Davis to E. M. Pease, July 14, 1866, R. Niles Graham–E. M. Pease Collection, Austin–Travis County Collection, Austin Public Library, Austin, Texas. Other sources include Gray, "E. J. Davis," pp. 1–112; *San Antonio Express*, December 28, 1867, July 31, 1868; *Daily Austin Republican*, January 4, 1869; *Handbook of Texas*, 1:469–470; William C. Nunn, *Texas under the Carpetbaggers*, pp. 19–22; William L. Richter, " 'We Must Rubb Out and Begin Anew': The Army and the Republican Party in Texas Reconstruction, 1867–1870," *Civil War History* 19 (December, 1973): 344; Sandlin, "The Texas Convention of 1868–1869," pp. 44–45; Francis B. Heitman, *Historical Register and Dictionary of the United States Army, 1789–1903*, 1:357.

[39] *Handbook of Texas*, 1:482; Degener correspondence, Newcomb Collection; R. L. Biesele, *The History of the German Settlements in Texas, 1831–1861*, p. 171.

most of his contemporaries to be a man of "Roman honesty" and "unyielding consistency," he denounced those who drew double salaries from the state. Nevertheless, he himself drew salaries both as state comptroller and as a delegate, plus per diem and travel to the convention of 1868–1869. He reputedly advocated the "plowing up of Jefferson Texas and other regions infested by Ku Klux, and sowing them with salt." Unlike his brother, he was not endowed with the gift of oratory or the ability to react instantly to unexpected situations, but he was a strong personality in the convention, and he threw his full support behind the move to create one or more new states out of Texas.[40]

James P. Newcomb ("Jimmie Lowdown" to his enemies), a votary of the radical program, was the party's unofficial publicist and whip. Born in Nova Scotia in 1837 but a Texan since 1839, Newcomb in 1854 established in San Antonio the *Alamo Star*. When this enterprise collapsed the next year, he began the *Herald*. In both papers, he supported the Know-Nothing party. A year later he sold the *Herald* to John D. Logan and went to Vermont and Canada. In 1858, the twenty-one-year-old Newcomb returned to San Antonio and edited the *Herald* for about a year during Logan's absence. He then published the *Alamo Express*, a very pro-Union voice, until it was destroyed in May, 1861, by a mob that included members of the Knights of the Golden Circle. Newcomb thereupon went to California. Except for two expeditions to Arizona—one with the California Volunteers to drive out the Confederates and one for mining—he remained for the duration of the war as a printer for the San Jose *Times* and part owner and editor of the *San Francisco Flag*, an ultra-Unionist voice. After both his son and wife had died, he returned in 1867 to San Antonio and acquired a one-third interest in the *San Antonio Express*, the *Freie Presse*, and the *Texas Farmer Zeitung*. He quickly converted the *Express* into the most pronounced voice of the radicals. Before the convention he editorialized: "The problem of Reconstruction is not a speedy restoration of the revolted State or States, but their restoration to the Union as Republican communities ruled by the Republican party, the party of liberty and progress. . . ." In 1867

[40] *Handbook of Texas*, 1:760; Sandlin, "The Texas Convention of 1868–1869," pp. 46–47, 254; "Bexar," *San Antonio Express*, July 20, 1867; A. J. Hamilton, "Speech," *Galveston News*, August 21, 1871; miscellaneous letters and items, Newcomb Collection; Waller, *Colossal Hamilton*, pp. 5, 6, 7, 112, 113, and 134.

Newcomb became a member of the board of registrars for Bexar County and a member of the San Antonio city council. As a delegate to the convention, he opposed the acceptance of any state constitution that did not provide for *ab initio*, disfranchisement of all former Confederates, and Negro suffrage. He fanatically advocated the creation of a new western state with San Antonio as the capital. He hoped that the restoration to the Union of eastern Texas, an area inhabited by detested rebels, could be delayed indefinitely.[41]

Possibly the next most prominent and influential radical in the convention, as well as in the state as a whole, was George T. Ruby, mentioned above. He was a New York–born and Maine-educated mulatto from Galveston, who apparently took his orders from the Union Leagues' national headquarters in New York City. For a time during the Civil War, Ruby was in Haiti as a reporter for a Boston newspaper. In 1864 he went to New Orleans to work for the education of the new freedmen, for a short time as a grade school principal and then as an agent to establish and visit schools throughout the state. In 1866 he came to Texas to continue his educational work with the Negroes. In the convention, he was one of the hard-core radicals and the leader of the black delegates, and afterward he served two terms in the Texas Senate.[42]

Some other radicals who participated prominently in the movement to reduce the size or divide the state included A. Jackson (A. J.) Evans, Dr. Robert K. Smith, William M. Varnell, A. T. Monroe, and James W. Flanagan. Evans, of McLennan County, was a thirty-three-year-old native of Mississippi. Having moved to Texas before the Civil War, he was a lawyer and the military reconstruction district judge at the time of the convention. Smith, a true carpetbagger from Pennsylvania, had served as a surgeon in the Union Army from 1861 to 1865. After the war, as mentioned earlier, he became a federal tax collector at Galveston. During the convention, he worked diligently to gain an advantage for Galveston in any division of the state and was frequently engaged in both verbal and physical confrontations. Var-

---

[41] *Handbook of Texas*, 1:275; Somers, "James P. Newcomb," pp. 449–469. The editorial is quoted in Somers, p. 465. More information on Newcomb, from various sources, is held in the Newcomb Collection.

[42] *Handbook of Texas*, 1:513. Other information on Ruby can be gleaned from items in the Newcomb Collection and from numerous references to him in the files of Texas newspapers, 1868–1869.

nell, a native of Alabama and a sixty-eight-year-old white farmer from the Victoria district, had lived in Texas about thirty years. He had been in the Constitutional Convention of 1866 and, afterward, had been a United States marshal and registrar of voters. Although apparently a person of very few words, oral or written, he was one of the leaders in the struggle to obtain a State of West Texas. Monroe, a merchant and the delegate from Houston and Trinity counties, had come from Virginia to Texas more than two decades earlier. He had been a justice of the peace and had served in the Confederate Army. Although a strong advocate of division, he disagreed with the framers of a constitution for a State of West Texas and urged the convention to adopt instead a three-state plan. Sixty-three-year-old James W. Flanagan, a native of Virginia who came to Henderson, Texas, from Kentucky in 1844, was a lawyer, farmer, real estate agent, merchant, and public official. In Kentucky he had been a justice of the peace and a circuit court judge. After moving to Texas, he had served in the 1850s in both houses of the Texas legislature and as a presidential elector. He had opposed secession, had owned and operated a tannery during the war, and had been a member of the Constitutional Convention of 1866. He had been one of the early advocates of the division of Texas, having introduced such proposals, as previously discussed, both in the legislature and in the convention in 1866. Although his reasons for wanting division were not the same, he strongly supported the efforts of Davis and his cohorts to establish a State of West Texas.[43]

In the interval between the election and the opening session of the convention, the conservative papers were filled with gloomy foreboding about the future of Texas. Veteran editor Charles DeMorse told his readers that the delegates would not reconstruct the state the way the people wanted. Nevertheless, he exhorted, the citizens should work with a will for the "redemption of the South by practical and peaceful forces," and thereby they could eventually regain control of their state government. A radical convention, he thought, was prefer-

---

[43] Sandlin, "The Texas Convention of 1868–1869," pp. 249–261, 52–53, 82, 92, 103–104, 113–119; Texas Legislature, House, *Journals of the House of Representatives of the State of Texas*, 4 Leg., 1851–1852, p. 867; Texas, *Journal of the Texas State Convention*, 1866, pp. 135–136, 188; *Handbook of Texas*, 1:608–609; and numerous items appearing in files of Texas newspapers, 1867–1876.

able to no convention, for the whites could regain control of the government from the radicals sooner than from the military.[44]

Seventy-eight delegates were on hand when the convention assembled in Austin in the Hall of the House of Representatives at 3:30 P.M. on June 1, 1868. The election of a president offered a preview of the forthcoming contest between the radicals and the moderate-conservative coalition. Morgan Hamilton nominated E. J. Davis, and A. J. Hamilton nominated Judge Colbert Caldwell; Davis was elected by a vote of 43 to 33.[45] The radicals were united behind Davis, but some conservatives considered Caldwell more dangerous than Davis. James B. Norris, the Austin correspondent for the *Galveston News*, preferred Davis to Caldwell. He knew very little about Davis, he explained, but he surely could not be as bad as Caldwell.[46]

The radicals also won all the other offices except those of secretary and an assistant doorkeeper. The officials chosen included Judge W. V. Tunstall, secretary; A. J. Bennett, first assistant secretary; and H. B. Taylor, second assistant secretary; none of these men was a delegate. The convention then created sixteen standing committees. A. J. Hamilton headed the Judiciary Committee; Morgan C. Hamilton, the Committee on General Provisions; A. J. Evans, the Committee on Federal Relations; Caldwell, the special Committee on Lawlessness; and Monroe, the Committee on Division.

The convention was now ready for work, but the delegates were slow in getting to the task for which they had been elected—making a constitution for Texas. A resolution to require the test oath was voted, but the subject was postponed indefinitely when it was found that a number of radicals would be excluded. The delegates spent most of their time debating *ab initio*, hearing complaints of lawlessness, investigating conditions in the state, chartering railroads and otherwise usurping legislative power, and debating proposals to divide Texas into two or more states.

The first serious debate in the convention was over *ab initio*. A resolution to incorporate *ab initio* in the new constitution was introduced on June 5 by A. J. Evans, but the majority favored a substitute

---

[44] *Standard* (Clarksville, Texas), March 6, 1868 (*Northern Standard* until 1852).

[45] *Daily Austin Republican*, June 1, 1868; *Texas Convention Journal*, 1868, 1 Sess., p. 3.

[46] *Galveston News*, June 3, 1868.

proposal, and the matter was never brought to a final vote. President Davis then proposed a modified *ab initio* declaration with a provision that measures enacted after 1861 of a purely private and domestic nature were valid. The proposal was defeated. By a vote of 45 to 28 a declaration was finally adopted that validated all wartime acts of the Texas government that were "not in violation of the Constitution and the laws of the United States, or in aid of the rebellion. . . ."[47] *Ab initio* was dead, but its supporters, unwilling to accept defeat, then set out to prevent the restoration of constitutional government in the former slaveholding area of Texas and to create a new state or states out of the section where the population had been predominantly Unionist. Their efforts to divide the state provoked the most time-consuming and most bitter debate in the convention.

[47] The foregoing discussion of the beginning of the convention is from *Texas Convention Journal*, 1868, 1 Sess., pp. 28, 241–242, 794–795, 797. The quote is from p. 797.

~(3)~

# THE DIVISION ISSUE DURING THE
# FIRST SESSION OF THE CONVENTION

.

E ven before the radicals had an opportunity to introduce the subject of division on the floor of the convention, Provisional Governor E. M. Pease, in his June 3 message to the convention, spoke
against division. Division, the governor claimed, would not be in the
public interest. To subject the impoverished population, estimated at
no more than 800,000, to the expenses of two or three governments
would not only be a great burden, but it would also hinder the establishment of a proper system of public education and of measures to
develop potential wealth. Furthermore, since Congress had provided
for the reestablishment of only one state government for Texas, a
proposal to divide the state undoubtedly would delay the restoration
of Texas to the Union. Division, if desired by the people, could be
achieved more easily, Pease insisted, after Texas had representatives
in Congress.[1]

As an alternative, Pease recommended that Texas negotiate to sell
to the United States the region west of a line connecting the mouth of
the Pecos River with the junction of the South Fork of the Red River
and the 100th meridian. The only two counties west of that line, El
Paso and Presidio, were too far removed to be properly governed
without excessive expenditure, and, besides, the inhabitants of those
counties, Pease believed, would favor the cession.[2] As an extension
of Indian Territory, the lands would be valuable to the United States,
and the compensation—"far greater than we can realize from it in
any other way"—could be used to improve education, to make internal improvements, and to promote immigration. Texas, Pease con-

[1] Texas, *Journal of the Reconstruction Convention* (hereafter cited as *Texas
Convention Journal*, 1868), 1 Sess., 1868, pp. 12–15.
[2] It was closer, easier, and safer for them to travel to Santa Fe than to Austin.

tinued, still would be large enough for three states.[3] The governor's recommendation was never taken seriously.

Five days later, on June 8, A. T. Monroe proposed that the portion of the governor's message pertaining to the sale of public lands be referred to the Committee on Public Lands. The committee would be instructed to report on the expediency of selling all the unappropriated public domain to the United States except a "sufficient portion" for public schools. Edward Degener, on the other hand, gave first priority to the erection of a new state out of the territory of western Texas and consequently opposed the sale of the western territory. He therefore countered with a substitute proposal for the appointment of a Special Committee on the Division of the State. The fifteen-member committee would be charged with reporting both a plan of division and procedures for its execution, if the committee judged such a plan expedient. The substitute motion was adopted, and Monroe's resolution relating to the sale of public lands was referred to the new Committee on the Division of the State. On the following day President Davis named to the committee eight divisionists, including Monroe as chairman, and seven antidivisionists.[4]

On the same day that Davis named the Committee on the Division of the State, the U.S. Congress also displayed an interest in the division of Texas. Congressman Fernando C. Beaman of Michigan reported from the Committee on Reconstruction a bill that was a refinement of the earlier proposal by Thaddeus Stevens. Beaman's bill would divide Texas into East Texas, Texas, and South Texas, with the Trinity and Colorado rivers as the basic divisional boundary lines. The bill was read a first and second time, then recommitted for perfection.[5]

---

[3] *Texas Convention Journal*, 1868, 1 Sess., pp. 15–16.

[4] Ibid., p. 44. The appointees, in addition to Monroe, were M. L. Armstrong of Lamar County, Edward Degener of Bexar County, James W. Flanagan of Rusk County, William H. Fleming of Red River County, S. M. Johnson of Calhoun County, Thomas Kealy of Collin and Denton counties, Jacob Kuechler of Gillespie County, W. H. Mullins of Cherokee and Angelina counties, H. C. Pedigo of Tyler, Liberty, and Chambers counties, Edwin C. Rogers of Fannin and Hunt counties, George T. Ruby of Galveston County, George H. Slaughter of Smith County, F. A. Vaughan of Guadalupe County, and Erwin Wilson of Brazoria County (ibid., p. 51).

[5] U.S. Congress, *Congressional Globe*, 40 Cong., 2 sess., June 9, 1868, p. 2971; *Daily Austin Republican*, June 12, 1868. The common boundary of

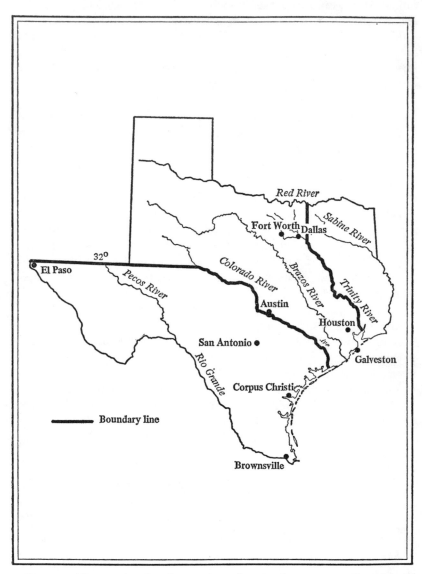

5. Beaman (Congressional) Plan, 1868 and 1869. Congressman Fernando C. Beaman's 1868 proposal, also known as the Congressional Plan, became the basis for several later division schemes.

The plan would have given East Texas considerably less area than the other two states but the largest population and the most wealth. South Texas was virtually uninhabited, and much of it was wasteland. The new Texas, the middle state, would have included some of the most desirable coastal area, much of the highly productive river-bottom land, and the vast Indian-inhabited plains.[6] Upon hearing that Congress was considering division, the Committee on the Division of the State asked for and received a copy of the Beaman bill before the division question came up in the regular order of business on June 19.[7]

The members of the convention, as well as many nonmembers, were already irreconcilably at odds not only on division but even on the question of the authority of the convention to consider the subject. Most radicals contended that the convention had unlimited authority. The *San Antonio Express* editorialized that it was both "stupid and wasteful" for the convention to continue without taking steps to divide the state. The convention, it argued, should adopt a division ordinance and divide into three conventions, with each drawing up a separate constitution, thereby avoiding the "expenses of subsequent conventions." The conservatives and many of the moderates, on the other hand, maintained that the power of the convention was limited to drafting a constitution for the State of Texas. A. H. Longley, editor of the *Daily Austin Republican*, a Unionist and a thoroughgoing Republican who still wanted to maintain party harmony, argued that the

---

East Texas and Texas was to begin in the middle of the channel between Galveston Island and Bolivar Point and thence run through Galveston Bay to the mouth of the San Jacinto River, up that stream and its East Fork to Polk County, north to the Trinity River, up the Trinity and its East Fork to the northwest corner of Kaufman County, thence to the southwest corner of Fannin County, and thence north to the Red River. The common boundary of Texas and South Texas would be a line extending from Pass Cavallo through Matagorda Bay to the mouth of the Colorado River, thence up that stream to its intersection with the 32nd parallel, and thence due west to the Rio Grande (*Texas Convention Journal*, 1868, 1 Sess., pp. 144–145).

6 Before the Committee on Reconstruction reported back to the House, Representative William P. Stokes, a Tennessee farmer, on June 15, offered a resolution which provided simply for the division of Texas and its readmission into the Union. This bill likewise was read a first and a second time and referred to the Committee on Reconstruction, where it was allowed to die (*Congressional Globe*, 40 Cong., 2 sess., June 15, 1868, p. 3164).

7 *Texas Convention Journal*, 1868, 1 Sess., pp. 106, 143.

convention could deal with local problems but not with ordinary legislation or with division.[8]

Some delegates wanted the convention to grant to the legislature the power to divide the state. To this end, Marshall Glenn, a conservative Democrat who represented Anderson and Henderson counties in deep east Texas, on June 22 proposed an ordinance that empowered the legislature to divide Texas into two or more states, to enact all laws necessary for the organization of any newly created state, and to allocate equitably among the new states the school fund and the public domain. The proposal was referred to the Committee on the Division of the State.[9]

On the same day, W. W. Mills of El Paso introduced a resolution that became entangled in the division issue. Mills, supported by a petition signed by a number of citizens of the El Paso area, proposed to cede to the United States the County of El Paso on the condition that it and the adjacent County of Doña Ana, New Mexico, would be granted a territorial government. Mills argued that, because of the county's location, it was "inconvenient and unwise" for El Paso to remain any longer a part of Texas and, further, that the cession would be beneficial to the people of Texas as well as to those of El Paso. The resolution was referred to the Committee on Federal Relations.[10]

Anticipating that division would become a reality, Degener, on the following day, introduced a resolution designed to ensure that the divided states would share equitably in both the assets and the liabilities of Texas—including the public domain, cash, and bonds on hand—since all were common property of all states that would be formed.[11]

On June 24, Monroe presented the majority report for the Committee on the Division of the State. The report recommended that, inasmuch as the great size of the state was an "obstacle to the enforcement of law and maintenance of order," to the economical administration of government, and to the growth of prosperity, the plan set forth in the Beaman bill should be adopted, except for some minor changes in the boundaries. The committee wanted the boundary be-

[8] San Antonio Express, June 13, 1868; Daily Austin Republican, June 16, 1868.

[9] Texas Convention Journal, 1868, 1 sess., pp. 136, 142, 147.

[10] Ibid., p. 135.

[11] Ibid., pp. 142–143. The proposal was referred to the Committee on the Division of the State.

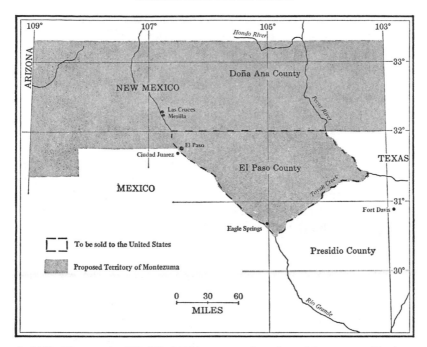

6. Mills Plan, 1868. W. W. Mills's proposal to form Montezuma Territory from El Paso County, Texas, and Doña Ana County, New Mexico, complicated division efforts in the Texas Reconstruction Convention.

tween the southern and middle states to extend from the mouth of the Colorado River due south to the Gulf, rather than through Matagorda Bay to Pass Cavallo. It also wanted the common boundary between the eastern and the middle states to follow the Elm Fork of the Trinity, rather than the East Fork, to the mouth of the Denton Fork, and then to run to the western boundary of Denton County and from there due north to the Red River.[12] Furthermore, the committee favored the passage of the Degener proposal (that the assets and liabilities of Texas should be common to all states created out of Texas) and recommended that the Glenn ordinance (that authorized the legislature to divide Texas into two or more states) not be passed.[13]

[12] This would add to East Texas on the northwest five counties: Dallas, Collin, Denton, Grayson, and Cooke.
[13] *Texas Convention Journal*, 1868, 1 Sess., pp. 146–147, 148.

51

When Monroe had finished, Ruby, who a few days before had declared at a mass meeting in the capitol that the major object of the convention should be the "formation of a constitution," reversed his earlier position with a minority report. He and Erwin Wilson of Brazoria favored division but with the boundaries exactly as specified in the Beaman bill. The majority report was accepted for later consideration.[14]

Two days later, on June 26, the Committee on Federal Relations sent to the floor its report on the proposal to cede El Paso County. Chairman A. J. Evans stated that the committee, having concluded that a separate government "is necessary for the people of that distant county and believing that the state will sacrifice no material interest," recommended passage of the resolution. The report was accepted indirectly when the convention voted that all resolutions and declarations originating in and reported favorably by its committees were to be printed and laid upon the desk of each member.[15]

On Saturday morning, June 27, the members of the convention read in the papers that on the preceding Wednesday the states of North Carolina, South Carolina, Georgia, Florida, Alabama, and Louisiana had resumed political relations as states with the federal government. Mississippi and Virginia were expected to adopt constitutions within a few days, thereby leaving Texas as the only unrestored state. The Texas press, in reporting the news to its readers, reminded the delegates that the people had sent them to Austin to make a constitution rather than to spend the time quarreling among themselves.[16]

If they read the admonition, the delegates gave it no heed. They debated at length the reports for the cession of El Paso County and for the division of the state. The Mills resolution came up for consideration first. The divisionists were united solidly in opposition. They wanted to hold the state intact until after the creation of a new western state so that that state would receive all the benefits from any sale or from the resources that might be developed. Thus, their strategy was to delay action on the resolution until after the final vote on division. For this reason, Morgan Hamilton moved to send the report

[14] Ibid., pp. 147–148.
[15] *Daily Austin Republican*, June 12, 1868; *Texas Convention Journal*, 1868, 1 Sess., p. 155.
[16] *Daily Austin Republican*, June 27, 1868.

back to the committee for further study.[17] Mills, however, blocked the return by obtaining and holding the floor until the appointed time for the next order of business. The cession of El Paso County to the United States, Mills claimed, was a matter of the utmost importance to the sixteen thousand people of the proposed territory. To postpone consideration until after a vote on division, if the vote were favorable, would kill his proposal. Some of the opponents from western Texas wanted to postpone the cession until after the formation of a new western state, Mills charged. Then they would sell a large area, including El Paso, to the United States for several million dollars, with which they would construct public buildings for the capital in San Antonio.

Mills then proceeded to give arguments in support of his resolution. The counties of El Paso, Texas, and Doña Ana, New Mexico, far removed from their respective centers of government, encompassed a fertile agricultural area, vast regions of fine-quality grass, and mountains rich in gold, silver, copper, iron, and lead. The proposed territory, generally referred to as "Montezuma," was about as large as Indiana and was capable of supporting a large and prosperous population. The people of El Paso labored under many disadvantages. They were separated from the nearest inhabited area of the state by six hundred miles of wasteland, "infested" by hostile Indians. They did not have regular mail communications and consequently were sometimes unable to participate in elections because notices to hold a vote did not arrive in time. As an example, because of his inability to ascertain when the convention would assemble, Mills himself had arrived in Austin a month beforehand. Judicial proceedings were severely hampered, and the state government was unable to give the region adequate protection from Indian harassment. He had brought with him, Mills continued, a petition, signed by four hundred registered voters of El Paso County, asking for the cession. In fact, he claimed, almost everyone in El Paso favored it. Texas would profit by the cession, because the state no longer would have the expense of administering the remote area, and it would enhance the possibility of selling the Panhandle region to the United States as an expanded Indian Territory. Finally, if they passed the measure, the members of

[17] *Texas Convention Journal,* 1868, 1 Sess., p. 160.

the convention would have the satisfaction of knowing that they had "acted generously and magnanimously" toward a people plagued with an "unfortunate situation."[18]

When Mills sat down, the president called for the report of the Committee on the Division of the State. Andrew McCormick's motion to postpone consideration until the next week lost by a vote of 43 to 43, with most divisionists and radicals voting against delay. After some parliamentary maneuvering, the convention, on the motion of Morgan Hamilton, resolved itself into a committee of the whole and heard chairman Monroe's arguments in support of the majority report. The written report, Monroe explained, set forth the chief reasons for division, but there were others to which he desired to call attention. Division, in his opinion, would have occurred prior to the Civil War had it not been for the likelihood of the establishment of another free state. The principal argument now for division was that a state as large as Texas could not administer government efficiently or provide protection to its people. The smaller the state, he maintained, the better the government. Rhode Island, Delaware, and New Jersey had better governments than New York and Pennsylvania; yet Texas was more than 6 times the size of New York. It was about 11 times the size of South Carolina, 7 times as large as Tennessee or Ohio, 27 times the size of Vermont, and over 176 times the size of Rhode Island. The government of Texas had failed disgracefully to protect the lives and property of its citizens. This could be done best by organizing three "loyal" states with three "loyal" constitutions that would keep the people "true to the great principle of Republicanism" (as viewed by the radicals). "Then all will be well." The people could organize "Republican" governments that would give protection to life, liberty, and property. Congress stood ready to aid with division, Monroe believed, but was hesitant to act until the convention passed the measure. The lines proposed in the majority report would give the eastern state 42 counties, an area larger than that of North Carolina or of New York and Connecticut combined. The middle or central state would have 57 counties plus an unorganized territory, an area larger than New York and Pennsylvania combined. Western

[18] Ibid., pp. 160–162; W. W. Mills, "Speech in Convention June 27 Regarding Ceding El Paso County," *Daily Austin Republican*, August 3, 1868; unidentified newspaper clipping in scrapbook, W. W. Mills Collection, Archives, Barker Texas History Center, University of Texas, Austin.

Texas would have 150 counties, an area larger than New York, Pennsylvania, Delaware, Maryland, and Connecticut combined. Division into six states would be even better, and eventually, he predicted, each of the three proposed would be divided into two or more.

The more states, the greater the competition among them for capital, laborers, and enterprise, and the quicker the vast unoccupied regions would become the homes of millions of happy and prosperous people. Citizens, he argued, were willing to pay more for a government that gave them protection and security. Then too, as the wealth and resources were developed, the additional tax burden would lessen. There were many precedents for division, all unquestionably acts of wisdom. Maine was formed out of Massachusetts; Kentucky, Ohio, Indiana, and Illinois, out of Virginia; Missouri and Arkansas, out of Louisiana; and Alabama and Mississippi, out of Georgia.[19] Without these divisions, Monroe insisted, the distant possessions would have remained unsettled territory. Finally, the division of Texas would bring the public records nearer the people and promote pride, security, and prosperity.[20]

On Monday, June 29, the convention heard the minority report from the Committee on Federal Relations on the cession of El Paso County. Edmund Bellinger of Gonzales and Jacob Kuechler of Gillespie County favored division but opposed the cession. They pointed out that, according to the 1860 census, El Paso County had 4,050 inhabitants, only 436 of whom had registered, and at the last election only 2 of 294 votes had been against the present convention. The formation of a new western state would attract an influx of immigrants who would quickly develop the coal, iron, lead, copper, and silver ores believed to be in the area in rather large quantities. Fur-

[19] Monroe did not include West Virginia, apparently because Virginia did not willingly relinquish it. Virginia and Georgia ceded to the United States their claims to western territory from which the respective states were formed.

[20] A. T. Monroe, "Speech on Proposition to Divide the State, Made in the Convention on June 27, 1868," *Daily Austin Republican*, July 13, 1868. On the evening of June 27 several members of the convention participated in a rally of the Republican party at the Capitol. Max Mobius served as secretary, A. J. Bennett and Scipio McKee served on the resolutions committee that drafted an endorsement of the nominees of the national convention, and W. C. Phillips, Judge W. V. Tunstall, and A. J. Hamilton all delivered what a strongly biased editor called "powerful," "eloquent," and "patriotic" speeches in support of the national platform and nominees (*Daily Austin Republican*, June 29, 1868).

thermore, the region contained "immeasurable" layers of rock salt, enough to furnish a continent and convert this region into one of the most desirable portions of western Texas. It would be unwise indeed, they maintained, for Texas to deprive herself of this potential wealth.[21]

At this point, A. J. Hamilton took charge of the antidivisionist forces in what the Brownsville *Daily Ranchero* called "some fine generalship." Aided particularly by Andrew P. McCormick, who had served both as a Brazoria County judge and in the Constitutional Convention of 1866, Hamilton resorted to parliamentary maneuvering to delay or prevent consideration of the committee's plan. To split the divisionists, he proposed division on a radically different geographical basis and a plebiscite on any division plan that might be adopted. If he could get the support of Degener and James Newcomb, who wanted the Brazos River as a dividing line, and L. D. Evans, who was anxious to have more counties in northern Texas placed in East Texas than proposed in the committee plan, a deadlock would result. His substitute plan likewise proposed to divide Texas into three states, but with the Brazos River as the boundary between the eastern and western states and the 32nd parallel as the southern boundary of the third state. This or any other plan of division would be subject to the final approval of the voters. The radical-divisionists could ill afford this, but to oppose would not sit well with the electorate. If the line were drawn at the Brazos River, West Texas would have a large conservative and moderate population that, Hamilton felt, could defeat the measure at the polls even if it was adopted by the convention. The plan placed the area between Dallas and the Red River with the northeastern region, an arrangement desired by the divisionists of both sections but not provided for in either the Congressional or the committee plan.[22] Morgan Hamilton's motion to lay the [Jack] Hamilton substitute on the table passed by a vote of 46 to 43, but his parliamentary maneuvering to kill the measure was blocked by a decision to adjourn for the day. Most of the radical bloc, joined by L. D. Evans, voted with Morgan Hamilton. On the other hand, M. L. Armstrong of Lamar, A. M. Bryant of Grayson, James W. Flanagan and his son Webster Flanagan, Livingston Lindsay, Colbert Caldwell, Monroe

[21] *Texas Convention Journal*, 1868, 1 Sess., pp. 170–172.
[22] *Daily Ranchero* (Brownsville), July 2, 1868; *Galveston News*, July 5, 1868; *Daily Austin Republican*, July 6, 1868.

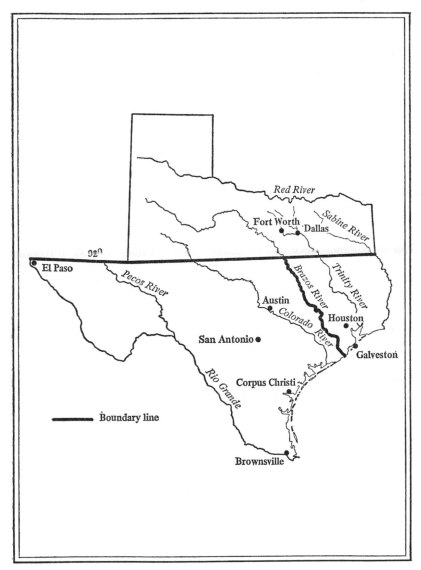

7. A. J. Hamilton Division Proposal, 1868. A. J. Hamilton proposed this division scheme as a diversionary tactic to split the divisionist forces.

(who had reported the original plan for division), Mills, and two extreme radicals, George Smith of Marion County and William Varnell, voted with A. J. Hamilton.[23]

On the following day, June 30, A. J. Evans of McLennan County, on his own initiative rather than for his Committee on Federal Relations, introduced a resolution calling for the sale of a part of the public domain along lines similar to those in Governor Pease's earlier suggestion. Evans' proposal would authorize the governor of Texas to sell to the United States, subject to the approval of the legislature, that part of Texas west and northwest of a line extending from the intersection of the 100th meridian and the Red River to the mouth of the Pecos River. The sale was conditional on the United States' agreeing to prevent the Indians in the ceded territory from making excursions into the remaining Texas. The convention referred the resolution to the Committee on Federal Relations and then voted to have both the report of the Committee on the Division of the State and Hamilton's substitute printed and placed on the calendar for the following Friday.[24]

When the convention on July 2 resumed consideration of the resolution to cede El Paso County, the radicals continued without abatement their efforts to defeat or delay action on the proposal until they had provided for the division of the state. J. W. Flanagan called for a proviso that would require the United States to pay Texas $1 million for the cession. This proposal was a clever political move: if division occurred and the sale was consummated, Flanagan's own state would share in the revenue. Caldwell, another delegate from eastern Texas, countered with a substitute that the United States would allow the El Paso cession to have a territorial government and would pay to Texas "just compensation." After Monroe and Degener failed in their respective efforts to get the matter postponed indefinitely, Morgan Hamilton moved unsuccessfully to refer the whole question to the Committee on the Division of the State, a proposal that, of course, would have been tantamount to sudden death since that committee had reported previously a plan of division. Mills's call for the main question (second reading) then carried by a vote of 47 to 35, the radical-divisionists voting solidly in opposition. However, parliamentary

[23] *Texas Convention Journal*, 1868, 1 Sess., pp. 174–175.
[24] Ibid., pp. 174–175, 180–190.

jockeying, led by J. W. Flanagan and Monroe, blocked for the day a vote on the question.[25]

In Washington that same day the Committee on Reconstruction, after more than two weeks' consideration and a number of letters and telegrams from the divisionists in Texas, reported back to the House the Beaman bill with only one very minor change. Thaddeus Stevens, the committee spokesman, stated that the members of the committee "were unanimously agreed" and that the Texans were anxious for Congress to enact the bill so that they could proceed legally with division while the convention was in session. Some members of the House who were not ready to vote, however, succeeded in getting the report recommitted.[26]

Next morning, in Texas, Davis, hoping to speed congressional action and to gain additional support for the radical program, moved that the convention send Morgan Hamilton and Colbert Caldwell to Washington without delay. The delegates would be instructed to report to Congress the condition of lawlessness and violence in Texas and to urge the immediate passage of a law that would assure the filling of offices with loyal and competent incumbents, the organization of loyal militia to be under the control of loyal provisional authorities, and the "expedition of such other matters" as might be desired by the convention. The motion was passed as an ordinance on July 6.[27] Caldwell, a Supreme Court justice, was primarily concerned with the rampant lawlessness in the state. Like Davis, he was a strong advocate of increased military control to curb it. He might even support division as a remedial measure, Davis reasoned, and, being from eastern Texas, he would carry weight among the congressmen. Morgan Hamilton was selected because he was an uncompromising radical and an advocate of division.

To strengthen the hands of the delegates, Degener, on the next day, July 7, moved a suspension of the rules to take up the report of the Committee on the Division of the State. Although he had the almost solid support of the radicals and several influential moderates, his motion failed by a vote of 36 to 40.[28] Caldwell and Hamilton, with-

[25] Ibid., pp. 205–206.

[26] *Congressional Globe*, 40 Cong., 2 sess., July 2, 1868, p. 3689.

[27] *Texas Convention Journal*, 1868, 1 Sess., pp. 212–213, 221, 222–224; Texas, *Ordinances of the Constitutional Convention at Austin, Texas, June 1, 1868*, p. 35.

[28] *Texas Convention Journal*, 1868, 1 Sess., p. 229.

out waiting for a vote on division, left the following day, July 8, for Washington.

Before leaving, Morgan Hamilton presented the report of the Committee on General Provisions and succeeded in getting the date for its consideration postponed until July 29. This would allow him time to be back and also would keep the convention in session should Congress act favorably or indicate that it preferred the convention to proceed with division.

Some of the divisionists, however, made an unsuccessful attempt to prevent the delay. On July 9, J. W. Flanagan, William Varnell, who represented four counties centered around Victoria, and Virginia-born William J. Phillips, a delegate from Matagorda and Wharton counties, argued that the "labor of the committee had been well matured." The convention either should proceed with preparing the constitution or adjourn *sine die*. To burden the state with the great expense of remaining in session, they argued, suggested motives other than drafting a constitution.[29]

For several days the convention engaged in parliamentary jockeying over Mills's resolution and A. J. Hamilton's division proposal. The radical divisionists desired to get both proposals either tabled or killed to clear the way for action on the plan proposed by the Committee on the Division of the State. On July 9, upon motion of James Thomas, the convention voted 42 to 38 to postpone indefinitely consideration of Hamilton's substitute.[30] Then, on the next day, when the time came to resume consideration of Mills's proposal, Dr. R. K. Smith of Galveston utilized the entire time to explain why he had previously opposed the committee plan of division and on what conditions he would now support it. Such a division, he explained, would be highly injurious to the port and people of Galveston, and it was his duty to protect the rights and interests of his constituents. The proposed line placed part of Galveston Bay within the jurisdiction of another state. Earlier, he had asserted that the convention had no jurisdiction to divide the state, for that power belonged exclusively to the legislature. Since then, however, he had concluded that the Reconstruction Acts of Congress placed the convention outside the limits of the constitution and that the state ought to be divided. Lawlessness, including

29 Ibid., p. 250.
30 Ibid., pp. 254–255.

threats upon his own person, was the determining factor in his decision to support division. (Ironically, during the convention, Smith was involved in more than one criminal incident.) Division, he now believed, would result in increased protection to the people, in redress for wrongs and outrages, and in the more rapid development of material interests. The courts would be purged of their treason and corruption, juries would be established upon a better foundation, law would be better observed, and government would be better administered. If the Committee on the Division of the State would amend its report to make the boundary conform to the interests of the citizens of Galveston, he would vote for its plan.[31]

On Saturday, July 11, the convention temporarily disposed of the proposal to cede El Paso by referring the subject to the Committee on the Division of the State. Two days later, on the motion of J. W. Flanagan, by a decisive vote of 49 to 33, it again laid Hamilton's plan for division indefinitely upon the table. The radical-divisionists, who voted solidly for both, were joined by some moderates, possibly with the approval of A. J. Hamilton.[32]

The radicals next moved to expedite division in case Congress should enact the Beaman bill or indicate its desire for the convention to proceed with division. Degener presented a substitute for the committee plan of division. The substitute differed in two ways: it reset the boundaries for the three proposed states in accordance with the Beaman bill, and it recommended the procedures to be followed in setting up the new states. The members of the convention were to organize into three separate conventions, each composed of the delegates from one of the proposed states. Each convention would then proceed to frame a constitution and submit it to the voters of the proposed state for ratification. When the constitution had been approved by Congress and when the legislature of the proposed state had ratified the Fourteenth Amendment to the Constitution of the United States, the state would be entitled to representation in Congress.[33] The radicals now needed only to get the Degener substitute adopted and

31 "Speech of Dr. R. K. Smith, of Galveston, on the Division of the State," *Daily Austin Republican*, July 11, 1868.
32 *Texas Convention Journal*, 1868, 1 Sess., pp. 286–287, 288–289, 309; John L. Waller, *Colossal Hamilton of Texas*, p. 115; Betty J. Sandlin, "The Texas Reconstruction Convention of 1868–1869" (Ph.D. diss., Texas Tech University, 1970), p. 114.
33 *Texas Convention Journal*, 1868, 1 Sess., pp. 309–312.

to delay the completion of the constitution for the unified Texas until they had a favorable nod from Congress.

Some members, however, had grown weary of the prolonged debate and were anxious to complete the constitution. Sensing this feeling, James W. Thomas of Collin and Denton counties, who was, as mentioned previously, editor of the *McKinney Messenger* and who was one of the most conscientious and businesslike delegates, on July 14 proposed that "no question relating to division of the State hereafter be entertained, unless by authority of Congress." The topic of division, he argued, had consumed a great deal of time, and, since the Reconstruction Acts did not authorize its consideration, the convention should henceforth confine itself to the business for which it was convened. Led by McCormick and J. W. Flanagan, the divisionists stalled for the day a vote on the proposal and on the next day attempted to substitute a favorable report on the Evans declaration.[34] However, A. J. Hamilton, in turn, managed to prevent an immediate vote on this measure. When, on July 16, the Thomas resolution again came up for consideration, Newcomb tried to frighten the delegates into voting against the measure by insisting that the people of his district would not favor any constitution that did not provide for a new western state. The members, however, ignored the threat and adopted the resolution by a decisive vote of 47 to 37. Joined by L. D. Evans, who consistently favored division, the radical stalwarts—including Davis, Newcomb, Degener, A. J. Evans, George Ruby, Monroe, C. W. Bryant of Houston, R. K. Smith of Galveston, and G. W. Smith of Marion—voted in opposition. A. J. Hamilton's motion for the final disposition of the question carried by a vote of 47 to 33.[35]

Hamilton, it appeared, had won his fight against division, partially by proposing a different plan. The proposal of the Committee on Federal Relations to sell an extensive area of western Texas had aided Hamilton, for some delegates wanted any newly created western state to be the sole recipient of the resulting compensation. The *San Antonio Express* claimed inaccurately that three-fourths of the delegates favored division, but that some had voted for the Thomas resolution

[34] Ibid., pp. 391–395. Evans' proposal was to sell all the territory lying west of a line connecting the intersection of Red River with the 100th meridian and the mouth of the Pecos River, with the approval of the legislature, and to apply all proceeds therefrom to school purposes only.
[35] Ibid., pp. 403–406, 409–411; *Daily Austin Republican*, July 17, 1868.

as a means of killing the Hamilton substitute.[36] To the contrary, such a majority, if it had existed, could have easily blocked any effort to revive the tabled Hamilton substitute. Editor Longley of the *Daily Austin Republican* thought that the vote on the Thomas resolution represented a "fair expression of the views" of the members of the convention. He expressed hope that the divisionists would accept their defeat gracefully and now turn their best abilities to the formation of a constitution that would meet the expectation of the loyal people of the state. Defeat of the measure, he insisted, was proper since the question of division did not enter into the election of the delegates. Furthermore, he believed that if division was connected with ratification, the constitution would be defeated.[37]

The final vote—in reality a vote on division—showed that the Republicans were nearly equally divided, 39 for the resolution or against division and 35 against the resolution or for division.[38]

After the victory of the antidivisionists, the convention devoted its efforts to the preparation of a constitution. By the end of July, all the committees had reported. The report of the Judiciary Committee had been printed; the Legislative Committee report had been sent to the printers; the report of the Committee on General Provisions had been made, and consideration would take place as soon as its chairman, Morgan Hamilton, returned from Washington; the Committee on State Affairs reported on July 30; and the Committee on the Executive Department had almost finished its section. Editor Longley was quite happy with the progress. "Thus we see that while the members have engaged in many long, and as we thought unnecessary discussions, they have been laboriously engaged as members of committees, and the greater part of the work is done. A few more weeks and the Constitution will be framed."[39]

[36] *San Antonio Express*, July 17, 1868.
[37] *Daily Austin Republican*, July 17, 1868.
[38] Those voting for the resolution included M. L. Armstrong, A. J. Hamilton, Lindsay, McCormick, Mills, Schuetze (German), Thomas, and Negro delegates McWashington, Watrous, and Williams. Those voting against the resolution included Davis, C. W. Bryant of Harris County, Burnett, Degener, A. J. Evans, both Flanagans, Kuechler, Monroe, Newcomb, Patten, Pedigo, Ruby, Slaughter, both Smiths, Varnell, Whitmore, and Yarborough. The other eight who voted for the Thomas resolution apparently were Democrats (*Texas Convention Journal*, 1868, 1 Sess., pp. 410–411; *Daily Austin Republican*, July 18, 1868).
[39] *Daily Austin Republican*, July 31, 1868.

Several factors, however, militated against an early completion of the constitution. From Wednesday through Saturday, August 12 through August 15, most members attended the Republican Party State Convention in Austin, where their differences on *ab initio* and other matters resulted in an official split in the party. On the first day, the delegates convened, organized, witnessed a parade at eleven o'clock, lunched on barbecue with "not less than fifteen hundred whites and five thousand blacks," and afterwards heard political orations by Judge James H. Bell, Jack Hamilton, and others.[40]

When the Republican convention adopted a platform favored by the moderates, the radicals, led by Davis, withdrew and held their own convention on August 14 through August 15.[41]

The major reasons for the delay, however, were the reports of widespread lawlessness, the belief that the final constitution would be too liberal toward the rebels, and the hope that Congress would act favorably on division. The Special Committee on Lawlessness and Violence, headed by G. W. Whitmore, first reported on July 2. The report made available information on only 60 of the 127 counties, but in these there had been 939 people murdered, including 470 whites, 429 Negroes, and 40 whose race was not specified. The report claimed that most of the victims were Negroes or loyal men who had died at the hands of former Confederates. Several delegates had been threatened and knew of other outrages against Union men.[42]

Their hopes kindled by the failure of *ab initio* and division in the convention, the platform of the national Democratic party, and the speeches of their nominees for president and vice-president, the Democrats in Texas were becoming increasingly bold. They organized Democrat Clubs throughout the state, including in them Negroes who

[40] Participating constitutional convention personnel included James H. Bell, chairman, the staff of secretaries who served here in a similar capacity, and on the platform committee Davis, A. J. Hamilton, Burnett, McCormick, W. R. Fayle, B. F. Williams, and B. O. Watrous (E. W. Winkler, ed., *Platforms of Political Parties in Texas*, pp. 112–115; *Daily Austin Republican*, August 11, 12, 13, and 14, 1868).

[41] A. J. Bennett and H. B. Taylor, assistant secretaries in the constitutional convention, served as secretaries, and for its State Executive Committee the Radical Republican Convention named constitutional convention delegates M. C. Hamilton, Degener, George W. Smith, C. W. Bryant, Arnold A. Bledsoe of Dallas, J. W. Talbot of Williamson County, Patten of McLennan County, and Ruby (Winkler, *Platforms of Political Parties*, pp. 115–116; *Daily Austin Republican*, August 14, 15, and 17, 1868).

[42] Sandlin, "The Texas Convention of 1868–1869," p. 71.

would vote with them. They warned the so-called loyal men in their respective communities to desist from their unwanted activities or to depart. As an illustration, Samuel R. Peacock, a military-appointed clerk of the District Court of Anderson County in deep east Texas, on August 12 sent the *Daily Austin Republican* a copy of a warning he and four others had received.

> Sirs:
> This is to notify you that your company at dinner [a Democrat rally and barbecue] to-day can be dispensed with. We want either negroes or white men, but as for damned mongrels, we want none. Your position in this country is such that no gentleman is willing to recognize or *intolerate* your company. You are known to be black-hearted negro lovers. Your *days is* numbered in this community. You nor your race cannot abide in this community much longer. Your [sic] are *damned* rascals, and are not worth a dog's notice. You *God damned* Radical set, you ought to be in hell, the last one of the Radical party, and I hope the day will soon come when you will have to leave this town and hunt a home in hell or some other seaport town. And this is notice for you to eat your dinners at home to-day. We have understood that a certain one of your Radical party has tried to buy over our party by *loaning* them money; but you can't come that; we are not to be led to Radicalism in this way.
> Respectfully,
> Many Citizens.[43]

Many of these resurgent Democrats, convinced that the Republican-controlled convention would not produce a document to their liking, wanted the delegates to adjourn without completing a constitution.

In response to the reports of lawlessness—specifically to the Houston editor's statement that Caldwell, Morgan Hamilton, and every member of the Union Leagues "ought to die"—and to the organization of Democrat Clubs throughout the state, editor Longley issued a call for the six hundred members of the Jack Hamilton Council No. 84, Union Leagues of America, to meet at their council room on Saturday evening, July 25. He declared that the members of this "splendid organization" could quickly clear the land of assassins, that the Grand Council of Texas was preparing to meet any issue, and that "everywhere the Council fires are being revived, and loyal columns being marshalled." Every member of the convention who was a "Loyal Leaguer" was urged to attend.[44]

[43] *Daily Austin Republican*, August 18, 1868.
[44] Ibid., July 23, 1868.

Having lost their fight for *ab initio* and division and confronted by lawlessness and the growing boldness of the Democrats, the radicals and some moderates feared that, if the constitution were completed in time for the state to participate in the November election, the conservatives might win control. If so, they felt, the monopoly of offices, the property, and even the lives of Unionists in Texas would be in jeopardy. Morgan Hamilton, while on his way to Washington, voiced this opinion. He told a reporter that the convention had expected to finish its work by July 4, but, in view of the lawlessness and the split in the ranks of the Republicans, the constitution could not be completed in time for the forthcoming election. Consequently, he favored abolishing civil government altogether, putting the state under military rule, and reconstructing it at the point of the bayonet in a way that would disfranchise the rebels and enfranchise the loyalists and Negroes.[45] From Washington he wrote that he was "persuaded that our very salvation depends upon division and that upon the line of the Colorado." He advised the convention to recess and the delegates to inform their constituents that Congress wanted division.

On August 9, Judge Caldwell, "a faithful servant," in editor Longley's estimation, returned from Washington with the "encouraging news" that Congress would give the "loyal men everything that is necessary for their protection and for the reconstruction of the state." However, he continued, Congress wanted the convention to take the initiative on division. The report inspired the radical-divisionists, despite the Thomas resolution, to try again. First, however, they must make a final disposition of the two proposals to sell a part of the public domain. Consequently, on August 17 they called for and defeated the proposal to cede El Paso by a final vote of 41 to 32, the radicals voting almost solidly against the proposal.[46] The Mills resolution was finally dead. Interestingly, A. J. Hamilton, soon to be Mills's father-in-law but an opponent of the diminution of Texas in any manner, abstained from voting. Having failed to achieve his major objective in the convention, Mills, "in great disgust," obtained a leave and left the next day for Washington.[47]

[45] Ibid., July 18 (from *Galveston News*, July 16), 1868.

[46] *Daily Austin Republican*, August 10, 1868; *Texas Convention Journal*, 1868, 1 Sess., pp. 758–761.

[47] *Texas Convention Journal*, 1868, 1 Sess., p. 777; *San Antonio Express*, August 21, 1868.

By this time the convention had exhausted its funds. Soon after it had convened, it had requested $125,000 for its expenses, but the military commander had authorized only $100,000. On August 20, it requested the balance of its original budget. "The $25,000 will be sufficient," the Committee on Contingent Expenses reported, "to meet the expenses of the present session of the Convention."[48] Apparently, the committee was already convinced that the delegates intended to postpone completion of their assignment.

To many delegates, the lack of funds provided a justifiable reason to recess. Nathan Patten of McLennan County immediately moved that the convention adjourn from August 22 to the first Monday in January next, but the majority still preferred to proceed with the business of forming a constitution. During the next few days progress was rapid. When, on August 24, it appeared fairly certain that the constitution would be passed to engrossment, the convention voted to recess from August 31 to the first Monday in December, subject to being convened at an earlier date by a duly invested committee.[49]

Before adjourning, however, the radicals, claiming that the reports by Caldwell and Morgan Hamilton provided sufficient justification, made still another effort to divide the state. On Saturday, August 29, Newcomb and J. W. Flanagan introduced resolutions that together authorized the establishment of a new western state and a new eastern state, both in accordance with the boundaries specified in the Beaman bill. The resolutions further authorized the people in each of the proposed states to adopt a separate constitution and submit it to Congress for approval.[50] The Newcomb-Flanagan proposals represented a more practical approach to division than earlier schemes. If this had been the original proposal in the convention, it is entirely plausible that the majority of delegates would have voted for a new western state. The convention, however, having decided already to wait until after the presidential election for more favorable support from Washington, refused to consider either proposal. On Monday morning, when it next convened, it promptly adjourned—by a vote of 33 to 27, most of the divisionists in the affirmative—until the first Monday in December.[51]

[48] *Texas Convention Journal*, 1868, 1 Sess., pp. 779–780, 798.
[49] Ibid., pp. 785, 851–853; *Daily Austin Republican*, August 25, 1868.
[50] *Texas Convention Journal*, 1868, 1 Sess., pp. 939–940.
[51] Ibid., p. 943.

# ~(4)~

# THE COYOTES CONTRIVE THE
# STATE OF WEST TEXAS

.

W hen they first convened, the delegates generally felt that the convention would finish its work by July 4. Two weeks passed, however, before they began working seriously. Then, for a time, they made good progress, and by the end of July all the major articles except education and suffrage had been approved or were ready for consideration.[1] Since it appeared that the constitution would soon be completed, the convention provided for the immediate publication of forty thousand copies of the completed portion.[2]

As would be expected, the press evaluations ranged from praise to condemnation. The *Daily Austin Republican*, the voice of the moderate Republicans, characterized the document as "a model specimen of organic law" that "meets the approbation" of a large majority of Texans. The *Houston Union*, generally radical, declared that it was "imminently Republican" and that the judiciary article "is incomparable."[3]

Some editors, both conservative and radical, disagreed. The conservative *State Gazette* felt, after "deliberation," that it would be better for Texas to remain under military rule "than to embrace, with pretending smiles and ardor," radical reconstruction. The radical *San Antonio Express* also felt that Texas had "better remain in military rule two years than accept such reconstruction."[4] The constitution did

[1] *Daily Austin Republican*, July 18 (from *Galveston News*, July 16), July 31, 1868.

[2] *Daily Austin Republican*, 5,000; *Freie Presse* (San Antonio), 5,000; *McKinney Messenger*, 5,000; *Paris Vindicator*, 5,000; *Tyler Index*, 5,000; *Union Republican* (Huntsville), 5,000; *San Antonio Express*, 5,000; *Flake's Daily Bulletin* (Galveston), 5,000 (H. P. N. Gammel, comp., *The Laws of Texas, 1822–1897*, 6:43–44; *Daily Austin Republican*, September 2, 1868).

[3] *Daily Austin Republican*, October 7, September 29 (from *Houston Union*, n.d.), 1868.

[4] *Daily Austin Republican*, October 5 (from *State Gazette* [Austin], Octo-

not incorporate the *Express'* radical desires, and the editor felt that a Republican victory in the November election would ensure the division of the state. Other journals that opposed the constitution included the *Galveston News, Civilian Houston Times,* and *Columbus Times.*

Officially, the convention had recessed because it had expended its allocated funds. To have money when it reconvened, it had authorized the collection by December 1 of a special property tax of $0.20 per $100.00 on the 1868 assessed valuation.[5] The real reasons for recessing were otherwise, and, for various motives, all three political factions favored the action. The Republicans, both factions, were frightened by the boldness and the aggressive resurgence of the Democrats. The *Daily Austin Republican* editorialized that the convention had acted wisely by recessing until after the presidential election, inasmuch as the Democratic party had as its aim the overthrow of the reconstruction laws.[6] If the convention had succeeded in drafting a constitution and getting the state readmitted, Texas' electoral votes might have tipped the election to the Democrats, who would have dismantled Republican Reconstruction. "Had the Convention completed its work and ordered an election before November," Longley wrote, "there is not a shadow of a doubt but that the election day would have seen us precipitated into a civil conflict." As evidence, Longley reported that one delegate (apparently, J. B. Boyd) had boasted that he and his friends intended to vote, if necessary, with a gun in hand. "We all know," Longley concluded, "that the work of the Convention hinges upon the presidential election."[7] The conservative *Columbus Times,* almost as defiant as Boyd, expressed its unabashed disgust with the delegates: "The Convention adjourned because it did not embody sense enough to frame a dog law, let alone a Constitution for a State. The men who composed that Convention never have done anything for the State of Texas, nor never will. As for the members of the scallawag [*sic*] concern being left alive for three months to

---

ber 2), September 29, and October 5 (from *San Antonio Express,* September 30), 1868.

[5] Texas, *Journal of the Reconstruction Convention* (hereafter cited as *Texas Convention Journal,* 1868), 1 Sess., pp. 858, 944; Gammel, *Laws of Texas,* 6:40.

[6] *Daily Austin Republican,* December 2, 1868.

[7] Ibid., August 31, 1868.

come, we don't suppose anybody cares, except their heirs at law. We don't; and never will."[8]

The interval between the sessions provided an opportunity for the public to assess the pros and cons of division. From the first, a majority of east Texans associated division with radicalism. Early in the summer, Dr. Ashbel Smith of Galveston, one of the best-educated and most prominent citizens of Texas, wrote that he opposed division because he favored one magnificent university to three small state colleges and because it would be more difficult to get a railroad across Texas with three legislatures than with one. The *Galveston News* apparently swayed many east Texas conservatives with its explanation that division was the scheme of Congressman Thaddeus Stevens "to crush and destroy." Despite delegate L. D. Evans' prodivision stand, early reports from northeast Texas indicated that the division question attracted only "mild attention" there and that the people were generally opposed.[9]

The radicals apparently gained a few converts as a result of Morgan Hamilton's report from Washington that Congress wanted division. In that same letter Hamilton advised the delegates to spread this information among their constituents during the recess. Although there is no indication that Hamilton directly promoted the cause either from the forum or in the press after he returned on September 13, a few days later the *Houston Union* observed that many who had previously opposed division had decided it was necessary in order to obtain law and order and that the subject would be a major issue in the reconvened convention.[10]

If the delegates heeded Hamilton's admonition to encourage divisionist enthusiasm, the press, which regarded the national election as

[8] Ibid., October 14 (from *Columbus Times*, n.d.), 1868. The editor of the *Houston Telegraph* revealed his ignorance of the subject when he explained to his readers that "the radicals by adjourning hoped to get Congress to adopt the Constitution without submitting it to a vote of the people" (*Daily Austin Republican*, September 7 [from *Houston Telegraph*, September 2], 1868).

[9] Ashbel Smith to President Hancock of the Teachers' Convention, June 22, 1868, Ashbel Smith Papers, 1823–1926, Archives, Barker Texas History Center, University of Texas, Austin; *Galveston News*, July 11 and July 18, 1868; DeWitt Brown to M. L. Armstrong, July 20, 1868, Texas, Reconstruction Papers, Archives, Texas State Library, Austin.

[10] Morgan Hamilton to J. P. Newcomb, n.d., J. P. Newcomb Collection, Archives, Barker Texas History Center, University of Texas, Austin; *Daily Austin Republican*, September 14 and September 28 (from *Houston Union*, n.d.), 1868.

the crucial issue, generally ignored it. James Newcomb and Edward Degener were exceptions. They persuaded the mayor of San Antonio to call a public meeting—in a new building near the Alamo—for Saturday evening, October 10, at which they would endeavor to arouse greater enthusiasm for the creation of a new western state. At the poorly attended meeting, both Degener and Newcomb talked at length. Degener reported the action of the convention and singled out the "Austin bunch of self and local interest politicians" as the major obstacle to division. He pointed out objections to A. J. Hamilton's plan and showed "conclusively," according to the *San Antonio Express*, that the Colorado River was the best eastern boundary for a new western state.[11]

Newcomb then spoke. Division, he declared, was a right secured by the Resolution of Annexation and, thus, was no revolutionary measure. It was the hinge upon which all the action of the convention turned. Only for that reason, the delegates had not completed a constitution. (Parenthetically, he added that it was good that the constitution remained unadopted, for he was strongly opposed to the document that was being framed.) Division would be beneficial to all, he continued, for in each resulting political entity the people would be more compatible in interests. Furthermore, the government would be more wieldy and more likely to restore law, order, and security, to promote "emigration" [*sic*] and internal improvements, and, in the State of West Texas, to provide for the equality of all men.[12]

On the eastern side of the state, the *Tyler Reporter* was also actively campaigning for division. At a meeting, called by the *Reporter*, in the courthouse in Tyler on Friday, December 4, some "prominent Citizens of Smith County" prepared a resolution addressed to the convention. The arguments set forth differed very little from those previously presented in the convention itself. Texas had three major geographical belts, each larger than the state of New York; the capital was too far from the extremities of the state, thereby hindering the prompt execution of the laws; and experience had shown that more compact states were better. The group did not specify its main reason —to get the capital of East Texas located at Tyler. The resolution called for division in accordance with the "Congressional Plan," which conformed to natural boundary lines more nearly than any

[11] *San Antonio Express*, October 15, 1868, clipping, Newcomb Collection.
[12] Ibid.

71

other proposed plan and allocated to each of the three states a stretch of seacoast, an essential requisite for the economic development of each state. On the other hand, some eastern antidivision editors concluded that further opposition was useless. William G. Barrett of *The Harrison Flag* wrote that he would no longer oppose it.[13] The divisionists appeared to be in a much stronger position when the convention resumed.

The convention reconvened on Monday, December 7, but there was no quorum until the next day. The composition of the delegation had changed. During the interlude three members had died, two violently, and four had resigned. Four simply did not return, and W. W. Mills was present only during the last week.[14] Furthermore, the breach between the moderates and the radicals had become irreconcilable.

Among the missing was carpetbagger and Loyal Union League leader George W. ("Dog") Smith. For three years, according to contemporary whites and more recent local historians, Smith had kept the people of Jefferson in a constant state of alarm. Although he never used liquor, tobacco, or profane language, he had a black mistress and purportedly had told the Negroes that they would not be able to govern Jefferson until it was burned. Not long afterward, part of the town's business section burned, and the conservative whites blamed Smith. Even Judge Colbert Caldwell and some other native Republicans refused to speak with him on the same platform. Before leaving for the convention in 1868, Smith was told emphatically that "his absence would be preferred to his return to Jefferson," but he ignored the warning. On Saturday, October 3, Smith, accompanied by four freedmen, went to the home of a white family to recover his saddlebag ("carpetbag"), which had been stolen from a fellow delegate, the Reverend Aaron Grigsby, who had brought it in his buggy from Austin. When Smith arrived at his destination, a shooting erupted; Smith wounded two of the guards. He and his companions surrendered to the military and were placed in the local jail. During the next evening, a mob that included some members of the Knights of the Rising Sun, a police force created by the county commissioners, broke into the jail and shot Smith to pieces.[15]

[13] *The Harrison Flag* (Marshall), December 24, 1868, February 4 (from *Tyler Reporter*, n.d.), 1869, and December 3, 1868.
[14] Betty J. Sandlin, "The Texas Reconstruction Convention of 1868–1869" (Ph.D. diss., Texas Tech University, 1970), pp. 249–261.
[15] C. Caldwell, "Account of the Affair at Jefferson," *Daily Austin Republi-*

The other delegate to die violently was thirty-four-year-old W. H. Mullins, a Democrat and "a gentleman of fine promise," who represented Cherokee and Angelina counties. Mullins died on the morning of October 24 after shooting himself through the heart. He had been the only member of the Committee on Lawlessness to oppose its majority report. He was replaced by M. Priest, who had served in the Confederate Army and afterward as Cherokee County judge.[16] William E. Oakes, a former captain in the Second Texas (Union) Cavalry who represented Bell, Falls, and McLennan counties and voted with the radicals on the division question, died on August 24 with a "violent congestive chill" and was replaced by Sheppard Mullins, a black.[17] Upon learning that General J. J. Reynolds, the military commander in Texas, had ordered an election for November 9 through November 11 to name Oakes's successor, editor Ferdinand Flake caustically commented that "by postponing these elections until after November, he [Reynolds] will be able at one election to fill the vacancies of those already dead and those yet to be killed."[18]

When the second session of the convention began business on Tuesday, December 8, both the delegates and the press generally recognized that division would be the major issue. The Austin correspondent for the *Galveston News* reported that division was "on the tongue" of at least two-thirds of the delegates and that thirty or more favored it. The divisionists took the initiative. During the organizational procedure, J. W. Flanagan, a divisionist, moved that the convention "act under the original regulations." Such a rule would have voided the Thomas resolution (adopted on August 16—"that no question relating to the division of the State be entertained, unless by

---

*can*, October 17, 1868; *Texas Republican* (Marshall), March 7, 1868; Traylor Russell, *Carpetbaggers, Scalawags & Others*, pp. 52, 99–100; *Jefferson Jimplecute* (100th Anniversary Ed.), June 17, 1965, 2:2; Lucille B. Bullard, *Marion County, Texas, 1860–1870*, pp. 92–93, 95–100; Allen W. Trelease, *White Terror*, pp. 140–141; Texas, *Journal of the Texas Reconstruction Convention, 1868–1869* (hereafter cited as *Texas Convention Journal, 1868–1869*), 2 Sess., p. 4.

[16] *Daily Austin Republican*, October 31 (from *Tyler Index*, October 24), 1868; Sandlin, "The Texas Convention of 1868–1869," pp. 79, 257; *Texas Convention Journal*, 1868–1869, 2 Sess., pp. 21–22.

[17] Sandlin, "The Texas Convention of 1868–1869," p. 258; *Texas Convention Journal*, 1868, 1 Sess., p. 862; *Daily Austin Republican*, August 25, 1868.

[18] *Daily Austin Republican*, October 8, October 19 (quoted from *Flake's Daily Bulletin*, n.d.), 1868.

authority of the United States"), but the delegates voted to abide by all regulations previously adopted.[19] This action, of course, should have put to rest the division issue, but the radical divisionists refused to concede. Two days later, on December 10, Newcomb, characterized by editor Longley as "a fanatic and venomous" deserter from the Republican party, proposed to rescind the Thomas resolution on the basis of Caldwell's report that Congress wanted the convention to take the initiative in dividing the state. Thomas countered with a resolution that bound the convention to complete a constitution before considering any other business, but he lost by a vote of 35 to 24. The vote and the comments indicated that the divisionists had a majority, but the opponents had two advantages: the filibuster and the support of most of the press.[20] On the following day when time came for consideration of the Newcomb resolution, A. J. Hamilton's request for a call of the house was sustained.[21] Realizing that he did not have

[19] *Galveston News*, December 15, 1868; *Texas Convention Journal*, 1868–1869, 2 Sess., p. 4.

[20] *Daily Austin Republican*, September 19, 1868; *Texas Convention Journal*, 1868–1869, 2 Sess., pp. 13–14; *Dallas Herald* (dateline, Austin, December 11, 1868), December 19, 1868; *The Harrison Flag* (dateline, Austin, December 11, 1868), December 24, 1868.

[21] *Texas Convention Journal*, 1868–1869, 2 Sess., pp. 21–27. Only fifteen votes were necessary to sustain a call of the house. If the call was sustained and any members were absent without leave, the question pending had to be laid on the table until the absentees appeared or until it came up again on the calendar order of business (Rule 55 in Texas, *Rules of the Constitutional Convention, Convened June 1, 1868*, pp. 11–12).
A hard-core group of twenty-three delegates consistently voted to sustain the call. They were J. T. Armstrong, John Bell of Austin County, Edmund Bellinger of Gonzales, A. M. Bryant, William H. Fleming of Red River County, A. J. Hamilton, C. T. D. Harn of Grimes County, Thomas Kealy of Collin County, William Keigwin of Leon County, J. G. Lieb of Washington County, John Mackey of Travis County, Titus H. Mundine of Burleson County, William Phillips of San Augustine County, W. H. Posey of Lavaca County, Edwin C. Rogers of Fannin County, Julius Schuetze of Bastrop County, C. J. Stockbridge of Washington County, Sumner, Thomas, Watrous of Washington County, B. F. Williams of Austin County, and Erwin Wilson of Brazoria County. All but three represented counties east of the Colorado River (Sandlin, "The Texas Convention of 1868–1869," pp. 121, 249–261).
On December 14, Davis announced the resignations of delegates David Muckleroy of Nacogdoches, Aaron Grigsby of Jefferson, Joseph W. Talbot of Georgetown, and J. B. Boyd of Robertson County, but the absence of Mills, H. H. Foster of Colorado County, C. E. Coleman of Harrison County, S. M. Johnson of Calhoun County, and Gilbert Yarborough of Upshur County still blocked action on a measure when a call of the house was sustained (Sandlin,

enough support to carry his resolution, Newcomb then tried unsuccessfully to adjourn the convention *sine die*.[22]

The antidivisionists thereupon resorted to the strategy they had used during the first session. Arvin Wright of Ellis County proposed a division with boundaries almost identical to those in the Hamilton proposal and with a stipulation that the measure must be approved by a majority of the voters in each state. The proposal was never given any consideration. On December 16, the correspondent for the *Dallas Herald* reported that all business other than division "is suspended." The divisionists were in a majority, according to the *Herald* reporter, but the minority was strong enough to prevent any action, and, the journalist concluded, as a compromise, the question might be submitted to the voters.[23] The reporter had not gauged well the stubborn determination of the radical leaders.

Faced with a stalemate, a group of the hard-core divisionists from west of the Colorado River held a caucus. Although they made no immediate announcement, the next morning there was a "rumor" that they had "laid the foundation for a constitution which they will complete, and send to Congress, a la West Virginia." The extreme divisionists thereby gave notice that for them the creation of a new western state took priority over the completion of a constitution for the State of Texas, and that, if such a constitution were made, they would allow no vote on it.[24]

About noon on Friday, December 18, President E. J. Davis announced that the subject of the division of the state was in order. The opponents during the next three days used a barrage of delaying tactics, especially calls of the house and motions to adjourn for the day.[25] But they gradually weakened, and on Saturday, December 19, Caldwell announced that he was ready to vote on the Newcomb resolution. He wanted to frame a constitution for Texas and to have a referendum on the Newcomb resolution at the same time as on the constitution.

---

"The Texas Convention of 1868–1869," p. 123; *Texas Convention Journal*, 1868–1869, 2 Sess., pp. 38–39, 42, 43).

[22] *Texas Convention Journal*, 1868–1869, 2 Sess., pp. 23–24.

[23] Ibid., p. 72; *Dallas Herald* (dateline, Austin, December 16, 1868), December 26, 1868.

[24] *Dallas Herald*, January 2, 1869, and December 22, 1868.

[25] Ibid. (dateline, Austin, December 18, 1868), January 2, 1869.

The divisionists, caught by surprise and "fearing some trick," called for adjournment until Monday morning. That night they held a caucus at the capitol, and, when the question came up on Monday, narrowly defeated Caldwell's motion by a vote of 33 to 32.[26]

Most antidivisionists, however, unlike Caldwell, were not yet ready for a vote on Newcomb's resolution, and they continued to filibuster. That evening the divisionists again held a strategy session; the next evening the antidivisionists did likewise. The divisionists appeared to be losing ground.[27] The excitement and interest over the subject, one observer wrote, was reminiscent of the secession days of 1861. The antidivisionists, he continued, seemed to be making headway with their argument that they had been authorized only to make a constitution for the state and with the charge that the divisionists were no less rebels and revolutionists than the secessionists. Furthermore, the antidivisionists felt that General Edward R. S. Canby, the new military commander in Texas, who had reached Austin on the preceding Sunday, would direct the convention to complete the constitution.[28]

Except for December 25 through December 27, when the convention took out for Christmas, the filibuster continued for another week. Finally, on Tuesday, December 29, Newcomb got the floor. The people of the west, he claimed, felt that they were ready for reconstruction. To delay statehood for them simply because the rest of the state was disloyal and rebellious did not seem fair. Division was the best solution and the shortest way to peace and order. A territorial government was the only other suitable arrangement.[29] When he finished and time came to vote, a call of the house failed; the antidivisionists had given up the fight. The convention then voted 37 to 28 to rescind the Thomas resolution. President Davis refused to sustain a point of order that the repeal of a previously adopted ordinance required a two-thirds-majority vote.[30]

[26] *Texas Convention Journal*, 1868–1869, 2 Sess., pp. 95, 98; *Dallas Herald*, December 23, 1868, and January 2, 1869.

[27] *Dallas Herald* (dateline, Austin, December 21, 22, and 23, 1868), January 2, 1869.

[28] *Galveston News*, December 23, 1868; Ronald N. Gray, "The Abortive State of West Texas" (Master's thesis, Texas Tech University, 1969), p. 49; *Dallas Herald* (dateline, Austin, December 22 and December 23, 1868), January 2, 1869.

[29] *Daily Austin Republican*, January 2, 1869.

[30] *Texas Convention Journal*, 1868–1869, 2 Sess., pp. 147–148; *Dallas Herald* (dateline, Austin, December 29, 1868), January 9 and January 16,

With the Thomas resolution rescinded, the divisionists lost no time. On the next day, L. D. Evans spoke in support of division. If the convention did not divide the state, he stated, then Congress "ought to be forced to do it."[31] He did not, however, explain how a Congress that had set aside presidential reconstruction and imposed its own plan could be forced to take such action. During the next morning's session, after Morgan Hamilton had condemned the "deplorable" lawless conditions in Texas and argued the need for the creation of a new western state, A. J. Hamilton denounced his brother and his state-making cohorts in a speech that editor Longley said "in true eloquence is unsurpassed" by any he had ever heard him make. Unlashing "withering invectives," Longley added, "he held up the secessionists . . . in their true character."[32]

Evans and A. J. Hamilton, at the time of their last speeches, may not have been aware of it, but some of the delegates—without any official authorization—had almost completed a constitution for a new western state. They had begun working on the document on the evening of December 16 in Morgan Hamilton's room in the Avenue Hotel.[33] There is no further information extant on its framing until Davis announced at the beginning of the new year that he and six other delegates were preparing a constitution for a State of West Texas to embrace the territory west of the Colorado River.[34] On Saturday

---

1869. In reporting the passage of the Newcomb resolution, editor Flake conjectured, incorrectly, that A. J. Hamilton ended the filibuster only after it appeared that any division ordinance would provide for ratification by the voters (*Dallas Herald*, January 16 [from *Flake's Daily Bulletin*, n.d.], 1869).

[31] *Dallas Herald* (dateline, Austin, December 30, 1868), January 16, 1869.

[32] *Daily Austin Republican*, January 2, 1869.

[33] Sandlin, "The Texas Convention of 1868–1869," p. 124; letter (unsigned), Palestine, Texas, to J. P. Newcomb, August 25, 1869, Newcomb Collection; *Dallas Herald* (dateline, Austin, December 17, 1868), January 2, 1869.

[34] The exact date of the announcement is elusive. On December 31 the *Daily Austin Republican* reported that seven delegates were planning to submit a petition to Congress for the creation of a new western state, leaving the impression that it was not aware that they were drafting a constitution. On Monday, January 4, 1869, editor Longley stated that "with profound regret we listened to the speech of General E. J. Davis on Friday last [January 1], in which he announced that he was engaged in the conspiracy of a little cabal of seven to frame a Constitution for that portion of the State west of the Colorado." The convention, however, did not meet on Friday, January 1. Either Longley (as well as Flake and some others) got the date wrong, or he

morning, January 2, after the convention had declared itself a committee of the whole for consideration of the report of the Committee on the Condition of the State, Davis spoke at great length. He unleashed a tirade against the conservatives and moderates and argued in favor of division. If the convention did not divide Texas, then Congress should do so. The Constitution of "West Texas," which would disfranchise enough people, he claimed, to ensure the loyalty of the new state, was being printed and would be submitted to the convention.[35] "Magnanimity to rebels," he declared, "was weakness or stupidity." Angrily he shouted, "They are not fit to govern, and they shall not again govern, so help me God!" They would pray to the legislature to change their name before they again would be allowed to hold offices, and they must "sit on the stool of probation" until they bore "fruits meet for repentance." He then turned his wrath on A. J. Hamilton for attempting to block division.[36]

In addition to Davis, the framers of the Constitution of the State of West Texas were Degener, Morgan Hamilton, Jacob Kuechler of Fredericksburg, Newcomb, sixty-eight-year-old W. M. Varnell of Victoria, who had been in the convention of 1866, and A. P. Jordan, also from south Texas. Of the twenty delegates from the proposed state of West Texas, only seven had a part in framing the constitution.[37]

On January 4, during a committee-of-the-whole consideration of the report on the condition of the state, Davis, to keep the support of the eastern divisionists, proposed, as a substitute for the majority report, that "Texas ought to be subdivided into states of more convenient size." Editor Longley was bewildered. "Who would have believed," he wrote, "that the junior member from Rusk [Webster Flanagan] would ever be found with Ruby sitting as his *vis-a-vis* in a beer saloon and with glasses raised, receiving the benedictions of the senior gentleman from Bexar [Degener] or carpetbag delegate from

heard Davis make the remark somewhere other than in the convention (*Daily Austin Republican*, January 4, 1869; *Flake's Daily Bulletin*, January 5, 1869).

[35] *Daily Herald* (San Antonio), January 8, 1869; E. J. Davis to James Newcomb, May 2, 1875, Newcomb Collection; *The Harrison Flag* (dateline, Austin, January 2, 1869), January 14, 1869.

[36] *Galveston News*, January 3, 1869; *Daily Herald*, January 8, 1869; *The Harrison Flag* (dateline, Austin, January 2, 1869), January 14, 1869.

[37] *Daily Austin Republican*, January 4, 1869; *Daily Herald*, January 8, 1869.

Titus [not identifiable; there was no carpetbag delegate from Titus County]—the stately, dignified bedfellow of the saddle-bagger [Morgan Hamilton] from Bastrop?"[38] Davis' proposal precipitated a long and bitter debate and another stalemate until Davis, almost three weeks later, again overrode the opposition by violating parliamentary rules. The debate began between the Hamilton brothers. Morgan Hamilton, it was reported, raved like a madman, accusing his brother of courting rebel favor. Jack countered by saying that Morgan was crazy and that he and the other framers of the constitution for a new western state were secessionists whose main object was the promotion of their own selfish interests.[39]

Former district judge B. W. Gray, representing Red River and Titus counties, Dr. Pleasant P. Adams, who represented Henderson and Anderson counties, L. D. Evans, and A. J. Evans spoke in favor of division. Gray argued that Congress had the power, even without consulting the people, to create as many as four additional states out of Texas. He favored allowing the people in the western area to organize a new state, for it would offer an asylum for the oppressed. Actually, he wanted Texas divided into three states with boundaries marked "by rivers that empty into the Gulf."[40]

Next morning, January 6, each delegate found a printed copy of the Constitution of the State of West Texas on his desk (see Appendix). L. D. Evans opened the debate with remarks in favor of the Davis substitute. The gist of his argument was that division would be a lawful and quick means of reconstruction. Newcomb then obtained

[38] *Daily Austin Republican*, January 5, 1869; *Texas Convention Journal, 1868–1869*, 2 Sess., p. 170. The remarks of delegates while the convention was acting as a committee of the whole were not published in the *Journal*.

The majority report of the Committee on the Condition of the State recommended that the convention appoint a delegation to visit Washington for the purpose of procuring legislation in the "interest of the loyal men of Texas." The two conservative members on the committee had dissented, and Newcomb had offered a minority report to the effect that the people west of the Colorado River had been loyal and should be allowed a separate state (*Texas Convention Journal, 1868–1869*, 2 Sess., pp. 107–110, 115, 116, 125–128).

[39] *Daily Herald*, January 5, 1869; *Daily Austin Republican*, January 8 and January 9, 1869.

[40] "Debates in the Convention, January 5, 1869," *Daily Austin Republican*, January 11, 1869; *Texas Convention Journal, 1868–1869*, 2 Sess., p. 222. Gray was badly confused. The Resolution of Annexation does not delegate to Congress the power to form additional states out of Texas; and, if the former Confederate states had reverted to territorial status, the legal status of Texas, never having been a territory, would have been uncertain.

the floor. He denied the charge that the framing of the constitution had been revolutionary but admitted that the document had been prepared without authorization. It had been drafted, he claimed, only after filibustering had blocked the possibility of division in the convention. Long before the convention first convened, he had informed Governor Pease and the commanding general in Texas of plans to divide the state.[41]

Edward "Baron" Degener spoke next. He was still of the opinion that the Brazos River should be the eastern boundary of West Texas. However, he said, Thaddeus Stevens favored the erection of a loyal German state on the Mexican frontier, and many Germans lived between the Colorado and Brazos rivers. Therefore, the Colorado River was the next best alternative. He then attempted to show that the State of West Texas could operate on a sound financial basis for less cost than the region could under a single Texas state government. The proposed state was "a trifle larger" than the remainder of Texas —96,100 square miles to 96,000 square miles. Thomas had estimated that the annual expenses for three states would be $500,000 for West Texas, $330,000 for East Texas, and $170,000 for Middle Texas. The amount for West Texas, Degener claimed, was grossly exaggerated. "We intend to govern our state," he said, "with something like $100,000 to $120,000. We . . . do not need quite as many officers . . . nor will our mileage run as high for legislative purposes." The assessment for 1867 in the proposed State of West Texas showed an income of $133,000. The public buildings in Texas had an estimated value of $2 million. West Texas' *pro rata* share of that would be $400,000, and "we do not want more for the erection of our public buildings. . . . If the territory out west is sold to the United States, say for $3,000,000, we believe we have a snug sum for education. . . ."

"You see, sir," Degener concluded, "that the State of Coyote or of Chaparral, as the Anti-Divisionists sneeringly call our western section, will manage to get along without calling for a loan . . ." and, he added, with a smaller tax assessment.[42]

[41] Degener's speech, January 6, 1869, *Daily Austin Republican*, January 9, 1869; L. D. Evans, *Speech of Hon. L. D. Evans on the Conditions of Texas, and the formation of new states*, delivered in the Constitutional Convention of Texas, on the 6th of January, 1869, pp. 22–28; *Daily Austin Republican*, January 9, 1869.

[42] *Daily Herald*, January 6, 1869; Degener's speech (January 6, 1869), *Daily Austin Republican*, January 9, 1869.

The editorial comment on Newcomb's and Degener's remarks generally was critical. The San Antonio *Daily Herald* replied that "Degener has shown that he does not know ABC's in American politics. Mr. Newcomb is too well known as an impudent upstart to need any description from us. . . ." The *Herald* blamed the two for arousing the ire of the Austin people who, in retaliation, were trying to have the Quartermaster Depot removed from San Antonio. To prevent this catastrophe, the paper asked its readers to pressure Degener and Newcomb to shelve all proposals for division.[43] It also disputed Degener's estimates of the cost of operating a State of West Texas. The state taxes in 1867 for the area west of the Colorado River, it stated, were $97,910.72; the total for the entire state was approximately $500,-000. If a new state were established, the estimated taxes for it would be $355,800 annually. Rather than being less, the taxes "will be nearly *four times more* than we pay at present."[44] The *Daily Austin Republican* charged that Degener's speech was "revolutionary indeed! If men in their leisure . . . prepared a constitution in a private room, which the entire body in the Capitol could not complete in four months. Revolutionary if they make the expense of a convention unnecessary for such a State, as they hope to erect with the assistance of Congress. . . ."[45]

When the time for consideration of the subject came on the following day, January 7, A. J. Hamilton, "the greatest man in the Convention," in a long, "great speech . . . tore to pieces all arguments for division" and urged the delegates to complete the constitution they had been elected to prepare. Contrary to Degener's claims, he pointed out, division would result in a tax increase and would delay the readmission of the state.[46]

After Hamilton's speech, editor Longley predicted that "today [8th] or tomorrow the Convention will, in all probability, rid itself of the Division quarrel and get to business." The Davis substitute would be defeated, and if so, the convention would proceed to frame a constitution for Texas, for neither the people of Texas nor Congress would "countenance a division of our territory, until we first erect a

43 *Daily Herald*, January 6, 1869.
44 Ibid., January 17, 1869.
45 *Daily Austin Republican*, January 9, 1869.
46 Ibid.; *Flake's Daily Bulletin*, January 11 and January 13, 1869; *Daily Austin Republican*, January 8, 1869; *Texas Convention Journal*, 1868–1869, 2 Sess., p. 232.

legal State Government."[47] Longley guessed wrong. The vote on the Davis substitute was not for another two weeks. The convention was doing absolutely nothing toward making a constitution, editor Flake reported, and Davis was attempting to harass the delegates into acquiescence to division.[48]

Meanwhile, the Constitution of the State of West Texas and its framers attracted considerable attention throughout the state. The constitution, thirty-five pages in length, revealed the names of no authors, no publisher, and no place or date of publication. Its preamble read: "We, the people of West Texas, acknowledging with gratitude the Grace of God in permitting us to make a choice of our form of Government, do ordain and establish this Constitution." The Bill of Rights, in addition to granting the normal Anglo-American guarantees, recognized the equality of all persons before the law, regardless of race, color, or previous condition of servitude. The constitution followed the normal Anglo-American pattern of providing for three branches of government—the legislative, judicial, and executive. The legislature was to consist of two houses, a Senate and a House of Representatives. The number of senators was limited to twenty-one, and the number of representatives to forty-two. There was nothing unusual in its composition or in its powers. In the judiciary, the judges of both the supreme and district courts were to be appointed by the governor; the supreme court justices were to hold offices for twelve years and the district judges for eight years. The appointive provision was obnoxious to the majority of Anglo Texans, who preferred to elect their judges for a short term. Most German Texans, on the other hand, having a tradition of bureaucracy, saw in it nothing seriously offensive. The justices of the peace, no fewer than five in each county, were to be elected. The judiciary article also violated Anglo-Saxon tradition by eliminating the grand jury system and by providing that in all jury trials only three-fourths (nine) of the jury votes were necessary for a verdict. The governor would hold office for a term of four years instead of the traditional two years but could hold office for no more than eight years of any twelve-year period.

The boundaries of West Texas commenced at a point in the Gulf of Mexico opposite the middle of the main channel of Pass Cavallo and ran up the middle of that channel and of Matagorda Bay to the

[47] *Daily Austin Republican*, January 8, 1869.
[48] *Flake's Daily Bulletin*, January 11, 1869.

8. State of West Texas, 1869. The proposed Constitution of the State of West Texas set different boundaries for division than earlier proposals had done.

mouth of the Colorado River, thence up the middle of that stream to the 32nd parallel (in northwestern Coke County, about fifteen miles northwest of the town of Robert Lee), thence along the 32nd parallel "to a point [blank] miles west," thence in a straight line to the junction of the Pecos River and the Rio Grande, thence down the main channel of the Rio Grande to the Gulf, and thence three miles from land to the place of beginning. The capital of the new state was to be at San Antonio until 1871, when it would be permanently located by the eligible voters.

The constitution contained several other unusual or controversial provisions. It prohibited the voter registration of any person who had voluntarily aided or abetted the "rebellion" against the United States in any manner, including editors of newspapers and ministers of the Gospel who had approved or aided it by writing, preaching, speaking, or publishing. It provided for a bureau of immigration and authorized the legislature to appropriate money to pay the expense, in part or in full, of immigrants from Europe. This proviso was especially desired by the westerners and strongly opposed by most easterners. The constitution also mandated the establishment of public free schools and compulsory attendance for at least four months each year. To support the schools, all monies derived from the sale of the public domain "shall be a perpetual fund" to be applied exclusively for the scholastic inhabitants of the new state.[49] Free, compulsory education was not a popular concept among many east Texas conservatives.

The press and public generally reacted with hostility. Even in the proposed capital and among some of the German communities, the proponents were unable to generate more than mild support. Editor Longley immediately denounced his former commanding officer and friend as "arrogant" and "obnoxious" for subordinating everything else to his plan for division and resorting to ways and means without historical precedent. "General Davis," he continued, "came to Austin with a hobby, which was the division of the State, and to the success of that measure, all else was made to yield." "Davis is a stubborn man" who "exhibited a sublime audacity."[50]

The most interest in the subject logically occurred in San Antonio, the proposed capital of the new state and the home of Degener, Newcomb, and the radical *Express*. The opposition was led by the con-

[49] *Constitution of the State of West Texas.*
[50] *Daily Austin Republican*, January 4, 1869.

servative *Daily Herald.* The editor of the *Herald* denounced the "wild and wicked attempt" to divide Texas. There probably were thousands of Texans, he continued, who would be willing to have division—if it was done at the proper time and in the proper manner—but "we venture the assertion that there are not twenty men in a single county (beyond those wishing fat offices) that favor the movement now going on in the Texas Convention." Degener, he asserted, supported the project because it would increase his chances of becoming a United States senator; the other leaders were likewise motivated by selfish considerations. "What an extreme folly it [division] would be when our State, through its miserable extravagance and misgovernment, is running deeper . . . into debt." [51]

The vehement denunciation of the division movement by the *Daily Herald* was due partially to the efforts of Newcomb and editor W. B. Moore of the rival *Express* to generate through public meetings greater interest and support—including financial support—for the establishment of the State of West Texas. On Thursday evening, January 7, responding to a call by the *Express,* about fifty citizens—including the mayor and, reportedly, ten antidivisionists—met in a casino in the Kampmann Building "to give aid and comfort to our delegates who are striving so earnestly to divide the State." The editor of the *Herald* dropped in "to see how the thing would be did." W. D. Gamble, county judge, presided; Peton Smythe, county clerk, was named secretary; and Moore served as master of ceremonies. Moore explained that he had learned from Newcomb that division undoubtedly would succeed, but the expenses of framing the constitution for the new state had been heavy and borne by only a few men. Consequently, if San Antonians wanted the capital, they must "plankup" a thousand dollars, "not to buy anybody" but to be used by the divisionists at their discretion. The divisionists intended to send a delegation to Washington to lobby their cause. If the convention failed to appropriate the necessary funds, they would be compelled to rely on private donations. Moore's proposal for a committee of three (a fourth person was later added) to raise the money carried. To start the contributions, Moore said he would deposit in a local bank one hundred dollars. To be able the next day to telegraph "our delegates" that the money was available, he urged nine others to make similar deposits.

[51] *Daily Herald,* January 3, 1869. Three days later, the *Daily Austin Republican* reprinted this editorial as an expression of its own views.

The original ten donors would have a *pro rata* share of their deposits refunded as the money was collected by the committee. When the amount promised reached five hundred and no other volunteers could be obtained, the city tax assessor promised the balance. (Either he had considerable faith that the committee would be successful or he was looking to the future with an unusual amount of optimism.) Before adjourning, the group voted to meet again the next Monday evening at the same place for a report by the finance committee.[52]

In the same issue, the *Daily Herald* expressed strong editorial opposition to the creation of a new western state. "Are the people so crazy as to think that Congress will encourage a revolutionary movement?" it asked and then proceeded to present an estimate of the cost for the "State of LaVaca." A convention would cost $200,000, and each state would pay not less than $1 million per annum in taxes compared to one-half of that amount currently being paid by the whole state. The *Express* men, it speculated, would get more than $40,000 in printing subsidies from the taxpayers.[53]

On Sunday, January 10, prior to the second "mass meeting," the *Daily Herald* published its major editorial on the Constitution of the State of West Texas. "It is the most vindictive, disfranchising, unjust, outrageous, visionary, detestable, wicked, unconstitutional, swindling, insurrectionary public document that ever emanated from a fevered brain; its effect will be to reward vice at the expense of virtue, offering a bounty to perjury and renegadism. [It was] prepared by seven revolutionists who ask Congress to establish it over a people not only opposed, but heartily disgusted with it."[54]

Apparently the *Herald*'s editorial inspired a Monday evening turnout of more opponents than supporters of division. After the meeting was called to order by Judge Gamble, the finance committee reported that it had deposited $1,000 in a local bank but only $670 had been collected. When the chair appointed only prodivisionists to a committee of five to draft resolutions expressing the sense of the meeting, "indignation was intense," and a new vote on division was demanded. The vote was "overwhelmingly" against division—55 to 32, ac-

[52] *Daily Herald*, January 9, 1869.

[53] Ibid.; *Flake's Daily Bulletin* (dateline, San Antonio, January 15, 1869), January 23 and January 24, 1869.

[54] *Daily Herald*, January 10, 1869. The editorial then denounced the "mass meeting" scheduled for the next evening.

cording to the *Daily Herald*, and 57 to 27, according to *Flake's Daily Bulletin*. Moore thereupon stated that he had announced twenty minutes before the door opened that there would be no meeting and that consequently many divisionists had left. He then proposed to adjourn until Wednesday evening; however, a motion to adjourn *sine die* carried "with a roaring cheer." The informant for the *Daily Austin Republican* felt that the divisionists had "most signally failed."[55]

The *San Antonio Express*, of course, defended the divisionists. The opposition, Moore claimed, consisted largely of "sore heads," who had been stirred up by the disfranchising clause in the proposed constitution and who had no more right to participate in public affairs than the "hosts of Satan to appear on the plains of paradise."[56]

When he learned of the San Antonio "mass meetings," Degener wired Moore to see if it was true that division was defeated. Moore wired back: "Called meeting a success. Raised $1,000. 60 or 70 present. No vote on division. Telegram is a rebel lie."[57] Technically, on the basis of the first resolution, Moore was correct, but on the basis of the second he was the greater prevaricator.

A few other small groups, all in the proposed western state, also favored the constitution and a State of West Texas. The convention received petitions from citizens of Bexar (despite the outcome of the "mass meeting"), Comal, Kendall, Starr, and Webb counties. The petitions, however, were not an accurate barometer of public opinion. Four of the counties were sparsely populated. In Bexar County the divisionists had been unsuccessful at the public meetings, and in Comal County the New Braunfels *Zeitung* spearheaded the opposition. On January 2, estimating that less than 10 percent of the population in the county favored division, the *Zeitung* called for a public meeting to consider the subject. A majority of those who attended opposed division.[58]

Most of the press, in east Texas and the nation, joined the San Antonio *Daily Herald* and the *Daily Austin Republican* in denouncing

---

[55] Ibid., January 13 and January 14, 1869; *Flake's Daily Bulletin*, January 23 and January 24, 1869; *Daily Austin Republican*, January 16, 1869.

[56] *San Antonio Express*, January 13, 1869.

[57] H. C. Logan to J. L. Haynes, January 11, 1869, E. Degener to Major Moore, January 12, 1869, W. D. Moore to E. Degener, January 12, 1869, all quoted in the *Daily Herald*, January 14, 1869.

[58] *Flake's Daily Bulletin*, December 29, 1869; *Dallas Herald*, January 23, 1869; *Daily Herald*, January 27, 1869.

"the Seven Wise Men" and their constitution. Editor Flake had strongly opposed the move from the first. When he learned that the document was being prepared, he wrote that "General Davis leads the secessionists in an effort to slough off from the State of Texas. . . . We cannot trust any man who pleads fealty to the federal government while working for secession." What Davis really wanted, he said, was offices and political gain. Flake later published two major editorials on the constitution and the "State of Coyote." "We are sorry to see such efforts made to create dissension . . . but when we see this document and hear the language of one of its authors upon the floor of the Convention, we are astonished that the treason avowed by the delegate was not at once made the cause of his expulsion from the body." The constitution, he stressed, was illegal, for its preparation was not within the jurisdiction of the convention and its framers had no authority to speak for the voters in the proposed western state.[59] To show its position, the *Dallas Herald* reprinted an editorial from the Austin *State Gazette*. These papers charged the architects of the newly proposed state with "flat rebellion" and "secession of the worst sort." The strongest advocates of states' rights and secession, they claimed, never considered it possible that the people of one part of the state would ever try to withdraw from the larger portion. "This is worse rebellion than anything of which the Southern States were guilty." The editor of the *Galveston News* on January 13 announced that he had received a copy of a "curious and somewhat rare pamphlet, purporting to be the Constitution of West Texas. . . . The whole thing is, in every respect, contemptible."[60]

The *Daily Herald* carried on its fight against division almost daily. The "seven delegates . . . offend Heaven and earth by proclaiming it [the constitution they prepared] as the work of 'We the people of West Texas'!" Since the proponents had decided against naming the new state for Lincoln (to avoid offending the conservative divisionists), the editor sarcastically suggested several appropriately descriptive names:

> The State of Lavaca (Cow State)
> The State of Sisterdale (in honor of our new lights)
> The State of Prickley-Pear (Cactaea)

[59] *Flake's Daily Bulletin*, January 5, 15, and 26, 1869.
[60] *Dallas Herald*, January 16 (from *State Gazette*, n.d.), February 13 (from *Galveston News*, January 15), 1869.

The State of Nueces (The State of Nuts)
The State of Cucola (Shepherd State)
The State of West-Texas (The State of Taxes)

Since no one of these names, nor "Tacata" (possibly a play on the word *Texas*), the preference of the *Express*, was likely to be acceptable, he preferred to keep the name of the great state of Texas and the Lone Star as the "brightest in the constellation of stars." More seriously, he continued, the erection of a new western state would destroy the possibility of getting the Southern Pacific Railroad. If built, on the other hand, this road, with its many branches, eventually would bring the people closer together and thereby destroy any desire for division. Furthermore, division would delay reconstruction and make necessary another convention, which would allow "the seven" to have "more pickings." [61] Then in a sarcastic, imaginary conversation, the editor had Davis, Degener, and Newcomb plot their respective political roles in the new state.

Mr. Degener—"Among friends we will . . . acknowledge that the principal reason why we want to divide is, that as long as we remain united with the balance of the State, short stock, like ourselves, will never succeed to go to Congress or become Governor or Judges of the Supreme Bench."

"Aye, Aye," responded Davis and Newcomb, "we understand each other perfectly. . . ."

"Yes," said Degener, "the Senatorial rank will become me. . . ."

"How I would like to be a member of the Lower House of Congress," wildly cried out Jimmy Lowdown.

"By Heaven, you shall both have what you want," exclaimed the Corpus Christian, "by the concoction I will prepare! And I shall be the first governor of West Texas, so we may start right, and when my four years have expired I shall be the Chief Justice of the State for life. But to succeed and protect my friends, we will abolish Grand Juries, that being the institution by which the rabble, the so-called honest man of the land, can bring the transgressors of the law to trial and we will delegate these powers to one of our own pets." [62]

Then again, in a later editorial, the *Herald* attacked the suffrage article in the proposed constitution. "No honest man in Western Texas who candidly wants to see civil law restored, and the wounds of war healed, can consent to division with such a constitution." Not

[61] *Daily Herald*, January 8, 12, and 16, 1869.
[62] Ibid., January 14 and January 19, 1869.

one white man of prosperity and education out of seventy-five, it continued, could vote or sit on a jury.[63]

The opposition press possibly helped sway public opinion by publishing a letter from Senator Henry Wilson, chairman of the Senate Committee on Military Affairs, to E. B. Turner, attorney general of Texas, dated January 4. "Concerning the project of dividing Texas," Wilson wrote, "I think you have no reason of apprehension on that score, for I hardly think there are twenty members of Congress who would look with favor upon the proposition."[64]

The *New York Times* was even less encouraging to the divisionists. It predicted that their opponents would "likely come off conquerors" through the direct intervention of General Grant, who had instructed General Canby to notify the convention that it had assembled to frame a constitution for the state, not to divide it. Also, the *Boston Post* reported, Grant had remarked that "one Texas was amply sufficient to have on hand for the present."[65]

[63] Ibid., January 17, 1869.
[64] Wilson's letter was in: *Flake's Daily Bulletin*, January 31, 1869; *Daily Austin Republican*, January 22, 1869; and *Dallas Herald*, January 30, 1869.
[65] *New York Times*, January 19, 1869; *Daily Austin Republican*, February 13 (from the Washington correspondent of the *Boston Post*, n.d.), 1869.

# ~(5)~

# THE COYOTES BREAK UP
# THE CONVENTION

.

Meanwhile, in the convention, the radical-divisionists were entirely insensitive to the mounting opposition to division and were increasingly determined to have their way. The first hurdle was to win over twenty-five-year-old James Russell Burnett, a former captain in the Confederate Army and a lawyer from Houston County, whose Committee on the Division of the State had reported already in favor of division into three states approximately in accordance with the Deaman Plan. Convincing Burnett required little more than a week. Burnett was in an awkward position, but he took the floor on January 11 to announce his acquiescence to the will of the "Coyotes." He still wanted Texas divided into three states, he stated, and he believed that to be the desire of a majority of the voters of Texas. Texas was too large to afford adequate protection to all its citizens, and the interests of the people were too diversified for unity. Although he preferred to have division on a "constitutional" basis, he would "bow to the will of the majority."[1]

During the evening session of the next day, the division issue became highly emotional. The delegates engaged in a six-hour, heated debate that continued until well past midnight. Erwin Wilson of Brazoria charged that a small group was determined to have division even though the convention in the first session had decided to the contrary. The convention had not been authorized to divide the state, he added, and there was no existing authority for such action. Furthermore, "the moment we divide the state, that moment we deal a death blow to the Republican party." The convention, acting as a committee of the whole, in spite of Wilson's objections, reported a resolution (proposed by E. J. Davis and hereafter referred to as the Davis substitute) that declared that Texas, due to its great size, conflicting in-

[1] *Daily Austin Republican*, January 13 and January 14, 1869.

terests, and disorganization, "ought to be subdivided into States of more convenient size" and that the convention through its commissioners would convey to Congress "a correct report" of conditions in the state and the sentiment of the convention.[2]

The resolution, after the normal filibuster tactics had been exhausted, came up for its second reading on January 16. The antidivisionists moved a call of the house, but to get a vote on the measure during the absence of some opponents Davis, in violation of the parliamentary rules, declared the house full, even though four delegates were absent without excuse. He also denied A. J. Hamilton's request to be allowed not to vote on the "unconstitutional" measure. Outraged at the action of the chair, A. M. Bryant of Grayson County resigned, and Hamilton and D. W. Cole of Hopkins County defied the ruling. Davis thereupon had Hamilton and Cole arrested, but he released them when they agreed to vote.[3] After rejecting Hamilton's move to adjourn for the day, the convention then passed to engrossment the division proposal by a vote of 38 to 33.[4]

Of the thirty-eight who voted for the Davis substitute (division), seven were the "revolutionist" framers of the Constitution of the State of West Texas, four were saddlebaggers, six were blacks, and twenty were proponents of *ab initio*. It was generally conceded that a majority of the nineteen absentees opposed division, including, certainly, Colbert Caldwell and Livingston Lindsay, who had both left to hold court; W. W. Mills, who had not yet arrived from El Paso; and A. L. Kirk of Erath County, who was ill. Three delegates (L. D. Evans, J. W. Flanagan, and Dr. Pleasant P. Adams of Henderson County) undoubtedly voted for division contrary to the wishes of the majority of their constituents. Editor Longley calculated that the vote of a full house would have been 39 for and 41 against. The *Advocate* speculated that "more than three-fourths of the constituents electing Adams are opposed to the division of Texas" and that, if the question of

[2] Ibid., January 14, 1869; Texas, *Journal of the Reconstruction Convention*, 1868–1869 (hereafter cited as *Texas Convention Journal*, 1868–1869), 2 Sess., pp. 267–268; *Flake's Daily Bulletin*, January 20, 1869.

[3] *Daily Austin Republican*, January 18, 1869. Bryant was reinstated after the vote was taken. Hamilton, anticipating Davis' refusal, hoped that it would influence some delegates to vote against the measure.

[4] *Texas Convention Journal*, 1868–1869, 2 Sess., pp. 267–268, 301–303; *Daily Austin Republican*, January 18, 1869.

division were presented separately, it would be voted down by "a majority unprecedented in the State."[5]

When the division resolution came up for final consideration on January 20, A. J. Hamilton's call of the house was sustained by sixteen votes. F. W. Sumner, an antidivisionist, and George H. Slaughter, a radical, were absent. Edward Degener then moved the expulsion of Sumner, but Hamilton argued correctly that no further business was in order because his call of the house had been sustained. Nevertheless, the convention voted 38 to 32 to expel Sumner, and Davis declared that the motion had carried. Thomas angrily challenged the ruling, pointing out that the vote was nine short of the two-thirds needed, but Davis replied that a simple majority was sufficient.[6]

In reporting the affair, "Fairplay," editor Flake's Austin correspondent, characterized Sumner as an "outspoken Unionist" and "a man of great firmness of character and moral habits," who during the Civil War had left Texas to serve the Union. Elected to the convention by a large majority, he had consistently taken a strong stand against division, an "unpardonable sin." Because he was in the way of their "pet scheme," Fairplay continued, the divisionists violated the rules and expelled an innocent member without trial.[7] Flake added the comment that Davis had resorted to "revolutionary" proceedings to divide the state but that his scheme would never be sanctioned by Congress. The *Dallas Herald* claimed that Sumner was no more at fault than Slaughter, but that Slaughter had not been expelled because he "was a divider."[8] The divisionists' use of a technicality to further their cause was unnecessary, for the convention then passed for final disposition the division article by a vote of 39 to 30.[9]

Upon learning that the convention had adopted the division article,

[5] *Daily Austin Republican*, January 18, February 18 (from *Advocate* [Trinity, Texas], February 3), 1869.
[6] *Texas Convention Journal*, 1868–1869, 2 Sess., pp. 323–326. Slaughter, who apparently had no better reason for his absence than Sumner, appeared in time to vote for the expulsion.
[7] *Flake's Daily Bulletin* (dateline, Austin, January 26, 1869), February 3, 1869.
[8] *Daily Austin Republican*, January 21 (from *Flake's Daily Bulletin*, n.d.), 1869; *Dallas Herald* (dateline, Austin, January 21, 1869), January 30, 1869. The *Herald* correspondent concluded that both delegates were absent for justifiable reasons.
[9] *Texas Convention Journal*, 1868–1869, 2 Sess., pp. 326–327.

the *Baltimore Gazette* charged the divisionists with promoting their own selfish ambitions and being derelict in their duty. In the *Gazette* reporter's view, every delegate who voted for division was an aspirant for office, "hence the necessity for triplicating all the machinery of a State Government, at a time, too, when the people of Texas are unable to bear the enormous taxation already upon them." The convention, it continued, was costing Texans $1,000 daily and in nearly one hundred days had accomplished nothing more than the passage of a resolution in favor of the division of the state.[10]

After the passage of the division ordinance, J. R. Scott, Lamar County justice of the peace, introduced a resolution to create a special committee. The committee, consisting of one delegate from each judicial district, would prepare an ordinance to define boundary lines that would divide Texas into three or more states, "as may be agreed upon," and to establish a fair and impartial division of the assets and liabilities. The resolution also provided that any action on division had to be ratified by both Congress and the voters of Texas. Since the adoption of the last proviso in all probability would have been tantamount to division's defeat, the divisionists gave the resolution no consideration.[11]

Davis then informed President-elect U. S. Grant that the convention, deeming it a convenient and logical time since there was no regular state government, had voted for the division of Texas. It was only a matter of time until Texas, "now a territory," would divide into states of more convenient size. The opposition to division, Davis stated, came largely from Austin and the "rebel" press with its Washington emissaries. He had the support, he claimed, of 90 percent of the "loyal" Texans, who had abandoned property and family to fight for the Union. He asked Grant to consider division favorably because it would demoralize the disloyal element and would give the peace and prosperity that the Unionists had struggled so long to secure.[12]

[10] *Flake's Daily Bulletin*, February 2 (from *Baltimore Gazette*, January 24), 1869. The *Gazette* underestimated the cost of the convention. In addition to the $100,000 for the first session, the convention during its second session appropriated more than $100,000 for its expenses (H. P. N. Gammel, comp., *The Laws of Texas, 1822–1897*, 6:50, 57–58, 121, 122, 123).

[11] *Texas Convention Journal*, 1868–1869, 2 Sess., pp. 338–339; *Flake's Daily Bulletin* (dateline, Austin, January 23, 1869), January 29, 1869.

[12] Letter from Edmund J. Davis to General U. S. Grant, January 28, 1869, in U.S. Congress, House, *Constitutional Convention of Texas. Letter from the Secretary of War*, 40 Cong., 3 sess., 1869, House Exec. Doc. 97, pp. 3–4.

Having finally settled the division question, the convention on January 22 began wrangling over the election of a delegation to lobby for division in Washington and over the amount of funds to appropriate for that delegation's use. It decided to elect two delegates-at-large and one from each of the four geographical regions. On the first ballot, Davis and J. W. Flanagan, with thirty-six votes each, were named at-large. As the district representatives, the convention elected G. W. Whitmore from the northern region, Burnett from the eastern, and Morgan Hamilton from the central. On the final ballot for the western member, W. M. Varnell received thirty-four votes, J. P. Newcomb twenty-four, F. A. Vaughan eight, and the "state treasurer" five. Davis refused to count the votes for "state treasurer" on the basis that no specific person was named. He then declared that Varnell, having received the necessary majority of the votes actually counted, had been elected. An observer for the *Harrison Flag* reported that it was understood that the votes for state treasurer were blank votes, and that Davis had "perpetuated one of his usual swindles." [13]

Ironically, Newcomb, one of the most diligent workers on behalf of division, was not elected because the moderates threw their support to Varnell. All six men elected favored division; three resided east of the Trinity River. Finally, on January 30, the convention approved $6,000 for the delegation. Upon learning who had been selected, editor Flake caustically commented that the $6,000 would "not be enough to liquor the committee." [14]

After the convention had named the Washington delegation on January 22, A. J. Hamilton presented a declaration, signed by thirty-two convention delegates, protesting the expulsion of Sumner. The convention quickly voted 35 to 34 to reject the declaration because, according to the *San Antonio Express*, it contained "epithets and incorrect statements." Instead, the members informed General Canby that Sumner had been expelled for misconduct. [15] The Sumner issue,

[13] *Texas Convention Journal*, 1868–1869, 2 Sess., pp. 343–345; *The Harrison Flag* (Marshall), February 11, 1869; *Flake's Daily Bulletin* (dateline, Austin, January 23, 1869), January 29, 1869; *Daily Austin Republican*, January 25, 1869; *Daily Herald* (San Antonio), January 29, 1869.

[14] *Texas Convention Journal*, 1868–1869, 2 Sess., pp. 424, 428; *Flake's Daily Bulletin*, February 4, 1869.

[15] *Texas Convention Journal*, 1868–1869, 2 Sess., pp. 330–331; *San Antonio Express*, January 23, 1869; *Flake's Daily Bulletin* (dateline, Austin, January

however, was not dead. Nathan Patten, a radical from Waco, sought and won approval for the appointment of a special committee of five to investigate and report on Sumner's conduct.[16] The committee had no measurable impact, for its report, signed by only three members and not made until the last full day of the convention, charged that Sumner—who claimed that his absence was accidental—had intentionally been absent to block a vote on the division ordinance. Regardless, the expulsion appeared to be in violation of parliamentary rules and a misuse of power. No action was taken on the committee report.[17]

Meanwhile, despite the efforts of the divisionists to the contrary, the convention was making some progress on the preparation of a constitution. Lindsay on December 29 and Sumner on January 8 attempted a return to the task for which the delegates had been elected, but it was not until January 12 that anything positive was accomplished.[18] On that date, B. W. Gray moved that a committee of eleven be appointed to revise, correct, and supplement the articles thus far adopted and to report a whole constitution with the least possible delay. The proposal was approved, and on the following day Davis named the members.[19] Thirteen days later, on Tuesday, January 26, the commit-

---

23, 1869), January 29, 1869; *Dallas Herald* (dateline, Austin, January 21 and January 22, 1869), January 30, 1869.

[16] Members of the committee were L. D. Evans, A. M. Bryant, W. H. Posey of Lavaca County, L. H. Wilson of Milam County, and Andrew Downing of Lampasas County.

[17] *Texas Convention Journal*, 1868–1869, 2 Sess., pp. 331, 346, 521–524. No provision had been made in the convention rules for expulsion, but Rule 71 states that "in all cases not provided for in the foregoing rules, *Jefferson's Manual* shall govern," and the *Manual* specified that two-thirds majority vote was required. The committee, however, contended that a simple majority vote prevailed "in all cases except where [the convention] had imposed on itself a contrary law" (Texas, *Rules of the Constitutional Convention*, 1868, p. 14).

[18] *Texas Convention Journal*, 1868–1869, 2 Sess., pp. 144–147, 235.

[19] Gray, Whitmore, W. F. Carter (of Ellis and Tarrant counties and a carpetbagger from Massachusetts), Anderson Buffington (of Grimes County, a veteran of the Santa Fe Expedition and the San Jacinto campaign), Newcomb, A. M. Bryant, C. W. Bryant, H. C. Pedigo (a former district judge from Tyler), Thomas Kealy (of Collin and Denton counties), James P. Butler (of Walker County), and A. T. Monroe. None of these men except Gray and Pedigo had any legal training, and only two of them, Gray and A. M. Bryant, could be truly classified as moderates (ibid., pp. 255–256; Betty J. Sandlin, "The Texas Reconstruction Convention of 1868–1869" [Ph.D. diss., Texas Tech University, 1970], pp. 195–196).

tee reported an almost completed constitution with very few changes in the articles that had been adopted in the first session.[20]

Having won approval of their division ordinance and named a pro-division delegation to Washington, the divisionists now determined to prevent the completion of the constitution. Perhaps, they reasoned, this could be done by adjourning the convention. To this end, Nathan Patten moved adjournment until February 1, subject to being reassembled by the commanding general or by a majority of the commissioners sent to Washington. J. W. Thomas, who had worked consistently to limit the convention to its authorized task, however, countered with a substitute motion that "no other business shall be in order other than the formation of a constitution until the same shall have been completed." After Degener's failure to have it tabled, the Thomas resolution was adopted by a vote of 34 to 25.[21] Thus, the convention, after wasting almost two months on extraneous matters, returned to the position it had taken more than five months previously. In his editorial the next morning, editor Longley remarked that the convention would devote the remainder of the session to the framing of a constitution "for the *whole* State, 'Coyote' included," and wondered what would be the reaction in Washington when the majority arrived with a constitution for the whole state and the minority with one for a new state.[22]

For several days the moderates were in control. Starting where it had left off in August, the convention began consideration of the constitution section by section and clause by clause. On Saturday, January 30, Longley jubilantly reported that it "is working lively now on the Constitution . . ." and, two days later, he announced that "the Constitution is nearly completed."[23] The most bitter contest during that interval, as might well be expected, was over the suffrage article. After

20 *Texas Convention Journal*, 1868–1869, 2 Sess., pp. 382, 384–388; Sandlin, "The Texas Convention of 1868–1869," p. 196. A minority report by Gray, A. M. Bryant, Buffington, and Kealy recommended two significant changes: leaving the details of creating a public school system to the legislature and enfranchising all adult males.

21 *Texas Convention Journal*, 1868–1869, 2 Sess., p. 379; also quoted in *Daily Herald*, January 31, 1869. Degener, Morgan Hamilton, and Newcomb were among those voting "nay" on the substitute.

22 *Daily Austin Republican*, January 27, 1869.

23 Sandlin, "The Texas Convention of 1868–1869," p. 196; *Daily Austin Republican*, January 30 and February 1, 1869.

delaying consideration of this controversial subject as long as possible, by a vote of 59 to 6 the convention defeated a substitute offered by Democrat James T. Armstrong to grant suffrage only to white men, and on February 3 it granted universal manhood suffrage. The preliminary draft of the entire constitution was then adopted and sent to the engrossing committee to be written in final form, but two days later the radicals succeeded in getting a partial disfranchisement article incorporated.[24]

Except for division and the commission to Washington, the radicals had lost every major controversial issue. They had failed to get the convention to divide into two or three groups and prepare constitutions for respective separate states; they had been defeated on *ab initio*; they had lost their fight to disfranchise enough former Confederates to guarantee Davis' declaration that the "rebels are not fit to govern, and they shall not again govern, so help me God!" and they had been unable to defeat the motion to have a final draft of the constitution prepared. Their best recourse, it seemed, would be to adjourn the convention before the constitution in its final draft could be returned to the floor and to transfer their fight for division to the nation's capital. Perhaps Congress and incoming President Grant would favor division and support Davis' pledge that the East Texas "rebels" would be required to "sit on the stool of probation until they brought forth fruits meet for repentance." To this end, Patten moved to adjourn *sine die*, but the majority of delegates preferred a declaration, as amended by Andrew McCormick, that provided for the submission of the constitution on July 1 to the registered voters for rejection or ratification and, assuming ratification, for the election of state officials.[25] The radical-divisionists, however, refused to concede to the will of the majority (charging that "Big Drunk"—A. J. Hamilton—and his backers had joined the rebels); somehow, some way, they would break up the convention.

Already in session far too long, the convention was petering out. Some of the original members had died; some had resigned; some had left without resigning; some had been expelled; and others were disgusted and ready to quit without a constitution. Pent-up emotions had reached the breaking point. During the debates on lawlessness, L. D.

[24] *Texas Convention Journal*, 1868–1869, 2 Sess., pp. 394–406, 412–416, 482–484, 512–528.
[25] Ibid., pp. 499–501, 506–510.

Evans had charged that there was more crime in Austin than in Jefferson. To that crime, the members of the convention had contributed more than their share. The spirit of violence became apparent even in the first session, not long after the convention convened. Several weeks before the recess, a number of delegates, unable to control their tempers, were involved in physical confrontations. On July 11 Newcomb and S. M. Johnson of Calhoun County resorted to a fistfight to settle a "personal difficulty." "Jimmy Lowdown" came out the winner; the convention did not consider the fracas worthy of an investigation.[26]

As the summer temperature climbed, so did tempers. The two carpetbag delegates from Galveston, G. T. Ruby and Dr. Robert K. Smith, on August 3 fought on the floor of the convention until stopped by the sergeant-at-arms. On the same day, sixty-four-year-old A. A. Bledsoe of Dallas flogged with his walking cane Arvin Wright of Ellis County, at sixty-nine the oldest delegate in the convention. Wright suffered a black eye, a lump on the head, and blows to the body after revealing that Bledsoe had a personal stake in a certain railroad he wanted chartered. Three days later, black delegate Wiley Johnson, of Harrison and Panola counties, got thrashed in a fistfight for calling black delegate Ralph Long, from Limestone County, a rebel. Both men were placed under arrest, and a committee was appointed to report on the incident, but, since the fight occurred outside the convention hall, they were released.[27] In mid-August, when W. H. Mullins made a minority report from the Committee on Lawlessness and Crime, M. H. Godkin, a carpetbag justice of the peace in Polk County, accused Mullins of being the leader of a "murderous gang." Mullins suggested that they settle their differences in the hall, but the hotheaded Godkin assaulted Mullins at his desk where the carpetbagger was forced to "eat so much dirt" that he withdrew his remark.[28]

During the recess several delegates were involved in conduct unbefitting the dignity expected of men chosen to frame a constitution. The violent deaths of George W. Smith at Jefferson and of Mullins have been mentioned already. Delegates C. E. Coleman, a carpetbag adventurer representing Harrison County, and H. H. Foster, of Colorado County, apparently left the state (at least their whereabouts were

[26] Ibid., p. 269; *Galveston News,* July 12 and July 18, 1868.
[27] *Galveston News,* August 7, 1868; Texas, *Journal of the Reconstruction Convention,* 1868, 1 Sess., pp. 681, 687–688.
[28] *Galveston News,* August 12, 1868.

unknown to their respective constituents). The committee that investigated their absence reported that "evidence not proper to embody in this report" indicated that the two would not return to the convention.[29] H. B. (Harry) Taylor, the second assistant secretary of the convention, during the recess fled to Ohio after being indicted for swindling by a Travis County grand jury.[30]

The feud between Ruby and Robert K. Smith did not end with their fight on August 3. A few days later Ruby, on the floor of the convention, charged Smith with remarks that were "wilfully false and malicious." Smith retaliated on August 18 in a personal-privilege speech that was highly inappropriate and venomous. The "source [Ruby] from which the insult emanated is so foul and unclean," Smith ranted, "that to touch such filth I would be befouled, especially, sir, when the insulter bears upon his brow the evidence of a violation of God's law. The offspring of a Jew, begotten by the body of a Negress . . . is a fraud upon the race he pretends to represent."[31] Editor Longley regretted that such remarks would be made in the convention and defended Ruby, who was "not responsible for his color, only his behavior and talents with which he is endowed." Ruby, who, he continued, had conducted himself with decorum, "is a gentleman of education, sober, quiet in his demeanor, and attentive to his duties."[32]

The feud between the two erupted again at a meeting of the Republican Association at the Colored Methodist Church in Galveston. During the meeting, Ruby claimed that a few days before he had been maligned by Dr. Smith, who had been disgracefully drunk at the time. Smith's assertion against him was a lie, he continued, and he felt obligated to vindicate his honor. At the door, after the meeting, Ruby apparently struck Smith, who pulled his pistol, but the alert chief of police snatched it before Smith could fire.[33]

During the second session of the convention scarcely a day passed without some delegate's being involved in unbecoming conduct. The most notable and deplorable case was that of black delegate C. W. Bryant, a minister from Harris County. On Saturday evening, January

[29] "The Convention" (dateline, January 15, 1869), *Daily Austin Republican*, January 18, 1869. Apparently they had left the state to avoid arrest.
[30] *Texas Convention Journal*, 1868–1869, 2 Sess., p. 4; *Daily Austin Republican*, March 16, 1869.
[31] *Daily Austin Republican*, August 29, 1868.
[32] Ibid.
[33] Ibid., September 12 (from *Flake's Daily Bulletin*, n.d.), 1868.

23, Bryant was arrested, charged with the rape of an eleven-year-old black girl, and jailed.[34] An Austin press correspondent reported that Davis, Morgan Hamilton, and Degener "made a terrible howl" when their great chaplain and leader was arrested on the affidavit of the child's mother. "Bryant is awful on praying and voting against 'the poor white trash,' and hence all the worshippers of the ebony idol are loud in their expressions of sympathy for the sufferings which Jack Hamilton and party have thrust upon him on account of his purity and great ability which they envy. I say emphatically, that he is guilty of the charge, to the extent of taking advantage of his Christian's position for the purpose of destroying one of his young lambs." Bryant's friends, the reporter continued, were attempting to raise money for the earthly salvation of the transgressing minister of the gospel. "I know that a radical judge has postponed the hearing from this evening until tomorrow evening—no legal reason—, possibly to allow the villain's friends an opportunity to compound the felony."[35]

Bryant's guilt was unquestionable, but, because his vote was needed, the Davis faction was reluctant to let him be expelled. According to black S. P. (Scipio) McKee, the convention's assistant doorkeeper, during the investigation Ruby and Newcomb unsuccessfully attempted to prevail upon the family of the victim to hush up the matter. After waiting for a week, the judge bound Bryant over to the next term of court.[36] Finally, after a bitter fight led by A. M. Bryant of Sherman, who on Sunday morning, January 31, "whipped" Smith of Galveston during an argument over the matter, the convention expelled C. W. Bryant by a vote of 33 to 30.[37]

The Bryant affair led to other bad situations. During the debate on it, James P. Butler, a carpetbag Huntsville prison warden and Freedmen's Bureau worker, unsuccessfully attempted to get Judge Caldwell expelled. Caldwell, he charged, while attending a party in Houston, had asked for a girl and a bed. He wanted to amend the Bryant reso-

[34] *Daily Austin Republican*, February 1, 1869; *Daily Herald*, January 29, 1869; *Dallas Herald* (dateline, January 26, 1869), February 6, 1869.

[35] *The Harrison Flag* (dateline, Austin, January 25, 1869), February 11, 1869.

[36] Ibid.; undated letter from S. P. (Scipio) McKee, *Daily Austin Republican*, February 16, 1869; *Dallas Herald*, February 13, 1869.

[37] *Daily Austin Republican*, February 3, 1869; *Daily Herald*, February 7, 1869; *Dallas Herald*, February 13 and February 20, 1869; *Texas Convention Journal*, 1868–1869, 2 Sess., p. 463.

lution to include Caldwell, on the basis of alleged "conduct unbecoming a gentleman."[38]

Another incident occurred at the courthouse on Monday evening, January 25, during the examining hearing of Bryant. Ralph Long, a black delegate representing Limestone, Navarro, and Hill counties, became "familiar" with Sumner. Sumner told him to behave himself in rather plain language, a witness reported, "whereupon the Hon. Long attempted to shoot Sumner. Two deputy sheriffs [grabbed] the copper colored delegate. Then Ruby, backed by a few other negroes, bustled up, but were informed that unless they behaved themselves they would smell something, and they behaved, leaving Long to his sad fate of going into the dungeon of the county jail, where he remained about two hours."[39]

Then, on Monday morning, February 1, while on his way to the capitol, Scipio McKee displayed his anger toward Ruby. According to McKee, Ruby had twice tried to have him replaced as assistant door-keeper with one of his own favorites, once for being an hour late because he had been detained at county court and again, during the consideration of the rape case, because "I remarked that it was a scandal to the Convention to have such a man remain a delegate." After Ruby asked Davis if the doorkeeper had any right to discuss the business of the members, "the President ordered me 'to shut my mouth.' I had only spoken outside the hall. On the next Monday I met Ruby. I gently doubled him up in the gutter and administered a mild chastisement to his person. As soon as I released him, he rushed off to the Capitol and whiningly reported me, and falsely charged an Austin conspiracy. 'Little Jimmy' went out of his way to attack me while defending Bryant; he claimed that the 'Austin Ring' prosecuted Bryant and connected me with it."[40]

Ruby wanted the convention to expel McKee, and the matter was referred to a committee—which also was to inquire into the fight between A. M. Bryant and Smith. The committee quickly reported that the attack on Ruby was indeed "without provocation" and recom-

---

[38] *San Antonio Express*, February 19, 1869; *Texas Convention Journal*, 1868–1869, 2 Sess., pp. 398–399, 441–444, 445, 459, 462–463.
[39] *The Harrison Flag* (dateline, Austin, January 25, 1869), February 11, 1869.
[40] Undated letter from S. P. (Scipio) McKee, *Daily Austin Republican*, February 16, 1869.

mended that McKee be dismissed. During the ensuing debate, Ruby charged that McKee had been put up to the "infamous crime" by the "Austin ring." When A. J. Hamilton denied involvement, brother Morgan called him a liar and accused him of causing this and some of the other fights in an effort to break up the convention because he had been beaten on division.[41]

On the same day that McKee whipped Ruby, Secretary W. V. Tunstall and President Davis became involved in a heated argument. The secretary presented a bill for copying the journal in excess of what Davis deemed reasonable, and Davis refused to approve it. Tunstall retaliated by refusing to sign Davis' per diem warrant. Davis thereupon asked the convention to dismiss the secretary, but instead it referred the controversy to the committee that investigated the Bryant-Smith and McKee-Ruby scraps. In the end, the convention refused to dismiss Tunstall, but it did adopt the committee's recommendation that the remuneration be less than requested and that Tunstall apologize to Davis.[42]

Longley editorialized that Davis "finds trouble closing in on him thick and fast." A reporter made a rather satiric comment about the convention's problem of maintaining law and order among its own membership: "As I started to the Capitol this evening," he wrote, "one waggish friend told me that the Convention did not assemble there. To my inquiry he replied that so many delegates were in jail that the Convention found it necessary to hold its sessions in the Courthouse nearby in order to have a quorum. Farther on, I asked another if the Convention had a quorum. He replied: 'I have not been up there for some time. If there are no more of them in jail than a short time ago, there is a quorum. The only way to know is to go up and count them.' "[43]

In the same story the reporter added, in a more serious vein, a pertinent commentary on the convention personnel and on traditional American ideology. "Could the history of this convention be written and believed, all readers of it would be astonished at the audacity and

[41] *Flake's Daily Bulletin* (dateline, Austin, February 1, 1869), February 2, 1869. The quotations are from McKee's letter in *Daily Austin Republican*, February 16, 1869.

[42] *Texas Convention Journal*, 1868–1869, 2 Sess., pp. 445, 460–462; *Daily Austin Republican*, February 3, 1869.

[43] *Daily Austin Republican*, February 3, 1869; *The Harrison Flag* (dateline, Austin, January 25, 1869), February 11, 1869.

impudence of mankind." American politics, in former days, he continued, had taught Americans to look upon the constitution as something sacred, and those who had the "proud privilege" of making a constitution "were considered as not only favored, but as possessing, in the highest degree the dignity and talent of man. . . . The wild wave of radicalism has the honor of destruction [of this ideal]. We have a constitutional convention composed of negroes and the balance of mankind."[44] Even the conservative Bonham *Texas News* had appealed already to General Canby "to disperse this mob. This loathsome, pilfering assembly continues to rant away for months, without accomplishing anything whatever, save the bankruptcy of the State Treasury and the disgrace of her people!"[45]

Without waiting for the interference of General Canby, Davis and his faithful cohorts engineered the final breakup of the convention on Friday, February 5. That morning the convention took under consideration the printing contract for the journal and the constitution. When it appeared that the *Daily Austin Republican*, the organ of the moderate Republicans, would be selected, Davis without a motion declared the convention adjourned until the usual hour that evening. At the evening session, according to the *Daily Austin Republican*, only "four or five" of his most loyal supporters were present.[46] During the afternoon the divisionists had conspired, their opponents claimed, to break up the convention for lack of a quorum. Nevertheless, a quorum of one was on hand, and Davis opened the meeting with an announcement that the *San Antonio Express* would print both the journal and the constitution in its final form. A. J. Hamilton and then Mills, who had arrived earlier in the week, vigorously protested. When the young customs agent spoke in terms regarded as inappropriate, Davis ordered his arrest. A. J. Hamilton protested that his soon-to-be son-in-law had a right to explain his conduct,[47] but Davis disregarded him and "poured the long pent up passions of his heart" upon Mills.[48] A motion to release Mills was made. Since the Hamilton-Mills group was in a majority, Davis was in a predicament. To break a quorum, New-

[44] *The Harrison Flag* (dateline, Austin, January 25, 1869), February 11, 1869.

[45] *Daily Austin Republican*, February 5 (from *Texas News* [Bonham], n.d.), 1869.

[46] *Daily Austin Republican*, February 8, 1869.

[47] *Texas Convention Journal*, 1868–1869, 2 Sess., pp. 527–528.

[48] *Daily Austin Republican*, February 9, 1869.

comb and Ruby, apparently at Davis' suggestion, tendered their resignations. A. J. Hamilton then argued that a quorum should be the majority of the number entitled to a seat in the convention rather than of the ninety. Davis, refusing to recognize Hamilton, declared that, for lack of a quorum, the convention was adjourned until the usual hour the next morning. Davis then started to leave the hall.[49]

Before Davis reached the door, the Hamilton forces made M. L. Armstrong of Lamar County president pro tem. Davis was taken into custody by the sergeant-at-arms and forced to remain in the hall. "Hamilton, 'the blow-gun,' being as usual drunk," according to A. J. Bennett, the assistant secretary, "said tha—— hic ——— . . . it was a good time to get through the bill on stealage, ——— hic, the printing bill." When the house was reported "full ——— of fools, the gentleman from Austin commenced an incoherent speech!"[50] Hamilton spoke for almost two hours, indulging in "vehement denunciation and personal abuse . . . for 15 minutes to the satisfaction of the delegates from Austin, and the disgust of the other delegates." When he relinquished the floor, he moved adjournment until 10:00 A.M. the next day.[51]

Next day, at the appointed time, the thirty-five Hamilton-Armstrong, proconstitution, antidivision delegates, holding that they constituted a majority of those who still were entitled to a seat, declared that the convention had a quorum. A messenger was sent to ask Davis to come to the hall and officially adjourn *sine die* the convention. Davis refused. The convention then designated Armstrong as president pro tem, named a committee to consult with General Canby in regard to the printing job (the "stealing proposition," according to Bennett) and the closing of the convention, and recessed until one o'clock.[52]

---

[49] Ibid., February 8, 9, and 10, 1869. In his official report, General Canby inferred that Davis had adjourned the convention to preserve order (letter from Edward R. S. Canby to Headquarters of the Army, February 11, 1869, in U.S. Congress, House, *Constitutional Convention of Texas. Letter from the Secretary of War*, 40 Cong., 3 sess., 1869, House Exec. Doc. No. 97, pp. 2–3).

[50] A. J. Bennett, Washington, D.C., to Newcomb, February 8 [*sic*], 1869, "Last Days Proceedings of the Reconstruction Convention," 10 pp., J. P. Newcomb Collection, Archives, Barker Texas History Center, University of Texas, Austin. Bennett was still in Austin on February 8.

[51] Ibid.; *Galveston News*, February 14, 1869.

[52] *Daily Austin Republican*, February 8 and February 10, 1869; *Galveston News*, February 14, 1869; Bennett, "Last Days Proceedings of the Reconstruction Convention," Newcomb Collection.

When the convention reconvened, thirty-six delegates answered the roll call. The first item of business was the report of the special committee sent to the commanding general. Canby, it reported, had advised them to go home. The delegates, however, determined to salvage the records and the constitution from Bennett, "a pliant tool of Davis," who had taken possession of them—including the engrossed declaration for the submission of the constitution to the voters. The convention (*junta* was the term preferred by the radicals) thereupon sent the sergeant-at-arms for the assistant secretary, who, when found, promised to report immediately with the records. Instead, he rushed to Canby's headquarters. When Bennett failed in due time to show, the convention again dispatched the sergeant-at-arms, this time with some aides ("some roughs," Bennett claimed), who soon returned with the errant secretary and the records. Given leave to state his case, Bennett defied the authority of the "Armstrong Convention" and stated that he was responsible only to General Canby—on what basis, he did not explain. Editor Longley commented, "That he acted under orders of his master [Davis] there is little doubt." Upon motion of A. J. Hamilton who, Bennett claimed, was again drunk, the convention by a unanimous vote dismissed Bennett from his job for contempt. It then named a committee of fifteen to take charge of the records and to deliver them to General Canby, heard the committee to investigate the Sumner affair report that the expulsion had been without trial and unwarranted, adopted a resolution to adjourn *sine die* at noon Monday, and then adjourned until 9:30 A.M. on that day.[53]

During the afternoon General Canby urged Davis to adjourn the convention in a decorous manner. Davis promised to do so and reportedly in the late afternoon issued a call for the convention to assemble that evening at the usual hour. At the appointed time he appeared with an officer of Canby's staff and had the roll called. According to Longley, only two delegates and three ex-delegates (probably C. W. Bryant, Newcomb, and Ruby) were present (Canby reported "only four or five"). Davis then, on the basis of Canby's request, directed Secretary

[53] Bennett, "Last Days Proceedings of the Reconstruction Convention," Newcomb Collection; *Daily Austin Republican*, February 8 and February 10, 1869; Canby to Headquarters, in House, *Constitutional Convention of Texas*, 40 Cong., 3 sess., 1869, House Exec. Doc. No. 97, pp. 2–3. The quotes about Bennett are from the *Daily Austin Republican*.

W. V. Tunstall to deliver the records to Canby and declared the convention adjourned *sine die.*[54]

The records were in unbelievable disorder. The Armstrong committee of fifteen had considerable difficulty in checking the material to see if it all was intact. Taking charge on Sunday, Canby appointed a commission, consisting of radical M. C. Hamilton, moderate James W. Thomas of Collin County, who had fought diligently throughout both sessions for a quick completion of the constitution, and Major C. R. Layton of Canby's own staff, to arrange the papers and prepare the engrossed constitution in its final form. According to Bennett, A. J. Hamilton, angered at Canby's action, "when drunk on yesterday [Sunday], swore that he would come into the hall this morning [Monday] and hold a session of his disfranchised Junta, and make a call of the House."[55]

When Hamilton and some of his supporters appeared at 10:00 A.M., on Monday, they were met at the door by "an exhibition of bayonets" in the hands of Canby's troopers and were informed that no more than five members of the convention would be permitted at any time to enter the hall. Thus foiled, they convened outside the chamber and adjourned *sine die*, as previously agreed, at noon. Sometime later in the day, Bennett wrote that "Old Call" Hamilton "has been *very* drunk ever since."[56]

Bennett defended Davis' action during the closing days of the con-

[54] Canby to Headquarters, in House, *Constitutional Convention of Texas,* 40 Cong., 3 sess., 1869, House Exec. Doc. No. 97, pp. 2–3; *Texas Convention Journal, 1868–1869,* 2 Sess., p. 529; *Daily Austin Republican,* February 8 and February 9, 1869.

[55] Canby to Headquarters, in House, *Constitutional Convention of Texas,* 40 Cong., 3 sess., 1869, House Exec. Doc. No. 97, pp. 2–3; Bennett, "Last Days Proceedings of the Reconstruction Convention," Newcomb Collection; William Lee Richter, "The Army in Texas during Reconstruction" (Ph.D. diss., Louisiana State University, 1970).

[56] Bennett, "Last Days Proceedings of the Reconstruction Convention," Newcomb Collection. There has been considerable argument as to the official date the convention adjourned—Saturday, February 6, or Monday, February 8. The question is academic, depending upon the interpretation of the number required for a quorum. The proconstitutionalists and antidivisionists, however, have in their favor a technicality that the convention adjourned on February 8. General Canby indirectly recognized this as the legal date by ordering that the delegates who remained until then be paid a per diem up to and including Monday (*Daily Austin Republican,* February 10, 1869).

vention by claiming that it saved the State of Texas "the ignomy [*sic*] of having fastened upon the Treasury, leeches of the [J. L.] Haynes order who would suck at it everlastingly."[57] A majority of the Texans, on the other hand, subscribed to the views expressed by the Marshall *Texas Republican* and the *Daily Austin Republican*. The first, contrary to its name, echoed the sentiments of many of east Texas Democrats: "Every good citizen of the state will rejoice to learn that the Austin Mongrel Convention has adjourned. A more villainous, depraved body of men never met within the bounds of a commonwealth for any ostensible purpose connected with governmental affairs. . . . [The delegates] outraged all decency, honesty, and self-respect, if they ever had any, and plotted at the state capital for months against the best interests of the country. . . ."[58] The feeling of the moderates, both Democrats and Republicans, was expressed quite accurately by editor Longley in the *Daily Austin Republican*: "General Davis has permitted himself to lose all sense of self-respect, to forget the gravity of the assemblage over which he presided, and to ignore the decency and decorum which were due to the Convention and for the cause for which they met. . . . He came with affection. He winds up a revolutionist." The constitution, Longley thought, would be approved by the voters; its few faults were due to a revolutionary faction. "The people of the state owe a debt to the noble band of thirty-five who stood so firmly by their interests. . . ."[59]

By February 15, the committee appointed by Canby to finish the work of the convention had "systematized and punctuated the whole constitution," and a few days later Longley announced that by order of General Canby he was printing 10,000 copies of it, post haste, in pamphlet form.[60] By then, however, a large number of both divisionists and antidivisionists were preparing to continue the battle over division in the national capital.

[57] Bennett, "Last Days Proceedings of the Reconstruction Convention," Newcomb Collection. J. L. Haynes, a former Union army officer under E. J. Davis, was the owner of the *Daily Austin Republican* and a supporter of A. J. Hamilton.

[58] James Curtis Armstrong, "The History of Harrison County, Texas, 1839–1880" (Master's thesis, University of Colorado, 1930), p. 202, quoted from *Texas Republican* (Marshall), February 19, 1869.

[59] *Daily Austin Republican*, February 8 and February 10, 1869.

[60] Ibid., February 15 and February 25, 1869.

# ⌐√6╭⌐

# THE DIVISIONISTS' FAILURE IN
# WASHINGTON

.

The adjournment of the convention did not terminate the bitter contest over division; the battleground merely shifted from Austin to Washington. Of the six official commissioners to Washington, five— E. J. Davis, J. W. Flanagan, Morgan Hamilton, George Whitmore, and William Varnell—favored division, contended that there was too much lawlessness in Texas to hold the election in July, and opposed the constitution they had helped to prepare. James Burnett, the sixth commissioner, agreed on wanting Texas divided into three states, but he approved the constitution and believed that a fair election could be held.

When the convention adjourned, the members of the commission went their respective ways. Davis left for Corpus Christi; Flanagan, after an unpleasantness with A. M. Bryant of Grayson, took the road to his farm near Henderson; Burnett rode eastward to Houston; Varnell headed for an unspecified port on the Gulf; Whitmore hastened to Tyler to avoid suspension as a registrar in bankruptcy cases; and the "amiable" Morgan Hamilton relaxed for a few days in Austin. Their only official meeting, according to the *Daily Austin Republican*, was to withdraw the $6,000 from the state treasury to defray their expenses.[1]

The official delegation was accompanied to Washington by a group of loyal supporters. This group, according to a partisan characterization by John L. Haynes (a former Union army officer under Davis, owner of the *Daily Austin Republican,* and chairman of the Republican party's state executive committee), included "philosophic" Edward Degener; James Newcomb, "the daddy of the bastard babies"; "rapist" C. W. Bryant; George Ruby, the "gem" and "immaculate martyr of virtue"; and A. J. Bennett, Davis' "yes-man." The last four should have been enough to destroy any influence the delegation might have,

[1] *Daily Austin Republican*, February 12, 1869; *Dallas Herald*, February 27, 1869.

Haynes continued, but their image suffered further when they were joined in Washington by indicted "swindler" Harry Taylor who had fled to Ohio. Haynes quipped that all the delegation lacked to make it complete was Jim Cassidy, the radical editor of the *Tyler Index*. Flake editorialized sarcastically:

> Lord! how delightful 'tis to see
> A whole assemblage worship thee,
> For each worships himself.[2]

On Tuesday evening, February 9, the day following the final adjournment of the convention, the third and largest San Antonio public meeting to consider division was held at the courthouse. The meeting, publicized by handbills, posters, and newspapers, in both English and German, was to obtain an expression of the opinion of the city and area residents on division. W. B. Knox was made chairman. Apparently very few divisionists attended. Alexander Rossy, an educated German Unionist, and Don Antonio Navarro, a longtime Texas patriot and one of the framers of the constitution of 1845, spoke against division. Samuel A. Maverick, who was also in the convention of 1845, could see no good reason for division, and the fourth speaker denounced the Constitution of the State of West Texas and its framers with withering sarcasm. No one spoke in favor of division.[3]

A resolution, drafted by a committee of seven, declared that the people of San Antonio did not consider the official commissioners to Washington qualified to represent the state fairly, since they had been "almost entirely taken from the most extreme men of the body." It further argued that the present was not favorable for the settlement of the question because the measure would retard, if it did not prevent, a proper reconstruction of the entire state. Furthermore, the resolution opposed setting the Colorado River as the eastern boundary of the proposed new state. It denounced the Constitution of the State of West Texas because it had been prepared without any authority, was anti-Republican in parts, and was in violation of Grant's admonition to "let us have peace." The statement repudiated the radical divisionists who would "seek to thrive on the misfortunes of the country" and recommended the ratification of the constitution prepared by the conven-

[2] *Daily Austin Republican*, March 16, 1869; *Daily Herald* (San Antonio), March 20, 1869; *Flake's Daily Bulletin*, March 28, 1869.
[3] *Daily Herald*, February 11, 1869.

tion. After adopting the resolutions, the assemblage then appointed Rossy to inform the national authorities of the "true condition" of the state and to protest against division at the Colorado River.[4]

Rossy was only one of several throughout the state who were either selected or decided upon their own initiative to go to Washington to lobby against division and for the constitution drafted by the convention. At 8:00 A.M. on February 10, a special stage pulled out of Austin for Brenham carrying a group of these "people's commissioners." The group consisted of Judge A. J. Hamilton and John L. Haynes of Austin, W. H. Fleming of Clarksville, Judge M. L. Armstrong of Paris, who had been the chairman of the convention during its last hectic hours, F. W. Sumner of Sherman, who had been expelled from the convention for missing a roll call, and W. H. Posey of Hallettsville, a carpetbagger. The unofficial delegation was to be joined en route by A. P. McCormick of Brazoria, Julius Schuetze of Bastrop, who in the convention had been chairman of the Committee on Education, Dr. R. N. Lane, collector of internal revenue for the Austin district, and Judge James H. Bell of Austin.[5] Altogether, a total of about fifty Texans went to Washington, a majority of whom were antidivisionists.[6]

Editor A. H. Longley was proud that Texas had such qualified men to represent her. A. J. Hamilton, he told his readers, was held in high

[4] A lengthy account of the meeting, including a copy of the resolution, was reported in ibid.

[5] *Daily Austin Republican*, February 11, 1869; *Daily Herald*, February 12 and March 20, 1869; "Delegates of the Constitutional Convention of 1868–1869," J. P. Newcomb Collection, Archives, Barker Texas History Center, University of Texas, Austin; *Daily Morning Chronicle* (Washington, D.C.), March 17, 1869.

[6] These also included Judge Donald Campbell of Jefferson, Governor Pease, Caldwell, George W. Paschal, G. H. Sweet ("Traveller," the correspondent for the San Antonio *Daily Herald*), C. T. Duval Harn of Navasota, Max Mobius, C. J. Stockbridge, L. E. Edwards, Dr. M. Boulds Baker of Houston, Judge B. O. Watrous, Dr. A. Krause, Dr. Levi Jones, Ben H. Epperson, W. E. Horne, A. P. Wiley, C. K. Hall of Galveston, Henry Himbler, James T. Kelher, A. F. Buffington, Jesse Stancel of Galveston, DeWitt C. Brown, the second assistant secretary of the convention, and "Morphis," the correspondent for the *Houston Telegraph* (*Daily Austin Republican*, February 13, 1869; *Daily Herald*, March 20, 1869; *Daily Morning Chronicle*, March 9 and March 17, 1869; *Flake's Daily Bulletin*, March 28, 1869). Flake, when naming the delegation, noted that Buffington, Sumner, and Brown "are a trio that run with the hares and hunt with the hounds, with both and in favor of none." Buffington, he continued, was the only person of the Texas delegations who did not want an office, and "we are not altogether sure of him."

esteem, particularly by President-elect Grant. Posey, a former Union soldier and a west Texan who opposed division, would attract the attention of the national officials and would be an "eye-sore" to Davis and Morgan Hamilton, who claimed that all Unionists west of the Colorado River favored division. Haynes, he felt, would be extremely influential because he had been the prime organizer of the Republican party in Texas and was the chairman of its state executive committee.[7] Rossy, who delayed his departure until the local finance committee had raised some expense money, started on February 19, with the "good wishes and ardent hopes of a great majority of our property holders and loyal citizens that he may be instrumental in thwarting the wild, visionary and ruinous schemes for the dismemberment of Texas."[8]

Because of the heavy rains, the moderates from Austin did not arrive in Brenham until late on the fourteenth. At 3:00 P.M. the next day, A. J. Hamilton, in a long and captivating speech at the Brenham courthouse, stated that he favored the constitution as the best that could be made, though not the best possible. He ridiculed Newcomb unmercifully and emphasized that he did not want his children to mix with those of any other race.[9]

The "people's commissioners" reached Houston two days later and on February 22 arrived in New Orleans, where they overtook some of the divisionists, including Degener and Varnell. Some of the Texans left by train the next day for Washington, but the others delayed their departure for a day or more. The *Daily Herald*'s "Traveller" (G. H. Sweet), in company with Bell, Harn, Rossy, Davis, and Robert K. Smith, traveled from New Orleans to Washington, a distance of 1,255 miles, in seventy-two hours. Bennett reached Washington on February 24 with instructions to make accommodations and to speak for the official delegation until it arrived. One group reached Washington three days later, two groups arrived on March 2, and other Texans continued to drift in for the next two weeks.[10]

The Texans encountered some difficulty in finding suitable lodging,

[7] *Daily Austin Republican*, February 11, 1869.

[8] *Daily Herald*, February 12 and February 21, 1869.

[9] *Daily Austin Republican*, February 19 and February 23, 1869.

[10] *Houston Times*, February 17, 1869; *Daily Austin Republican*, February 22, 1869; *Daily Herald* (dateline, Washington, March 8, 1869), March 19, 1869; *Daily Austin Republican*, March 3, 1869; James R. Burnett to Mark Miller, March 12, 1869, Texas, Executive Correspondence, Texas State Library, Austin; *Daily Morning Chronicle*, February 24 and March 4, 1869.

because there "are 500 delegations here" and an estimated 100,000 persons. Bennett joked that he had gone ahead to set up a grocery store with suitable retiring rooms for his group. He actually obtained rooms at the National Hotel. Varnell quipped that the official commissioners were placed on the first floor—from the roof—and informed the management that, if the hotel became any more crowded, he would get on the roof as an accommodation. "Old Morg" Hamilton complained vigorously. The delegation did not long remain at the National Hotel; Davis moved to 449 C Street, and the others found lodging at 389 Third Street. According to Haynes, the "people's commissioners" finally managed to obtain "tolerably comfortable" quarters—A. J. Hamilton at the Kirkwood House, one of the more desirable lodging places.[11]

The first reaction of the Washington *Daily Morning Chronicle* to the official commissioners was favorable. "Earnest and true Republicans," the commissioners, in the *Chronicle*'s view, wanted reconstruction upon the basis decided in the last presidential election, namely, "that loyalty shall govern what loyalty conquered."[12] The paper soon expressed a different opinion, however.

As soon as they arrived in Washington, the Texans began meeting with government officials. On March 1 some of the divisionists had an initial meeting with Grant, who only three days later would be president. G. W. Whitmore of Tyler, the vice president of the Union Leagues in Texas, acted as their spokesman.[13] Two days later the "people's commissioners" got off to what Haynes optimistically thought to be an "abundant success." After their presentation to Grant by General J. J. Reynolds, who had served a short time as military commander in Texas during Reconstruction, A. J. Hamilton, as the rump delegates' spokesman, told Grant that the constitution prepared by the convention was good and was acceptable to the people. Grant, seemingly quite satisfied, said that he would send Reynolds back to Texas.[14] Division,

[11] J. L. Haynes to A. H. Longley (March 4, 1869), *Daily Austin Republican*, March 16, 1869; *Daily Herald*, March 20, 1869; *Daily Morning Chronicle*, February 24, March 4, and March 8, 1869.

[12] *Daily Morning Chronicle*, March 4, 1869.

[13] *Daily Herald*, March 5 (from *San Antonio Express*, March 4), 1869.

[14] *Daily Austin Republican* (dateline, Washington, March 3, 1869), March 5, 1869. According to the *Dallas Herald* (dateline, Washington, March 3, 1869), March 13, 1869, those calling upon Grant included A. J. Hamilton, Haynes, Armstrong, Lane, Sumner, Stockbridge, Ira M. Camp, Edwards, Baker, and Stancel.

113

Haynes wrote the next day, "is a dead cock in the pit. You can rest in peace. It will not find a single advocate in Congress, and could not get twenty votes if the issue could be presented." If anyone besides Andy Johnson felt miserable in Washington on inauguration day, Haynes continued, it was the Coyote delegation. On that morning he had met Newcomb and Ruby on the avenue, locked arm in arm and protected from a drizzling shower by a partnership umbrella. "Only think of it," he quipped, "$6,000 and only one umbrella to two such important adjuncts of the delegation." [15]

The *Daily Morning Chronicle* felt that the Texans would be pleased with the return of Reynolds, a favorite with the "earnest men" because he was reported to have said that the dismemberment of Texas "would be folly." A. J. Hamilton, Governor E. M. Pease, Judge Bell, and Haynes had assured Grant that Texas was peaceful and that the "firm, wise guardianship" of Reynolds was necessary for her "thorough and quick redemption." [16] Little then did they realize that Reynolds' return to Texas would result in their own political extirpation.

The news that the divisionists had seen Grant was slow in reaching Austin, for on March 4 editor Longley asked if anyone knew what had happened to Ruby and the "rest of the Hebrew children." Four days later he reported that the telegraph had not brought a single word about the "nondescripts" who had gone to Washington to lobby for division. The "people's commissioners," on the other hand, he remarked, were being so remarkably successful that "the howling of the Coyotes" was no cause for alarm. [17]

The "howling of the Coyotes," however, was in fact being heard on Capitol Hill. During the evening of March 7, "Old Morg" Hamilton, Davis, and five other divisionists informed former Vice President Benjamin F. Wade that they intended to oppose the ratification of the proposed constitution of Texas and that A. J. Hamilton and a majority of the delegates in the Texas convention had gone over to the rebels. [18] They were aware, however, that they had a "hard road to travel." Wade was politically obligated to A. J. Hamilton for supporting his

---

[15] Haynes to Longley (March 4, 1869), *Daily Austin Republican*, March 16, 1869; *Dallas Herald* (dateline, Washington, March 3, 1869), March 13, 1869.

[16] *Daily Morning Chronicle*, March 8, 1869; *Dallas Herald*, March 27, 1869; *Daily Austin Republican* (dateline, Washington, March 2, 1869), March 4, 1869.

[17] *Daily Austin Republican*, March 4, 5, and 8, 1869.

[18] *Daily Herald* (dateline, Washington, March 8, 1869), March 14, 1869.

candidacy for vice president at the Chicago convention in 1868. Then, on March 9, President Grant, with whom they had gotten an interview through the courtesy of General Reynolds, repeated that in his opinion one Texas was enough. By March 11, "Traveller" felt that Flanagan and Varnell were inclined to "jine" the Hamiltonians.[19] There is no evidence that Flanagan ever had second thoughts as to the merits of the division of the state. However, on March 15 Varnell, one of the "seven wise men" who made the Coyote constitution and "one of the immortal six" official commissioners, wrote editor Longley that he was now anxious to support the proposed Texas constitution. He authorized Longley to sign his name to the document.[20]

The divisionists, however, refused to concede. On March 11, the convention's commissioners presented to both houses of Congress a memorial (known as the "Davis Memorial") "respecting conditions and the remedy" necessary to reconstruct Texas on a "loyal basis." Basically, the Davis Memorial described eastern Texas as deplorably lawless and disloyal and the newly framed constitution as failing to meet the requirements set forth in the Reconstruction Acts. The memorial's proposed remedy called for the postponement of the election on the constitution, congressional intervention, the immediate admission to the Union of the state west of the Colorado, and the retention of military rule over the area east of the Colorado River until its citizens had proved their loyalty. The memorial contained the complete report on lawlessness presented to the convention on June 30, 1868, which showed a total of 939 killed in the state in three years—429 freedmen and 470 whites. The memorial quoted General Reynolds' remark, made on December 4, 1868, that "the civil law east of the Trinity is almost a dead letter." In some counties, according to the memorial, "the civil officers are all, or a portion of them, members of the Ku Klux Klan." Free speech and a free press, it continued, had never existed in Texas. Civil courts could not punish the outlaws, and freemen were kept from voting by threats of violence.

The memorial then denounced the moderates and the constitution prepared by the convention. Although drafted by Republicans (a con-

---

[19] *Daily Austin Republican*, March 16 and April 2, 1869; *Daily Herald* (dateline, Washington, March 11, 1869), March 23, 1869.

[20] Wm. M. Varnell to A. H. Longley (March 15, 1869), *Daily Austin Republican*, March 29, 1869. The constitution had been printed before Longley received the letter.

siderable number of whom did not adhere to party principles), the constitution provided no security to the loyal people of either color. It recognized the validity of rebel legislation (so far as not contrary to the Constitution or laws of the United States), thus putting legislation during the rebellion on the same footing as that of the most loyal states. The proposed constitution also destroyed the state school fund and enfranchised the rebel majority. Without federal interference—General Canby was not strong enough to assure a fair canvass of the voters—it would be adopted. Therefore, it should not be submitted for ratification.

The Davis Memorial had a solution. The military commander must order a postponement of the election until the national government had restored genuine peace and Congress had intervened to get a revision of the Constitution. Reconstruction could best be completed in accordance with the convention's resolution—that because the state was of such great size, had such diversified interests, and was plagued by lawlessness, it should be subdivided into three states in accordance with the (congressional) Beaman Plan. East Texas with 32,813 square miles had a population of 239,300; Middle Texas was 63,423 square miles and was the home of 242,448 people; and West Texas contained 96,628 square miles and 121,276 persons. Since there was a marked difference in the political attitudes of the people east and west of the Colorado River, West Texas could be entrusted at once with self-government. The remainder of Texas, however, should be kept for some time under the control of the national government. If Congress deemed it improper to permit the immediate organization of a state government for West Texas, Texas should be subdivided into three territories and each placed under a separate territorial or military government.[21]

The press was almost unanimously hostile toward the Davis Memorial. The Washington *Daily Morning Chronicle*, in a lengthy editorial, noted that the memorialists claimed that division would result in three

---

[21] "Memorial" to the Senate and House of Representatives of the United States, Washington, D.C., March 11, 1869, reprinted in *Flake's Daily Bulletin*, March 27 and March 31, 1869; *Daily Austin Republican*, March 31 and April 2, 1869. Burnett claimed that he neither signed nor authorized his name on the document, and he submitted a separate "Memorial" on March 18 (*Daily Morning Chronicle*, March 24, 1869; *Flake's Daily Bulletin*, March 27, 1869; J. L. Haynes to Major Longley, March 17, 1869, in *Daily Austin Republican*, March 30, 1869).

This building served as the State Capitol in Austin from 1853 to 1881. The Reconstruction Convention of 1868–1869 met here. Courtesy, Texas State Library

This view of Congress Avenue in Austin, 1867, shows, on the right, the Avenue Hotel, where the Constitution of the State of West Texas was drafted. Courtesy, Austin Public Library

Charles Colbert Caldwell, who opposed the division of Texas, was a leader of the moderate delegates in the 1868–1869 convention. Courtesy, Texas State Library

Edmund Jackson Davis, probably the most prominent radical in the 1868–1869 convention, masterminded the movement to establish the State of West Texas. Courtesy, Texas State Library

Andrew Jackson Hamilton, the dominating personality of the 1868–1869 convention, was the acknowledged leader of the moderates and of the fight against
division. Courtesy, Texas State Library

Morgan Calvin Hamilton opposed his more popular brother's stands; "Old Morg" was an outspoken prodivision radical. From Dudley G. Wooten, ed., *A Comprehensive History of Texas, 1685–1897*, 1898, 2:175.

James P. Newcomb, who worked strongly for division of the state, was the radicals' unofficial publicist and whip. Courtesy, Southwest Collection, Texas Tech University

# CONSTITUTION

OF THE

# STATE OF WEST TEXAS.

᥊᥊᥊

We, the people of West Texas, acknowledging with gratitude the grace of God in permitting us to make choice of our form of Government, do ordain and establish this Constitution:

## ARTICLE I.
### BILL OF RIGHTS.

That the general, great and essential principles of liberty and free government may be recognized and established, we declare:

SECTION 1. All political power is inherent in the people, and all free governments are founded on their authority, and instituted for their benefit; and the people of this State have at all times the unalienable right to alter or reform their form of government, in such manner as they may think expedient, subject to the Constitution and Laws of the United States.

SEC. 2. All freemen, when they form a social compact, have equal rights; and no man, or set of men, is entitled to exclusive separate public emoluments or privileges, but in consideration of public services.

SEC. 3. No religious test shall ever be required as a qualification to any office or public trust in this State.

SEC. 4. All men have a natural and indefeasible right to worship God according to the dictates of their own consciences; no man shall be compelled to attend, erect, or support any place of worship, or to maintain any ministry against his consent; no human authority ought, in any case whatever, to control or interfere with the rights of conscience in matters of religion; and no preference shall ever be given by law to any religious societies or

This is the first page of one of the few extant copies of the proposed Constitution of the State of West Texas. Courtesy, Texas Tech University Library

## Shall We Make It Five Flags?

### Why Not Form New Republic, Is Query

This cartoon from an unidentified newspaper clipping of April, 1921, reflected the interest in division of Texas at that time. From the Royston Campbell Crane Papers, 1916–1937, courtesy, Southwest Collection, Texas Tech University

"DON'T LEAVE THE OLD HOME, DAUGHTER!"

This antidivision cartoon expresses a sentiment common in many newspapers from the time of the earliest division proposals. From the *Austin American*, April 10, 1921

loyal states and in the election of loyal Congressmen. However, the editorial continued, Burnett, who had been chairman of the Committee on Conditions in the State, had emphatically stated that nearly every official report indicated an increasingly better feeling toward loyal men, that lawlessness was on the decline, and that, had there been a plebiscite, a large majority of the voters would have been against sending commissioners to Washington. The *Chronicle* felt that the official commissioners, except Burnett, were wedded to division rather than to reconstruction, and it challenged the assertion that an unsound whole could be cut into three sound parts. Division should be considered upon its merits, the editorial concluded, after the state government had been restored under the recently prepared "Republican, enlightened, and progressive" constitution.[22]

In two editorials, editor Longley denounced the Davis Memorial and its authors' claim to have authority to speak for a majority of Texans. The "delectable" document was "vulgar" in its style, "acrimonious" in its spirit, "villainous" in its objectives, and a "compound of falsehood and malice." In it could be seen the "lowdown" of Newcomb, the "bile" of Morgan Hamilton, the "virtue" of rapist Bryant, and the Germanic "philosophy" of Degener. The document's claim that division had been endorsed by the people in many public meetings was a "malicious falsehood." The aggregate attendance at divisionist meetings had not exceeded five hundred, and not more than fifty, Longley claimed, had expressed themselves in favor of the Colorado and Trinity boundaries.[23]

The presentation of the Davis Memorial, however, encouraged Congressman Fernando C. Beaman of Michigan to renew his efforts to have Texas divided. On March 16 Beaman offered two bills, drawn by "some gentleman" from Texas—HR 131 to divide Texas into three states (in accordance with his former proposal) and HR 132 to divide Texas into three territories, again with the Trinity and Colorado rivers as boundaries.[24] It was the intent of the divisionists, of course, to get

[22] *Daily Morning Chronicle*, March 24, 1869. The *Daily Austin Republican*, April 5, 1869, reprinted the *Chronicle* item.

[23] *Daily Austin Republican*, March 30 and April 2, 1869. Several other papers followed the theme of the *Daily Morning Chronicle*. The San Antonio *Daily Herald*, April 7, 1869, charged that the divisionist leaders wanted division, not reconstruction.

[24] U.S. Congress, *Congressional Globe*, 41 Cong., 1 sess., March 16, 1869, p.

the "State of Coyote" organized quickly and to keep the remainder of Texas under the control of the national government. "Bexar" assured the *San Antonio Express* that Texas certainly would be divided—into territories, at least.[25]

Beaman's action made it necessary for the antidivisionists to take countermeasures immediately. Consequently, during the evening of the same day that Beaman introduced his bills, the "people's commissioners" met at 500 Ninth Street.[26] The meeting was called to order by Haynes, Hamilton was named chairman, and Max Mobius was made secretary. Bell, having been previously designated, submitted a draft of a memorial. The memorial (generally referred to as the "Bell-Hamilton Memorial") was adopted and signed by those present and other Texans who were "so disposed." Presented by A. J. Hamilton on March 18 to Benjamin Butler, chairman of the House Committee on Reconstruction, it gave an account of the progress of reconstruction in Texas, an explanation of the temper of the people, and a "sound policy" to be pursued in completing the task of reconstruction. It presented reasons why division of Texas would be detrimental and too great an expense to the public. This second memorial insisted that the people were disposed to submit to national authority and recommended that the vote on the constitution be permitted as provided by the convention.[27]

---

100. Both bills were read twice and referred to the Committee on Reconstruction.

[25] *Daily Austin Republican*, March 24, 1869; *Daily Herald*, March 24, March 25 (from *San Antonio Express*, n.d.), 1869.

[26] Those present included Armstrong, Baker, Bell, Buffington, Burnett, Campbell, Edwards, Epperson, Fleming, A. J. Hamilton, Harn, Haynes, Jones, Krause, McCormick, Mobius, Paschal, Rossy, Julius Schuetze, and Watrous (*Daily Morning Chronicle*, March 17, 1869; Haynes to Longley [March 17, 1869], *Daily Austin Republican*, March 30, 1869).

[27] *Daily Morning Chronicle*, March 24, 1869; *Flake's Daily Bulletin* (dateline, Washington, March 16 and March 17, 1869), March 26 and March 27, 1869; *Daily Austin Republican*, March 26, March 30, and April 8, 1869; *Daily Herald*, March 26, 1869.

The "Bell-Hamilton Memorial" was signed by Armstrong, Bell, Buffington, Caldwell, Campbell, Edwards, Fleming, Hall, A. J. Hamilton, Harn, Haynes, Himbler, Horne, Jones, Kelher, Lane, McCormick, Mobius, G. W. Paschal, Rossy, Schuetze, Stockbridge, Watrous, and Wiley. Twelve of the signers (including Max Mobius, who had served as an assistant secretary) had been members of the Texas Convention (*Daily Morning Chronicle*, March 17, 1869; *Flake's Daily Bulletin* [dateline, Washington, March 16, 1869], March 27, 1869).

With very few exceptions, the press applauded the Bell-Hamilton Memorial. The *Daily Morning Chronicle*, reporting that the memorial was written with "clearness, dignity, and temper," urged Congress and President Grant to heed its recommendations. Governor Hamilton, Colbert Caldwell, Bell, G. W. Paschal, and Haynes it regarded as "true and tried Republicans," and, the *Chronicle* went on, "we wish them success in their efforts to restore loyal civil government to their state." Flake found that the memorial had two faults—its unpardonable length and its embellished rhetoric. Apart from these, he asserted that it was skillfully written—the "clearest history yet written of reconstruction in Texas . . . charitable and conciliatory in tone." Its recommendations, Flake concluded, were creditable. Longley claimed that Bell handled *ab initio* in a "masterly manner, and fully exposed those who placed division above reconstruction." [28]

The next move by the divisionists was an effort to present their case on the floor of the House. They almost got the opportunity. On March 19, Congressman Halbert E. Paine of Wisconsin, at Butler's request, sought to get Davis, Flanagan, Morgan Hamilton, Varnell, and Burnett admitted, but he was prevented by the objection of Fernando Wood of New York.[29]

That same day, Newcomb wrote a lengthy appeal to Republicans in Congress to divide Texas. East of the Colorado River conditions were appalling; it was land "where loyal men have fallen like leaves of the forest in the autumn wind" and where no fair election could be held at an early date. The terms of the newly prepared, "slip-shod" constitution, if adopted, "will be an invitation to all the disaffected disloyal" element from the other reconstructed states, and Texas will "indeed become the Botony [*sic*] Bay of the South." The restoration of the "revolted" states should not be speedy, he continued, and then only "as Republican communities, ruled by the Republican party, the party of liberty and progress . . . ." Congress must see that the work of redemption of the South should not be "ruined in its finishing strokes." Inasmuch as submission of the constitution to the people for ratification would be "preposterous," the best solution, Newcomb concluded,

---

Sumner and "others," it was reported, had joined the divisionists (*Daily Herald*, March 25, 1869).

[28] *Daily Morning Chronicle*, March 24, 1869; *Flake's Daily Bulletin*, March 28, 1869; *Daily Austin Republican*, March 20, 1869.

[29] *Congressional Globe*, 41 Cong., 1 sess., March 19, 1869, p. 174.

would be to divide Texas into territories and admit them as states when their "good behavior would warrant."[30]

The divisionists finally found a member of Congress who agreed to help. On March 22 Congressman Joel F. Asper of Missouri introduced a bill (HR 196) to form the territory lying west and south of the Colorado River into the State of Lincoln and to retain the remainder of Texas under military control. The bill was read twice and referred to the Committee on Reconstruction.[31]

During the evening of March 22, Ruby and Degener attended a meeting of the Executive Committee of Colored Men to enlist support for the Asper bill. Division was a major topic of discussion. The two Texans told their audience that life was not safe in eastern Texas and that it was the "unanimous wish of all Republicans" that eastern Texas should be kept under military government until the entire loyal element could vote without intimidation. On the other hand, they continued, western Texas was loyal and ready for restoration. The proposed constitution for the whole state should not be accepted, they argued, for it would place the ballot in the hands of the disloyal, who would make life and property unsafe for the loyal. The executive committee, despite the plea, refused to take a stand on the division question.[32]

While the Texans waited for a hearing before the Reconstruction Committee, "Snooks," in a dispatch entitled "Things Social," reported that Ruby and Bennett, "bully boys with glass eyes," were industriously working to introduce Texas politics into the Washington ward meetings, which in turn would bring pressure on Congress to provide for the division of Texas. Ruby, "in all his glory, like Falstaff, was a man of mark and sought after." "Snooks" had seen the president of the Texas Union Leagues walking along Pennsylvania Avenue, "gallanting a very handsome quadroon. With a plug hat, claw-hammer coat,

---

[30] James P. Newcomb, "An Appeal in Behalf of the Republicans of Texas," March 19, 1869, 4 pp., Newcomb Collection.

[31] *Congressional Globe*, 41 Cong., 1 sess., March 22, 1869, p. 194; U.S. Congress, House, *Journal* (hereafter cited as *House Journal*), 41 Cong., 1 sess., 1869, p. 87. "Bexar" optimistically predicted its passage. Texas would be divided, at least, into territories, he wrote, "with the West having a good chance for immediate reconstruction [statehood]" (*Daily Herald*, March 25, 1869 [from *San Antonio Express*, n.d.]).

[32] *Daily Morning Chronicle*, March 24, 1869.

and lavender kids, he appeared irresistible to the Washington belle, to judge from her pleasant aspect." Bennett, "Snooks" added, was about to "commit matrimony." [33]

On Tuesday, March 30, Benjamin F. Butler's Committee on Reconstruction began its hearing on the Texas situation. Fifty Texans were present. A. J. Hamilton, the first to be heard, argued that the proposed constitution was in conformity with the reconstruction laws and that it should be submitted to the voters for ratification or rejection on the date designated by the convention. Varnell, according to "Traveller" a "vulgar," "vindicitive [*sic*]" "person of coarse language" and Davis' candidate for Congress from his district, spoke next. His remarks were mainly an attack on Burnett for not supporting the Davis Memorial. Burnett had presented his own memorial, Varnell explained, not because he disagreed with his fellow commissioners but "to save himself from the Rebels and the Ku Klux Klan." Most of the remainder of the session was devoted to a general discussion of disfranchisement. A "gut-shot" at his opponents by Jack Hamilton brought brother Morgan to his feet, but "Old Morg" was quieted by Davis just as Butler was about to bang his gavel.[34] Without waiting until the hearings with the Texans were finished, the Committee on Reconstruction began taking action on Texas matters. Later that day, it sent to the House a copy of the proposed constitution. Then, with the unanimous consent of the committee, Congressman B. F. Whittemore, a radical carpetbagger from South Carolina, on the next day, March 31, introduced a resolution (HR 66) to postpone the election in Texas. The resolution was read twice and referred to the Committee on Reconstruction.[35] In a major editorial the following morning (April 1), the *Daily Morning Chronicle* strongly objected to the Whittemore resolution and urged Congress to dispose of the Texas problem before adjournment. The Texans, it stated, were "aroused" and inspired with the spirit of

[33] *Daily Austin Republican*, April 3, 1869.

[34] J. L. Haynes to Major Longley (April 4, 1869), *Daily Austin Republican*, April 15, 1869; letter from "Traveller" (April 4, 1869), *Daily Herald*, April 16, 1869; *Daily National Intelligencer* (Washington), April 5, 1869; *New York Herald*, March 21, 1869; *Flake's Daily Bulletin*, April 3, 8, and 27, 1869; *Daily Austin Republican*, March 31 and April 2, 1869; *Daily Herald*, April 2, 1869; "Washington Correspondent" (April 3, 1869), *Flake's Daily Bulletin*, April 13, 1869.

[35] *House Journal*, 41 Cong., 1 sess., 1869, p. 140.

progress and "only ask to be left alone." With Reynolds as the military commander, Texas, the *Chronicle* argued, would be almost assured of a fair election, the proposed constitution would be adopted, and normal relations with the federal government would be restored by the time Congress next met.[36]

There is no way to determine if the editorial had any influence on the congressmen, but at 11:30 A.M., Saturday, April 3, when the Committee on Reconstruction met, chairman Butler announced that the hearing on Texas affairs would resume. He informed Davis that he could have forty-five minutes to make his statements. Following fairly closely the theme of his memorial, except for interspersing his remarks with excerpts about lawlessness from Texas newspapers (principally the *San Antonio Express*), Davis explained that he was against the proposed constitution, that the election should be postponed, and that Texas should be divided. He opposed the constitution because its enfranchisement article was too liberal; disfranchisements, he claimed, should "insure the subjection of the State to Radical rule." In response to a question, he stated his opinion that at least thirty thousand whites should be disfranchised. He objected to holding the election in July because of the lawless conditions. If the election were held then, one hundred lives, he predicted, would be lost by violence.

Unable to answer satisfactorily when members of the committee wanted to know if the crimes he mentioned had political bearings, he became nervous and irritated. He insisted that because of Texas' unwieldy size, one single loyal state could not be formed. Thus, Texas should be divided; the area west of the Colorado River, where the citizens were loyal, should be admitted as a state, and the remainder kept under military rule. Division, he realized, was no longer possible during the current session of Congress (Congress had agreed to adjourn on April 10), but the election must be postponed indefinitely. Harassed by a shower of questions from A. J. Hamilton and committee members, Davis admitted that he was simply asking Congress to maintain military rule over Texas until a new western state could be established or until enough conservatives could be disfranchised to place the entire state under the control of the radical Republicans. A. J. Hamilton and his Republican followers, he charged, in order to gain political control, had sold out to the Democrats and conservatives and were

36 *Daily Morning Chronicle*, April 1, 1869.

themselves the "equivalent of rebels." Texas rebels today, he continued, "are as fierce and bitter, and equally strongly opposed to reconstruction as two years ago.

When the "crimination and recrimination" between Davis and Hamilton became rather unpleasant, Degener rose to Davis' defense, but Butler ordered him to hush and to take his seat. Only one committee member, carpetbagger Whittemore, championed Davis, and only one Republican, John F. Farnsworth from Illinois, spoke against him. Butler denounced the convention's action on division as rebellion, but he said he did not like the suffrage article in the proposed constitution, either. Some of those present thought that Davis, who was "not a forcible speaker," made a poor presentation, and that he was "vindictive, malignant, and revengeful, and . . . seriously . . . damaged his cause." [37]

At the conclusion of the hearings, the "people's commissioners" were optimistic upon learning from a committee member that reconstruction would be allowed to proceed in accordance with the Hamilton proposal, although the date of the election would be left to the President's discretion. Disappointed over defeat on the election date, Haynes reported to his newspaper in Austin that "it is useless to deny and ought not to be concealed from the people of our state that the Davis delegation . . . and their following of scullious [scullions] and scavengers, [have] made a considerable impression here upon the more extreme and radical members of Congress, and they are not to be despised as having no influence." [38]

While waiting for Butler's committee to make its decision regarding the future of Texas, the Philadelphia *North America* editorialized that division, "a project originated by Thaddeus Stevens, should be made as it would give us three new Republican states." [39] Most of the press, however, strongly opposed division and urged Congress to permit the

[37] The account of Davis' appearance before the committee is compiled from the following: Haynes to Longley (April 4, 1869), *Daily Austin Republican*, April 15, 1869; "Traveller" (April 4, 1869), *Daily Herald*, April 16, 1869; *Daily National Intelligencer*, April 5, 1869; "Washington Correspondent" (April 3, 1869), *Flake's Daily Bulletin*, April 13, 1869; *Daily Herald*, April 10, 1869; *Flake's Daily Bulletin*, April 7, 1869; *Daily Austin Republican*, April 16, 1869; *The Harrison Flag* (Marshall), April 22, 1869.

[38] Haynes to Longley (April 4, 1869), *Daily Austin Republican*, April 15, 1869; "Traveller" (April 4, 1869), *Daily Herald*, April 16, 1869.

[39] *Flake's Daily Bulletin*, April 6 (from *North America* [Philadelphia], n.d.), 1869.

immediate restoration of Texas to the Union. The San Antonio *Daily Herald* denounced "those disturbers of the peace in Texas, whose careers is, thank heaven, about coming to a most timely end." It repeated the conclusion of the *Daily Morning Chronicle* that it seemed "paradoxical to assert that an unsound whole can be cut into three sound parts." "The divisionists," it continued, "are interested in division not in reconstruction. To reconstruct is the supreme duty at the present time. . . ." [40]

On April 7, the Committee on Reconstruction agreed to allow elections in Virginia, Mississippi, and Texas. On the next day Butler reported a resolution (HR 405) that authorized the president to designate a date "at such time as he may deem fit for the public service" for a vote in Texas on the constitution and for the election of members of Congress. That same day, in the House the bill was read twice, engrossed, and passed by a vote of 125 to 25, with 47 abstaining. A day later the Senate concurred by a vote of 44 to 9, and on April 10 the bill was signed into law by President Grant.[41] The issue of division—after a fierce and bitter struggle that had lasted unabated for more than a year—was dead.

[40] *Daily Herald*, April 16, 1869.
[41] *House Journal*, 41 Cong., 1 sess., 1869, pp. 196–197; U.S. Congress, Senate, *Journal*, 41 Cong. 1 sess., 1869, p. 165; *Daily Herald*, April 10, 1869; *Daily National Intelligencer*, April 9, 1869.

# TEXAS: ONE AND INSEPARABLE

.

Although the Coyotes had lost their fight in Washington, the law authorizing President Grant to set the date for the election left the gate slightly open. They would get the president to postpone the election as long as possible, and, when it did occur, they would defeat the proposed constitution and convene a new constitutional convention (or conventions) that they hoped would adopt *ab initio*, disfranchisement, and division. As a secondary measure, in case the constitution were ratified, they would elect a complete slate of officeholders.

On the other side, A. J. Hamilton, on behalf of the delegation he headed, appealed to President Grant to allow the election on the ratification of the constitution to be held in July as provided by the convention. The constitution had been framed, he pointed out, in compliance with the Reconstruction Acts, and the only serious objection for Republicans was its suffrage clause, which "disfranchises none but lunatics and felons. We have tendered our late opponents the olive branch. . . . Since the subject has been referred to the wisdom and justice of your Excellency, we . . . pray your Excellency to order" the election to be held as provided by the convention. He got no encouragement.[1]

The official delegation, on the other hand, was encouraged. Grant apparently promised them to postpone the election until November, at least, on the grounds that, because of the vast size of Texas, preparations could not be completed by July. Grant's decision was confirmed when General J. J. Reynolds, who arrived at Galveston on April 6, stated as he passed through Brenham on his way to Austin that there would be no election in July. Edward Degener, as a result,

---

[1] *Flake's Daily Bulletin* (dateline, Washington, April 10, 1869), April 20, 1869.

125

thought that "our mission to Washington has not been entirely in vain."[2]

Meanwhile in Washington, the two factions engaged in bitter rivalry to win federal patronage. Again, the Coyotes were the temporary losers. In Galveston, the site of some of the richest plums, G. T. Ruby lost his bid for postmaster, H. C. Pedigo got the job as assessor of internal revenue, and J. L. Haynes was named the collector of customs. For the Northern District of Texas, Sumner was appointed federal internal revenue assessor. A. H. Longley, who became collector of internal revenue at Austin, gloated that the only thing the Davis group could boast of was the $6,000 compensation from the state treasury.[3]

Some members of the Texas delegation left for home immediately after Congress adjourned on April 10; a few lingered in Washington, hoping either to influence Grant regarding the date of the election or to obtain patronage appointments. On Sunday, April 4, J. W. Flanagan and two antidivisionists, James Burnett and C. T. D. Harn, arrived in Galveston on a Morgan steamer. Judge James H. Bell arrived in Austin on Monday, April 12, and Morgan Hamilton reached home on April 21.[4] A report from Washington stated that Degener left the day after Congress adjourned and that Degener's friends should give him a public reception as he had been working very hard to defeat anything that would lead to an early reconstruction.[5] On May 6, Degener was back in San Antonio at a Loyal Union League meeting in the Hertzberg store, expressing his annoyance at the failure of *ab initio* and dwelling at length upon the sacrifices he had made—including paying his own expenses to Washington—on behalf of Negroes and Unionists.[6] Haynes and Colbert Caldwell reached Galveston on Sunday, April 25. Caldwell proceeded immediately to Tyler to attend court, and Haynes, three days later, arrived in Austin, where he remained a couple of weeks before leaving to take over his new job as collector of customs at Galveston.[7] Ruby, before returning to Texas,

[2] *Daily Herald* (San Antonio), April 16, 1869; *Flake's Daily Bulletin*, April 6 and April 9, 1869; *Daily Austin Republican*, April 12, 1869.

[3] *Daily Austin Republican*, April 10, 1869.

[4] *Daily Herald*, April 14, 1869; *Flake's Daily Bulletin*, April 6, 1869; *Daily Austin Republican*, April 14 and April 22, 1869.

[5] *Daily Herald* (dateline, Washington, April 14, 1869), April 23, 1869.

[6] Ibid., May 8, 1869.

[7] *Daily Austin Republican*, April 27, April 29, and May 17, 1869; *Dallas Herald*, April 29, 1869.

went to New England and then to New York City, where he visited the headquarters of the Union Leagues. Upon returning to Galveston, he spoke on the evening of May 6 at a "crowded colored church." There he gave an account of his elaborate banquet in Maine and of a big reception in New York City, where he was given the freedom of the Union League club rooms. The major portion of his speech, however, was a denunciation of A. J. Hamilton.[8]

A. J. Hamilton remained in Washington for several days. After his conference with the president concerning the election, he still had work regarding some federal appointments. On April 25, he called upon Attorney General George F. Hoar to protest the nomination of a person who, in Hamilton's opinion, was "a bad man, and not fit to hold office."

"I had heard you were opposed to him, and was not surprised," countered Hoar, "as I also hear that you are going over to the Copperheads."

"G——d d——n you, or any man who impugns my political motives," Hamilton angrily retorted. "Where were you when the war was raging? . . . Dispensing the only law you know—Massachusetts law—whilst I was risking my life in behalf of the Union. As you know what is decent or well-bred in your intercourse with gentlemen, I will not trouble you further, but will go to your master." And that he did, leaving the attorney general "in a state of rage and astonishment."[9]

Upon his return to Texas, Hamilton brought with him from New Orleans the remains of his son, who had died in that pestilence-plagued city. Reaching Galveston on April 30, he proceeded to Austin, arriving there on May 6, and on the following day the remains of his son were interred in the Austin cemetery. "Friends are invited to attend the funeral of Mr. and Mrs. A. J. Hamilton's son, John, this afternoon at 4 o'clock." " 'Jonnie' died nearly two years ago, in New Orleans, of yellow fever."[10]

It is not the purpose of this treatise to describe the ensuing political campaign. The dramatic events, the questionable tactics associated

8 *Daily Austin Republican*, May 7, 1869.
9 The account of the Hamilton-Hoar incident is from the *Dallas Herald* (dateline, Washington, April 29, 1869), May 8, 1869; Gray, "The Abortive State of West Texas" (Master's thesis, Texas Tech University, 1969), p. 127.
10 *Dallas Herald* (dateline, Galveston, April 29, 1869), May 15, 1869; *Daily Austin Republican*, May 7 and May 10, 1869.

therewith, and the resulting long-lingering bitterness provide adequate material for a significant and interesting historical study. A brief account of events leading to the election is essential, however, inasmuch as the ratification of the constitution doomed any surviving or lingering hope of the Coyotes for the erection of a State of West Texas.

A. J. Hamilton, while on his way to Washington, had unofficially opened his campaign for governor at Brenham on February 15. In a speech there he appealed to the blacks for their support. Later, lest he might alienate the white conservative voters, he announced that he wanted no integrated schools. On March 18, while in Washington, he officially announced his candidacy. A Republican State Executive Committee meeting in Austin was poorly attended, but afterward chairman Haynes announced that the Republican party would not hold a state convention and that its candidates would be A. J. Hamilton for governor, A. H. Latimer for lieutenant governor, A. T. Monroe for comptroller, and James W. Thomas for treasurer. All of these candidates had been members of the Reconstruction Convention.[11]

Ten days after returning to Austin, Hamilton launched in earnest his campaign, for the ratification of the constitution as well as his try for the governor's office. On Saturday night, May 16, he "bearded" Degener and Newcomb before a "large attendance" in San Antonio, the stronghold of the Coyotes, whose leaders—like drowning persons at sea, continuing to hold to the sinking ship—hoped to defeat the constitution and get a new convention, or conventions, that would divide the state. Hamilton stressed that, because he desired for Texans a quick recovery from the effects of the war, he had opposed disfranchisement. Degener, Morgan Hamilton, and others, he emphasized, had attempted to disfranchise an estimated thirty thousand and to adopt *ab initio*. Failing this, they had worked diligently for division, and, having been blocked in this as well, they had succeeded in getting the election postponed. Hamilton explained that he wanted to enfranchise every male citizen, twenty-one years of age or older, except those disbarred for crime, and he insisted that there was no longer any need for a military government in Texas. With sarcastic humor he referred to Newcomb as a "wet nurse for all the fatherless babies in Texas." The

[11] A. J. Hamilton to Ferdinand Flake (March 18, 1869), *San Antonio Express*, March 26, 1869; E. W. Winkler, ed., *Platforms of Political Parties in Texas*, p. 117.

editor of the *Daily Herald* characterized the speech as "most effec-
tive."[12]

Dissatisfied with his share of the patronage, Edmund Davis lingered in Washington until late April. His request for the removal of
the political disabilities of some disfranchised Republican clients had
received congressional approval. A Washington correspondent of the
*San Antonio Express*, probably Newcomb, heralded this insignificant
bit of success as evidence that "Davis and Morgan Hamilton have the
ear of Congress" and rejoiced that "the day of Jack Hamilton's influence at Washington had passed."[13]

Davis returned to Corpus Christi by way of Galveston. By the time
he arrived, he had decided to get himself elected governor, just in case
the electorate should ratify the constitution. But the radicals were in a
dilemma. The Republican Executive Committee, without holding a
nominating convention, had endorsed Hamilton. As a result of their
defeat on *ab initio*, division, and disfranchisement and their failure to
break up the convention and to prevent a vote on the constitution, the
radicals concluded that to oppose the constitution meant certain defeat. To join the moderates, on the other hand, meant liquidation of
their party. Thus, they decided to hold their own convention. To this
end, Morgan Hamilton, chairman of the newly created Radical Republican State Executive Committee, issued a call for a state convention to be held in Galveston on May 10. He and Davis prepared and
sent to the counties a platform resolution and called upon all loyal
Texans to attend. By May 3, however, Davis realized that the call was
premature and that the convention would be poorly attended. There
was no great hurry, for by now he knew there would be no election
until the fall. At Galveston, the Morgan Hamilton convention met
only long enough to praise Davis, condemn A. J. Hamilton, and issue
a call for the delegates to reassemble on June 7 in Houston.[14]

During the interval, Davis' supporters worked diligently to assure
for him the gubernatorial nomination. Ruby felt that, if the campaign
were "properly managed, we [would be] sure of victory." Before

[12] *Daily Herald*, May 18, 1869.

[13] *San Antonio Express*, April 20, 1869.

[14] *Flake's Semi-Weekly Bulletin* (Galveston), May 12, 1869; Morgan C.
Hamilton to James P. Newcomb, May 14, 1869, J. P. Newcomb Collection,
Archives, Barker Texas History Center, University of Texas, Austin; Winkler,
*Platforms of Political Parties*, pp. 117–119.

leaving for Washington, he had boasted in a radical caucus that he could command 45,000 colored voters and that he would, therefore, demand that his name be put on the next ticket for lieutenant governor. To this the editor of the *Daily Herald* quipped: "Davis and Ruby! Oh, what a happy pair they would be hung upon a tree together." Editor Longley, after noting that the *Houston Union* was advocating Ruby for a high office on the radical ticket, sarcastically asked: "Why not entrust their standard to him? Who is so worthy as he? Who so lovely to look upon with his plug hat, his claw-hammer coat, and his lavender kids?"[15]

When the Radical Republican party met on the first Monday in June in the Harris County courthouse at Houston, J. G. Tracy, one of its prime movers and the editor of the *Houston Union*, presided. Tracy later stated that forty-five self-appointed delegates (thirty of whom were black) from thirty counties attended.[16] Recognizing the exigencies of the political situation, the convention's platform omitted any reference to *ab initio* and division, endorsed the Fourteenth and Fifteenth amendments, demanded equal civil and political rights for male adults, and, reversing the previous radical stand, called for the ratification of the proposed constitution. The convention unanimously nominated Davis for governor—the "official promulgation of a fact which was settled in the hearts of the loyal people of Texas more than a year ago"—and J. W. Flanagan for lieutenant governor.[17] Strange as it may seem, Davis promised to campaign for the constitution he had hitherto vigorously condemned and to govern a people he had denounced as unfit for statehood. He now had one major advantage over Hamilton—he was the nominee of a convention. Furthermore, on July 7, the national executive committee recognized the Davis group as the official Republican party in Texas.[18]

The Democrats, fearing that organized participation in the contest

---

[15] George T. Ruby to James P. Newcomb, May 6, 1869, Newcomb Collection; *Daily Herald*, March 28, May 11 (from *Daily Austin Republican*, n.d.), 1869.

[16] J. G. Tracy, "Address at the Republican Convention in 1872," in Winkler, *Platforms of Political Parties*, p. 119. The estimates vary widely, from thirty-four to ninety-five delegates and from eleven to ninety-eight counties (*San Antonio Express*, June 11 and June 20, 1869; A. J. Hamilton, "Address to the People of Texas" [June 29, 1869], *Dallas Herald*, July 31, 1869).

[17] Winkler, *Platforms of Political Parties*, pp. 120–121; *San Antonio Express*, June 23 and June 15, 1869.

[18] *San Antonio Express*, July 21, 1869.

would result either in victory for the radicals or rejection of the constitution, put forward only legislative and county candidates. They generally favored the constitution, as a lesser evil than military rule, and supported Hamilton, "a man of ability and natural generosity."[19] Most state newspapers, including the *State Gazette, Galveston News, Houston Telegraph*, and *Standard*, threw their full support to Hamilton.

During the campaign, the radicals gradually gained strength. They claimed that they had the support of the radicals in Congress and emphasized that their nominees had been selected in a regular convention. After the national Republican Executive Committee recognized the Davis faction, radical Republicans pressured Grant to endorse Davis. Finally, on July 15, the president issued a proclamation postponing the Texas election until November 30 and the three following days; one week later he expressed a preference for Davis.[20]

Thereafter, the campaign became more intense. Democrats and moderate Republicans called the radicals a carpetbagger-black-supremacy party and accused them of favoring adoption of the constitution for the sake of convenience. The radicals, in turn, charged that the Hamiltonians had "sold out to the rebels."[21] Although strongly supported by only six newspapers, the radicals had, in addition, two powerful allies—George T. Ruby, the president of the Loyal Union Leagues of Texas, and General J. J. Reynolds, a friend and former West Point classmate of President U. S. Grant. Ruby diligently marshaled the Texas subordinate councils into action with circulars that urged black members to participate vigorously in the campaign and that maintained that the furtherance of liberty, union, and equality depended upon their alignment with the "soldier-hero, General E. J. Davis." *The Harrison Flag*, as early as June, reported that the Union Leagues had been "thoroughly perfected. The President of the district of Texas, the notorious nondescript G. T. Ruby, . . . had not been idle by any means."[22] The same issue of the paper carried a complaint

---

[19] *Standard* (Clarksville), March 20 and March 21, 1869; Ernest Wallace, *Charles DeMorse*, p. 164; Winkler, *Platforms of Political Parties*, pp. 122–123.
[20] James D. Richardson, ed., *A Compilation of the Messages and Papers of the Presidents, 1789–1897*, 7:17–18; *San Antonio Express*, August 10, 1869; *Dallas Herald*, August 4 and August 11, 1869.
[21] S. S. McKay, *Seven Decades of the Texas Constitution of 1876*, p. 23.
[22] George T. Ruby, "To the Subordinate Councils—Union League of Amer-

by a black citizen that his church, near Marshall, was too preoccupied with holding meetings of the Union League and endeavoring to convert the blacks to vote for the radicals in the forthcoming election to leave any time for religious services.

Reynolds had been led to believe (or promised outright) that, if Davis won, he would be sent to the United States Senate, so he carried out his part of the bargain.[23] On September 4, he sent President Grant a personal letter in which he endorsed Davis, for, he wrote, the election of Hamilton "will put the State in the hands of the very men who, during the rebellion, exerted every nerve to destroy the Union, and who have uniformly opposed the reconstruction laws with a persistency worthy of a better cause." Offended by the letter, Provisional Governor E. M. Pease tendered his resignation.[24] Then, on September 25, the general began removing Hamilton supporters from office and replacing them with radical Republicans. Before the election, he had made almost a clean sweep, including supreme court judges Caldwell and Latimer; Latimer was the candidate for lieutenant governor on the moderate Republican ticket. W. W. Mills, collector of customs at El Paso, was replaced by a carpetbag supporter of Davis. W. B. Moore, the editor of the radical *San Antonio Express* during the convention and a leading advocate of division, got Longley's job as collector of internal revenue at Austin. Haynes, the collector of customs

---

ica, Texas," n.d., Newcomb Collection; *The Harrison Flag* (Marshall), June 24, 1869.

[23] Reynolds, in April, 1869, apparently proposed to John L. Haynes that he would use the power of his position as military commander to ensure A. J. Hamilton's election in return for his own appointment to the United States Senate. Haynes and others favored acceptance, but Hamilton refused. Reynolds then gave his support to the radical Republicans (A. J. Hamilton to W. W. Mills, July 1, 1869, W. W. Mills Collection, Archives, Barker Texas History Center, University of Texas, Austin; A. P. McCormick to My dear Friend, April 28, 1869, James H. Bell Papers, Archives, Barker Texas History Center, University of Texas, Austin; Charles W. Ramsdell, *Reconstruction in Texas*, p. 274; Betty J. Sandlin, "The Texas Reconstruction Convention of 1868–1869," p. 231).

[24] J. J. Reynolds to U. S. Grant (September 4, 1869), *New York Times*, September 27, 1869; *Daily Austin Republican*, October 8, 1869; E. M. Pease to J. J. Reynolds, September 30, 1869, R. Niles Graham–E. M. Pease Collection, Austin–Travis County Collection, Austin Public Library, Austin, Texas; Texas, Executive Records, Register Book 283, Archives, Texas State Library, Austin; *Dallas Herald*, October 16, 1869.

at Galveston, was replaced by Nathan Patten, who had been one of the hard-core radical divisionists throughout the convention and in Washington. By the time of the election, practically all federal positions, including postal officials and federal marshals, were held by Davis supporters.[25] On October 1, Reynolds issued an order, in compliance with a proclamation of the president, for the election to be held on November 30, December 1, 2, and 3. At the same time, he ordered a revision of the voter registration lists. The revision increased the registration from 109,995 to 135,553 (81,960 whites and 53,593 blacks). Some 2,166 whites and 383 blacks were removed from the lists.[26]

The turnout on election day was relatively light. Only 58.5 percent of the registered voters went to the polls; more than 56,000 registrants failed to vote. The miserable weather throughout most of the state and the presence of soldiers at polling places (ten soldiers were stationed at each county seat where a disturbance was thought possible) were, no doubt, partially responsible.[27] The major reason, though, was that many old-line Democrats simply could not bring themselves to support either a Republican-made constitution or a ticket composed of moderate Republicans.

The returns, particularly from northern Texas, filtered in slowly, and there were a number of irregularities. General Reynolds notified President Grant on December 14 that the "Davis ticket for state officials is elected beyond all doubt," but it was not until January 8, 1870, that he officially announced that Davis had won. Three days later, he reported the vote: Davis, 39,901; Hamilton, 39,092; Hamilton Stuart (the Democratic nominee), 380. The constitution had been ratified by an overwhelming vote of 72,466 to 4,928. Davis received only about 10 percent of the white vote. He carried, on the other hand, almost three-fourths of those counties where over 40 percent of the regis-

---

[25] *Daily Austin Republican*, June 15 and September 27, 28, and 30, 1869.

[26] "General Order No. 174, Fifth Military District," printed in *Austin Record*, October 8, 1869; *New York Times*, November 29, 1869; "General Order No. 73, Fifth Military District," in Texas, *Tabular Statement of Voters (White and Colored) Registered in Texas in 1867, and at Revision of the Lists in 1867–1868–69*, pp. 1–8; Ronald N. Gray, "Edmund J. Davis" (Ph.D. diss., Texas Tech University, 1976), p. 176.

[27] *State Gazette*, December 3, 1869. A total of eleven officers and six hundred troops were placed on duty on the election days (Robert W. Shook, "Federal Occupation and Administration of Texas, 1865–1870" [Ph.D. diss., North Texas State University, 1970], p. 401).

trants were Negro, and he received between 80 and 90 percent of the total black vote.[28]

With such a close vote, charges of fraud could be expected. General Reynolds refused to count the votes in Milam County, where the polls were closed after the first day because of a fight, or in Navarro County, where the chairman of the registration board absconded with the list of registered voters. Both of these counties were claimed by Hamilton. In Hill County the ballots were removed to an adjoining county and counted by only one member of the election board. Hamilton and many of his supporters were convinced that Reynolds had fraudulently awarded the election to Davis. There was never any reported official tabulation. Later, a committee of the Democratic-controlled Constitutional Convention of 1875 reported that it had been able to find all the election returns since the Civil War except those of 1869. Presumably they had been sent or taken out of the state or destroyed by Reynolds.[29]

On January 8, 1870, Reynolds appointed the successful candidates to assume provisionally the offices to which they had been elected. The legislature, controlled by the radicals, convened on February 8, as provided by the April 10, 1869, act of Congress. The elected body ratified the Fourteenth and Fifteenth amendments on February 17, and on February 22 it named Morgan Hamilton and J. W. Flanagan as United States senators. On March 30 Congress approved the act that permitted the senators and representatives from Texas to take their seats, and on April 16 General Reynolds formally terminated military rule in Texas.[30] The restoration of Texas to the Union settled, perhaps forever, the fate of division.

The Coyotes failed in their 1868–1869 major effort for several rea-

28 *San Antonio Express*, January 22, 1870; Texas, Executive Records, Register Book 284, Archives, Texas State Library, Austin; U.S. Secretary of War, "Election Returns" (Texas), Fifth Military District, Record Group 393, National Archives, Washington, D.C.; McKay, *Seven Decades of the Texas Constitution of 1876*, p. 23. The percentages used are from Gray, "E. J. Davis," pp. 178–179.

29 Ramsdell, *Reconstruction in Texas*, p. 284; *Dallas Herald*, January 15, 1870; Gray, "E. J. Davis," p. 179; *Daily Ranchero* (Brownsville), January 4 and January 12, 1870; Ernest Wallace, *Texas in Turmoil, 1849–1876*, p. 209.

30 Texas, *Journals of the House of Representatives of the State of Texas* (hereafter cited as *Texas House Journal*), 12 Leg., prov. sess., 1870, pp. 3, 40–41, 61–65; Texas, *Journals of the Senate of the State of Texas*, 12 Leg.,

sons. They handled a respectable and logical cause in an undemocratic and an extralegal manner, violating parliamentary rules when it was to their advantage. They tried to scuttle a constitution that did not suit their political whims and to create a state with a constitution not strictly in accord with Anglo-Saxon traditions—primarily, a majority of Texans felt, to further the personal ambitions of its principal proponents. The *Corpus Christi Advertiser* stated this point less kindly. The Coyotes are a "lean, lank, snarling, hungry, mangy pack who would snap at the shadow of a mule's tail to satisfy their cravings. . . . These prowlers after offal . . . go for the enfranchisement of darkies and scalawags, and the disfranchisement of any white man, Indian, or Negro who don't vote their ticket. They are rampant for division of the State. . . ."[31] The movement became inextricably associated with the radicals, a minority group composed largely of carpetbaggers, scalawags, Negroes, and some Germans, whose political views were not shared by a majority of Texans. Nonetheless, it seems safe to conclude that the major reason for the failure of division was history. Shared historical experiences, encompassing adversity and success in the face of difficult odds, have provided through the ages a common denominator for the unification of peoples, regardless of geography, economics, language, and race. In the case of Texas, this feeling was beautifully stated by United States Senator Joseph Weldon Bailey:[32]

> Texas was not divided in the beginning . . . and under the providence of God she will not be divided until the end of time. . . .
> While from her proud eminence today Texas looks upon a future as bright with promise as ever beckoned a people, it is not so much the promise of that future as it is the memory of a glorious past which appeals to her against division. She could partition the fertile valleys and broad prairies; . . . she could distribute her splendid population and her wonderful resources, but she could not divide the fadeless glory of those days that are past and gone. To which of her daughters could she bequeath the names of Houston, and Austin, and Fannin, and Bowie, and Crockett? The fame of these men and their less

---

prov. sess., 1870, pp. 9, 28–30, 42, 46; "An Act to Admit the State of Texas to Representation in the Congress of the United States," *Texas House Journal*, 12 Leg., 1 sess., 1870, pp. 4–5.

[31] *Dallas Herald*, May 1 (from *Corpus Christi Advertiser*, n.d.), 1869.

[32] Joseph Weldon Bailey, extracted from a speech during the debate over the admission of New Mexico and Arizona as a single state and a proposal to divide Texas into four states, U.S., *Congressional Record*, 58 Cong., 3 sess., February 7, 1905, p. 1981.

illustrious, but not less worthy, comrades cannot be severed; it is the common glory of all. . . . The story of their mighty deeds . . . which rescued Texas . . . and made her a free and independent republic still rouses the blood of her men like the sound of a trumpet, and we would not forfeit the right to repeat it to our children for many additional seats in this august body. . . .

Mr. President, . . . I would say of Texas: She is one and inseparable, now and forever.

# ⌇8⌇

## EPILOGUE: BAYING AT THE MOON

·

Since 1869, the "Coyotes" have been heard occasionally on the western horizon, but the noise has been from a lonely few baying at the moon rather than from a ravenous pack intent on tearing to pieces its helpless victim. The first episode involved a few of the 1868–1869 radical diehards both in Congress and in the state legislature who, encouraged by the results of the election, clung to the illusion that the division of Texas was possible. In Congress, Senator Jacob M. Howard of Michigan on February 25, 1871, three days after the Texas legislature had named senators, introduced a bill (S 593) to divide the State of Texas and to establish the territories of Jefferson and Matagorda. The eastern portion, denominated the State of Jefferson, was apparently meant to be the portion of the original state east of the Trinity River, although the boundary provisions in the bill were contradictory. The area between the Colorado and Trinity rivers was to be the State of Texas, and all area to the west of the Colorado River was to be the Territory of Matagorda. The population estimates given by Howard were, respectively, 230,000; 250,000; and 130,000 (Indians not included). Howard's basic argument was that because of Texas' size, "the people within its limits are of such a peculiar character, that I should despair hereafter of seeing a State government established in the State, as now organized, that will be competent to the protection of life and property and all the other interests which pertain to civilized, regular government." The bill was referred to the Committee on Territories, but it was never reported out, for both the Congress and the president felt that a decision had been made already against division.[1]

Undismayed by the action of Congress and encouraged by his election as governor, Davis and some of his divisionist supporters initiat-

[1] U.S. Congress, *Congressional Globe*, 41 Cong., 2 sess., February 25, 1870, pp. 1555–1556.

137

ed their division scheme in the state legislature. To prepare for its passage at the forthcoming regular session, some proponents offered a resolution calling for division during the 1870 provisional session, but it was given no consideration.[2] Then, when it met in regular session, the Twelfth Legislature received a memorial, prepared by a convention at Tyler in November, 1870, at which twenty-one counties were represented, asking for division of the state. To deal with the subject, the legislature named a joint committee of ten. About two months later, the committee, with only one dissenter, E. L. Dohoney of Paris, recommended division into smaller states, but it was unable to agree on boundary lines. Because no agreement could be reached, a substitute on May 8, 1871, proposed the creation of one additional state, but both the bill and the substitute were allowed to die in committee. Another bill, by Representative W. G. Robinson of Jefferson, provided for the division of Texas into North Texas, Southeast Texas, Central Texas, and West Texas; this was the first plan ever offered for division into four states.[3]

The Robinson proposal had several attractive advantages. It placed with northeastern Texas all the organized counties north and west of Dallas, an arrangement that the congressional plan (Beaman bill) and the convention's committee-majority plan had failed to provide. North Texas would have a water outlet at Jefferson, then a booming city with extensive commerce. Perhaps even the Trinity and the Colorado, in time, might be developed. Southeast Texas would get all the Galveston waterway, thereby overcoming the objection delegate Smith

[2] Texas, *Journals of the Senate of the State of Texas* (hereafter cited as, *Texas Senate Journal*), 12 Leg., prov. sess., 1870, pp. 34, 104; W. J. McConnell, *Social Cleavages in Texas*, pp. 104–105.

[3] North Texas was to be bounded on the north by the Red River, on the east by Arkansas and Louisiana, and on the south by the southern line of Panola and Henderson counties. Thence the boundary was to follow a direct line to the southeast corner of Hamilton County, the southern boundary of Hamilton, Brown, Coleman, and Runnels counties, and, on the west, the western line of Runnels, Taylor, Jones, Haskell, Knox, and Hardeman counties. Southeast Texas and Central Texas would have as a common boundary the western line of the counties of Brazoria, Fort Bend, Austin, Washington, Burleson, Williamson, Bell, and Coryell. The western boundary of Central Texas would be a straight line from the mouth of the Pecos River to the southwestern corner of Runnels County (McConnell, *Social Cleavages in Texas*, pp. 107–110; Texas, *Journals of the House of Representatives of the State of Texas* [hereafter cited as *Texas House Journal*], 12 Leg., reg. sess., 1871, p. 212).

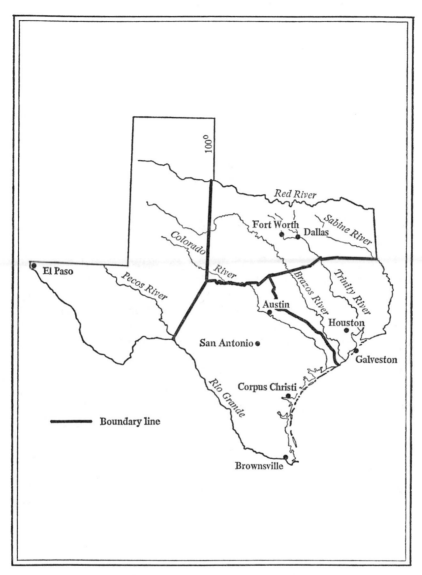

9. Robinson Division Plan, 1871. Representative W. G. Robinson of Jefferson made the first proposal for division into four states.

from that city had voiced in the convention of 1868–1869 against the congressional plan. Central Texas would be almost identical to the State of West Texas projected in 1869 by the Coyotes, except its eastern line would be between the Brazos and Colorado rivers, thereby including, as Degener had wanted, many additional Germans. The western state, still inhabited, except for El Paso, by unconquered Comanche, Kiowa, and Apache Indians, would be almost the same area as Degener, Governor Pease, and A. J. Evans previously had proposed to sell to the United States. Robinson's plan, however, attracted no interest and was never brought out of committee.[4] Thus, Davis lost his last hope of getting a new western state carved out of Texas. The increasing unpopularity of his administration, resulting from the obnoxious and unconstitutional acts of the Twelfth Legislature and his arbitrary exercise of power, had by September, 1871, alienated many of his strongest radical supporters, including Morgan Hamilton.

Disgruntled over the failure to get the gubernatorial nomination for James W. Throckmorton, the *Dallas Herald*, in July and August of 1878, while not suggesting any specific boundary, called upon Texans to allow the northern and western sections of the state to "depart in peace." The tremendous increase in population, the astonishing economic development, the growing antagonism between the sections, and the inability, because of the state's size, to have an efficient administration of general laws and a good school system were the major reasons cited for division.[5] Sentiment throughout the state, however, condemned the *Herald*'s stand. The Third Congressional District Convention of Democrats at Fort Worth on August 7 applauded and then adopted a resolution that opposed division—"ever" —and reaffirmed the doctrine that "united we stand, and divided we fall." The press was unanimously opposed, including the previously prodivision *San Antonio Daily Express* and the Jacksboro *Frontier Echo*, whose editor claimed that by division "all quarters of the Old State will have nothing."[6]

[4] *Texas House Journal*, 12 Leg., reg. sess., 1871, p. 212; *Daily Austin Republican*, March 9, 1871.
[5] *Dallas Herald*, July 30, 1878; *San Antonio Daily Express*, August 3, 1878; *Galveston Daily News*, July 31, August 2, 4, and 8, 1878; *Fort Worth Daily Democrat*, August 4, 1878.
[6] Resolution quoted in *Fort Worth Daily Democrat*, August 8, 1878; *Galveston Daily News*, August 8, 1878; *San Antonio Daily Express*, August 8,

After 1878, the calls for division were first from the northwestern and central-western, then, more recently, from the southwestern regions of the state. A number of factors contributed to uniting the people of those regions in moves to secure either a new state or more equitable treatment by the legislature. The west Texans resented the legislature's perceived favoritism toward the eastern section. Largely stockmen, they wanted predatory game laws, but the legislature consistently refused to enact them; they wanted state colleges, but the legislature ignored their pleas. When the grass-leasing legislation was not in accordance with the region's best interests, some west Texas editors argued that the only remedy to their problem was the division of the state, and in 1891 a west Texas legislator suggested that the best solution would be the annexation of east Texas to the State of Arkansas.[7]

After several public meetings, the resentment climaxed with a mass meeting at Vernon on April 10, 1893. There, a resolution, adopted with "deafening applause," declared that the state capital was distantly located, the legislature consistently ignored the welfare of northwest Texas, the west Texans paid annually $300,000 more in taxes than they received in return, and the interests of the two sections differed widely. Those at the meeting favored a convention for the purpose of creating out of northwestern Texas a new state. Though opposed to division, several editors felt that the west Texans had good reason to be unhappy and called upon the legislature to adopt a more liberal policy in their behalf.[8]

After that fairly insignificant flurry of discontent, the division issue lay dormant both within the borders of Texas and in the halls of Congress until next stimulated by the discussion surrounding the admission of Arizona–New Mexico and Oklahoma to statehood. As a ploy to gain support for the admission of these states, Congressman J. Adam Bede of Minnesota on April 10, 1906, proposed the division of Texas into four states (North Texas, East Texas, South Texas, and West Texas) by the projection of lines from Austin outward to the border. All states would have a common governor and lieutenant gov-

---

1878; *Frontier Echo* (Jacksboro, Texas), August 9, 1878. The *Fort Worth Daily Democrat*, August 6 and August 23, 1878, also strongly opposed division.

  7 W. C. Holden, *Alkali Trails*, pp. 120–121.

  8 *Dallas Morning News*, April 11, 1893; *Galveston Daily News*, April 13 and April 15, 1893; *San Antonio Daily Express*, May 1, 1893; Holden, *Alkali Trails*, p. 121.

ernor, but each would have its own legislature, two United States senators, and representatives in Congress. In support of his plan Bede argued that, because of its proud historical heritage as an independent nation and its having entered the Union under its own volition with the right to divide and have ten senators in Congress, Texas should have the advantages of division without dismemberment. Furthermore, he argued, the state was too large and its interests too diverse for efficient governmental administration. North Texas had been settled largely by native American prohibitionists; south Texas, by antiprohibitionists of European extraction. The people of east Texas were farmers and gardeners from the Old South who wanted low tariffs, and west Texas was still only partially occupied by cattlemen, who needed military protection.[9]

Congressmen regarded Bede's presentation more as a bit of humor than as a serious proposal. Senator Joseph Weldon Bailey of Texas, however, had already spoken against division on the basis of the state's historical heritage, and most of the press either opposed or ignored the "comic resolution."[10]

The prohibition issue, which by 1908 had become the all-absorbing political issue, inspired a few politicians in 1909 to suggest the creation of two new states (Northeast Texas and Northwest Texas) where statewide prohibition could be adopted at once, but the noise they made was prohibitionists' whimpers rather than Coyote howls.[11]

The muffled howls of the Coyotes were next heard in 1915, this time over the inequity in legislative representation. On January 28, state Senator W. A. Johnson of Memphis introduced a resolution (SJR 7) that called for a special election in July on a constitutional amendment that, if passed, would have authorized the creation of a State of Jefferson out of the area encompassed by 117 counties of western Texas. In defense of his resolution, Johnson maintained that his proposed state, since the last federal census, was entitled to twice its representation in the Texas senate and to the two additional congressmen-at-large, but that two regular and five special sessions of the legislature had refused to redistrict. Although the Senate Committee on

[9] U.S. Congress, *Congressional Record*, 59 Cong., 1 sess., April 10, 1906, pp. 5021–5023; McConnell, *Social Cleavages in Texas*, pp. 113–116.

[10] *Congressional Record*, 58 Cong., 3 sess., February 7, 1905, p. 1981; *Dallas Morning News*, April 11 and April 12, 1906; McConnell, *Social Cleavages in Texas*, pp. 116–118.

[11] *Dallas Morning News*, August 27, 1909; Holden, *Alkali Trails*, p. 122.

Constitutional Amendments reported favorably, the proposal was never debated on the floor. Senator Johnson was merely trying to prod the legislature into action on redistricting.[12]

Two other division proposals were made in the same session of the legislature. In February, Senator W. L. Hall of Galveston proposed (SJR 9) the creation of three states (North Texas, South Texas, and Jefferson), and in the House L. H. Bates of Brownsville proposed (HJR 40) the creation of the state of South Texas, but neither proposal received favorable committee action.[13] The proposals attracted very little public attention and no strong emotional reaction for or against from the press. The *Austin American* felt that the division of Texas into two or more states was inevitable, for patriotic sentiment would eventually succumb to the will of ambitious politicians and business expediency.[14] The editor of the *Memphis News* disagreed. "Although there is enough room in the Panhandle to lose several of the smaller states of the Union," he wrote, "the people of Texas, so long as there is a drop of the Alamo blood in their veins, will resent to their last breath the division of Texas or the excision of a foot of, to them, hallowed territory."[15]

After concentrating their attention on World War I and the problems of readjustment that followed, the Coyotes in 1921 resumed where they had left off in 1915. This time their painful howl was more pronounced than at any other time since 1869. The immediate cause was Governor Pat M. Neff's veto of a bill providing for the location of an agricultural and mechanical college in western Texas. On the same day as the veto, April 2, 1921, an estimated five thousand west Texans, meeting in Sweetwater, adopted resolutions, drafted by

[12] *Texas Senate Journal*, 34 Leg., reg. sess., 1915, pp. 99, 298, 1204; Holden, *Alkali Trails*, pp. 122–124; McConnell, *Social Cleavages in Texas*, pp. 120–123.

[13] *Texas Senate Journal*, 34 Leg., reg. sess., 1915, p. 249; *Texas House Journal*, 34 Leg., reg. sess., 1915, pp. 375, 755; Holden, *Alkali Trails*, p. 124. Hall did not designate boundaries. Bates specified that the northern and western boundary of his proposed South Texas would be an extension from the Sabine River along the northern boundary of the counties of Orange, Hardin, San Jacinto, Walker, Grimes, Brazos, Burleson, Lee, Williamson, Burnet, Llano, Mason, and Menard, and thence south along the west line of Menard, Kimble, Kerr, Bandera, and Uvalde counties, and thence west along the northern boundary of Maverick County to the Rio Grande (*Austin American*, February 9, 1915).

[14] *Austin American*, February 18, 1915.

[15] Quoted in McConnell, *Social Cleavages in Texas*, p. 126.

R. M. Chitwood and O. H. Roberts, that set forth their grievances and threatened to call for the creation of a new western state unless the legislature at its next special session complied with the group's demands. Of more fundamental importance than the veto, however, was equality of representation. For twenty years Texas had violated its own constitution by failing to redistrict the state for purposes of representation in the legislature and in Congress. Other demands included a more equitable adjustment of taxes and the establishment of adequate educational facilities and other institutions for the region's citizens. Intense anger was evident over the governor's veto of the agricultural and mechanical college bill.[16]

Two nights later more than two hundred representatives of Chambers of Commerce and commercial organizations from throughout west Texas gathered at a dinner meeting at the Wright Hotel in Sweetwater. After hearing an angry and emotional narration of injustices imposed on the people of western Texas, they endorsed a number of strongly worded resolutions. Although there was no reference to creating a new western state, possibly because on the previous day Governor Neff had promised to call a special session of the legislature for the purpose of correcting the injustices, the tone of the meeting indicated that west Texans no longer would permit their grievances to be overlooked.[17]

Most of the press ignored the howls of the west Texans or else, in reporting them, expressed opposition to division. The *Dallas Morning News* editorialized that "west Texas does have its grievances," especially inadequate representation in the legislature, but that in the long run it "would be better off to stay a part of Texas."[18]

For the next three years west Texans assumed a militant attitude

[16] *Austin American*, April 3 and April 4, 1921; *Dallas Morning News*, April 3 and April 4, 1921; R. C. Crane, "The West Texas Agricultural and Mechanical College Movement and the Founding of Texas Technological College," *West Texas Historical Association Year Book* 7 (1931):21; Holden, *Alkali Trails*, pp. 124–125. The resolutions are quoted in McConnell, *Social Cleavages in Texas*, pp. 128–129.

[17] *Austin American*, April 6, 1921; *Dallas Morning News*, April 6, 7, 8, and 10, 1921; Crane, "The West Texas Agricultural and Mechanical College Movement," 7:21.

On the previous day, April 5, "several hundred residents" of Plainview and the surrounding area had adopted resolutions that condemned Governor Neff, charged discrimination against west Texas, and threatened dismemberment of the state (*Austin American*, April 6, 1921).

[18] *Dallas Morning News*, April 6, 1921.

both in and out of the legislature. Hoping to attain sectional peace, the legislature provided for the establishment of Texas Technological College. This token appeasement quieted the division sentiment in north and northwest Texas. Thereafter, the division movement was in the southwestern part of the state, sustained at first almost single-handedly by a lone Coyote, whose yelps were really directed at other political objectives than at division itself.

The first such yelp came from Congressman John Nance Garner of Uvalde in 1930. Angered by New England's domination of Congress for its own advantage, particularly in the enactment of tariff measures, Garner suggested that Texas, if so disposed, could transfer the balance of political power from New England to the South. The industrial advancement of the South and Southwest, he asserted, had been retarded by the Northeast's control over the political policies of the nation, including the Hawley-Smoot and Fordney-McCumber tariff bills. Every industry of the North Atlantic region, he claimed, had been granted special privilege to exploit Southern and Southwestern producers of raw materials. Garner threatened that Texas might divide into five states (the first proposal for five): North Texas, East Texas, South Texas, West Texas, and Central Texas, each of which, he asserted, was a logical geographical, political, and agricultural region.[19]

The *New York Times*, apparently taking him seriously, editorialized that "Mr. Garner must not foster this calamitous thing. Contrasted with his proposed revenge on New England, Sherman's march would seem pastoral." Elsewhere, however, the public and press regarded Garner's remarks as a ploy to attain from Congress more favorable treatment of the South and Southwest. Federal judge William H. Atwell of Texas stated that by division Texas would have nothing to gain politically and would suffer the "loss of a great deal from a sentimental and patriotic standpoint." A Texas congressman remarked that Garner "is merely kidding the boys in Washington."[20] With that, the subject passed into oblivion with no more effect than a small west Texas whirlwind on a hot summer afternoon.

Eight years later a small group of citizens in south Texas, to relieve

[19] *Congressional Record,* 71 Cong., 2 sess., May 8, 1930, pp. 8642–8643, and June 9, 1930, pp. 10308–10; *New York Times,* May 16, 1930; *Dallas Morning News,* May 16, 1930; *Austin American,* May 16, 1930.
[20] *New York Times,* May 17, 1930; *Dallas Morning News,* May 17 and May 18, 1930.

their burden of bond indebtedness, suggested the possibility of creating a State of South Texas. Led by Gordon Griffin, a McAllen attorney, and P. E. Montgomery, a local publisher, the group proposed to form the new state from the territory comprising Hidalgo, Willacy, and Starr counties, an area about the size of Connecticut and with a population of 176,452 persons. The sponsors of the movement advocated a unicameral legislature, no ad valorem taxes, and raising revenue from state-owned liquor stores, state-controlled horse and dog racing, and easy divorces. Although the sponsors named promotional committees for several cities and had the endorsement of several prominent residents of the proposed state, the move was opposed by Harbert Davenport, the foremost local Texas historian. Outside the area, Texans generally regarded the whole affair as amusing, humorous, and ridiculous.[21] With that single outburst, the south Texas Coyotes faded into oblivion. Since 1938, the dismemberment of Texas has seldom been mentioned. After the lapse of nearly four decades, a congressman from Dallas drew some public attention in 1975 by replaying the discarded 1930 record of John Nance Garner.[22]

Like the unpopular animal for which they were derisively named, the Coyotes—after an all-out effort in 1868–1869 to create out of Texas a State of West Texas—gradually vanished with the growth of population and the development of technology until the sound of a "loner" yelping in pain or baying at the moon no longer arouses in those who happen to hear any sense of alarm but instead a feeling of amusement and patriotic romanticism.

[21] *Dallas Morning News*, January 19 and January 21, 1938; *Lubbock Evening Journal*, January 20, 1938.
[22] *Congressional Record*, 94 Cong., 1 sess., February 27, 1975, p. 1129; *New York Times*, March 1, 1975; *Dallas Morning News*, February 28 and March 1, 1975.

# CONSTITUTION
# OF THE
# STATE OF WEST TEXAS.

We, the people of West Texas, acknowledging with gratitude the grace of God in permitting us to make choice of our
form of Government, do ordain and establish this Constitution:

## ARTICLE I.

### BILL OF RIGHTS.

That the general, great and essential principles of liberty
and free government may be recognized and established, we
declare:

SECTION 1. All political power is inherent in the people,
and all free governments are founded on their authority, and
instituted for their benefit; and the people of this State have
at all times the unalienable right to alter or reform their form
of government, in such manner as they may think expedient,
subject to the Constitution and Laws of the United States.

SEC. 2. All freemen, when they form a social compact,
have equal rights; and no man, or set of men, is entitled to
exclusive separate public emoluments or privileges, but in
consideration of public services.

SEC. 3. No religious test shall ever be required as a qualification to any office or public trust in this State.

SEC. 4. All men have a natural and indefeasible right to
worship God according to the dictates of their own consciences; no man shall be compelled to attend, erect, or support any place of worship, or to maintain any ministry against
his consent; no human authority ought, in any case whatever,
to control or interfere with the rights of conscience in matters
of religion; and no preference shall ever be given by law to
any religious societies or mode of worship. The Legislature
shall pass laws to protect all persons in the peaceable enjoyment of their mode of worship, free from all disturbances
whatever, but shall make no laws prescribing a special obser-
vance of any religious days or customs.

SEC. 5. Every citizen shall be at liberty to speak, write, or
publish his opinions on any subject, being responsible for the
abuse of that privilege; and no law shall ever be passed cur-
tailing the liberty of speech or of the press.

SEC. 6. In prosecutions for the publication of papers investigating the official conduct of officers, or men, in a public
capacity, or when the matter published is proper for public
information, the truth thereof may be given in evidence. And
in all indictments for libels, the jury shall have the right to determine the law and the facts, under the direction of the court,
as in other cases.

SEC. 7. The people shall be secure in their persons, houses,
papers and possessions, from all unreasonable seizures or
searches; and no warrant to search any place, or to seize any
person or thing, shall issue, without describing them as near
as may be, nor without probable cause, supported by oath or
affirmation.

SEC. 8. In all criminal prosecutions, the accused shall have
a speedy public trial, by an impartial jury; he shall not be compelled to give evidence against himself; he shall have the right
of being heard by himself or counsel, or both; shall be con-

fronted with the witnesses against him, and shall have compulsory process for obtaining witnesses in his favor; and no person shall be holden to answer for any criminal charge, but on presentment or information, except in cases of offences against the laws regulating the militia.

SEC. 9. All prisoners shall be bailable by sufficient sureties, unless for capital offences, when the proof is evident; but this provision shall not be so construed as to prohibit bail after presentment or information, upon an examination of the evidence by a Judge of the Supreme or District Court, upon the return of the writ of *habe s corpus*, returnable in the county where the offence is committed.

SEC. 10. The privileges of the writ of *habeas corpus* shall not be suspended, except when in case of rebellion or invasion the public safety may require it.

SEC. 11. Excessive bail shall not be required, nor excessive fines imposed, nor cruel or unusual punishment inflicted. All courts shall be open, and every person, for an injury done him in his lands, goods, person, or reputation, shall have remedy by due course of law.

SEC. 12. No person, for the same offence, shall be twice put in jeopardy of life or limb, nor shall a person be again put upon trial for the same offence after a verdict of not guilty; and the right of trial by jury shall remain inviolate.

SEC. 13. Every person shall have the right to keep and bear arms, in the lawful defence of himself or the government, under such regulations as the Legislature may prescribe.

SEC. 14. No bill of attainder, *ex post facto* law, retroactive law, or any law impairing the obligations of contracts, shall be made, and no person's property shall be taken or applied to public use, without adequate compensation being made, unless by the consent of such person, nor shall any law be passed depriving a party of any remedy for the enforcement of a contract which existed when the contract was made.

SEC. 15. No person shall ever be imprisoned for debt.

SEC. 16. No citizen of this State shall be deprived of life, liberty, property, or privileges, outlawed, exiled, or in any manner disfranchised, except by due course of the law of the land.

SEC. 17. The military shall at all times be subordinate to the civil authority.

SEC. 18. Perpetuities and monopolies are contrary to the genius of a free government, and shall never be allowed—nor shall the law of primogeniture or entailments ever be in force in this State.

SEC. 19. The citizens shall have the right, in a peaceable manner, to assemble together for their common good, and to apply to those invested with the powers of government for redress of grievances, or other purposes, by petition, address, or remonstrance.

SEC. 20. No power of suspending laws in this State shall be exercised, except by the Legislature, or its authority.

SEC. 21. The equality of all persons before the law is herein recognized, and shall ever remain inviolate; nor shall any citizen ever be deprived of any right, privilege, or immunity, nor be exempted from any burden, or duty, on account of race, color, or previous condition.

SEC. 22. Importations of persons "under the name of coolies," or any other name or designation, or the adoption of any system of "peonage," whereby the helpless and unfortunate may be reduced to practical bondage, shall never be authorized, or tolerated by the laws of this State, and neither slavery nor involuntary servitude, except as a punishment for crime whereof the party shall have been duly convicted, shall ever exist in this State.

SEC. 23. To guard against transgressions of the high powers herein delegated, we declare that every thing in this "Bill of Rights" is excepted out of the general powers of government, and shall forever remain inviolate, and all laws contrary thereto, or to the following provisions, shall be void;

and we declare that the powers herein granted to the different departments of the government of this State are based upon the equality, in civil and political rights, of all human beings within the jurisdiction of this State; and should any department (either executive, legislative or judicial) attempt, in any manner, to deprive any person or persons of their herein guaranteed civil and political rights, such attempts shall be considered as a violation of the compact under which this State entered the Union.

## ARTICLE II.
### DIVISION OF THE POWERS OF GOVERNMENT.

SEC. 1. The powers of the Government of the State of West Texas shall be divided into three distinct departments, and each of them be confided to a separate body of magistracy— to wit: those which are Legislative to one, those which are Executive to another, and those which are Judicial to another; and no person, or collection of persons, being of one of those departments, shall exercise any power, properly attached to either of the others, except in the instances herein expressly permitted.

## ARTICLE III.
### LEGISLATIVE DEPARTMENT.

SEC. 1. Every male person who shall have attained the age of twenty-one years, and who shall be (or who shall have declared his intention to become) a citizen of the United States, or who is, at the time of the acceptance of this Constitution by the Congress of the United States, a citizen of West Texas, and shall have resided in this State one year next preceding an election, and the last six months within the district or county, in which he offers to vote, and is duly registered, (Indians not taxed, excepted,) shall be deemed a qualified elector: and should such qualified elector happen to be in any other county, situated in the district in which he resides, at the time of an election, he shall be permitted to vote for any district officer, provided that the qualified electors shall be permitted to vote anywhere in the State for State officers, and provided, further, that no soldier, seaman, or marine in the Army or Navy of the United States, shall be entitled to vote at any election created by this Constitution; provided, further, that the residence within the limits of the old State of Texas, of persons who, within six months from the acceptance of this Constitution by the United States Congress, may remove into this State, shall be counted in estimating the residence required previous to voting.

SEC. 2. Electors in all cases shall be privileged from arrest during their attendance at elections, and in going to and returning from the same, except in cases of treason, felony, or breach of the peace.

SEC. 3. The Legislative powers of this State shall be vested in two distinct branches; the one to be styled the Senate, and the other the House of Representatives, and both together the "Legislature of the State of West Texas." The style of all the laws shall be, "Be it enacted by the Legislature of the State of West Texas."

SEC. 4. The members of the House of Representatives shall be chosen by the qualified electors, and their term of office shall be two years from the day of the general election; and the sessions of the Legislature shall be annual, at such times as shall be prescribed by law.

SEC. 5. No person shall be a Representative, unless he be a citizen of the United States, a resident of the county or district from which he may be chosen, for the last year previous to his election, and a qualified elector at the time of his election.

SEC. 6. All elections by the people shall be held at such

time and places, in the several counties, cities or towns, as are now, or may hereafter be designated by law.

SEC. 7. The Senators shall be chosen by the qualified electors for the term of four years; and shall be divided by lot into two classes, as nearly equal as can be. The seats of Senators of the first class shall be vacated at the expiration of the first two years, and of the second class at the expiration of four years; so that one-half thereof shall be chosen biennially thereafter.

SEC. 8. Such mode of classifying new additional Senators shall be observed, as will as nearly as possible preserve an equality of number in each class.

SEC. 9. When a Senatorial district shall be composed of two or more counties, it shall not be separated by any county belonging to another district.

SEC. 10. No person shall be a Senator, unless at the time of his election he shall be a citizen of the United States; shall have attained the age of twenty-five years; shall have resided in the district from which he may be chosen for one year immediately preceding his election, and shall be a qualified voter of the State.

SEC. 11. The House of Representatives, when assembled, shall elect a Speaker and its other officers, and the Senate shall choose a President of the Senate and its other officers. In case of absence or inability to serve, for any cause whatever, of the President of the Senate or the Speaker of the House of Representatives, a President of the Senate, for the time being, or a Speaker *pro tem.* of the House, may be chosen by their respective bodies. Each House shall judge of the qualifications and elections of its own members, but contested elections shall be determined in such manner as shall be directed by law: two-thirds of each House shall constitute a quorum to do business, but a smaller number may adjourn from day to day, and compel the attendance of absent members, in such manner, and under such penalties as each House may provide.

SEC. 12. Each House may determine the rules of its own proceedings, punish members for disorderly conduct, and, with the consent of two-thirds, expel a member, but not a second time for the same offence.

SEC. 13. Each House shall keep a journal of its own proceedings, and publish the same; and the yeas and nays of the members of either House, on any question, shall, at the desire of any three members present, be entered on the journals.

SEC. 14. When vacancies happen in either House, the Governor, or the person exercising the power of the Governor, shall issue writs of election to fill such vacancies.

SEC. 15. Senators and Representatives shall, in all cases, except in treason, felony, or breach of the peace, be privileged from arrest during the session of the Legislature, and in going to and returning from the same, allowing one day for every twenty miles, such member may reside from the place at which the Legislature is convened.

SEC. 16. Each House may punish, by imprisonment, during the session, any person not a member, for disrespectful or disorderly conduct, in its presence, or for obstructing any of its proceedings: provided such imprisonment shall not at any one time exceed forty-eight hours.

SEC. 17. Neither House shall hold secret sessions, except the Senate, when acting on appointments.

SEC. 18. Neither House shall, without the consent of the other, adjourn for more than three days; nor to any other place than that in which they may be sitting, without the concurrence of both Houses.

SEC. 19. Bills may originate in either House, and be amended, altered, or rejected by the other; but no bill shall have the force of a law, until on three several days it be read in each House, and free discussion be allowed thereon, unless, in case of great emergency, four-fifths of the House in which the bill shall be pending may deem it expedient to dispense with this rule; and every bill, having passed both Houses, shall be

154

signed by the Speaker and President of their respective Houses.

SEC. 20. After a bill or resolution has been rejected by either branch of the Legislature, no bill or resolution containing the same substance shall be passed into a law during the same session.

SEC. 21. Each member of the Legislature shall receive from the public Treasury a compensation for his services, which may be increased or diminished by law; but no increase of compensation shall take effect during the Legislature at which such increase shall be made.

SEC. 22. No Senator or Representative shall, during the term for which he may be elected, be eligible to any civil office of profit under this State, which shall have been created, or the emolument of which may have been increased during such term: the President of the Senate and the Speaker of the House of Representatives shall be elected from their respective bodies.

SEC. 23. No Judge of any Court of law or equity, Secretary of State, Attorney General, Clerk of any court of record, Sheriff, or Collector, or any person holding a lucrative office under the United States, or this State, or any foreign government, shall be eligible to the Legislature; nor shall at the same time hold or exercise any two offices, agencies or appointments of trust or profit, under this State: provided, that officers of militia, to which there is attached no annual salary, the office of Notary Public, or the office of Justice of the Peace, shall not be deemed lucrative; and that one person may hold two or more county offices, if it be so provided by the Legislature.

SEC. 24. No person who at any time may have been a Collector of taxes, or who may have been otherwise entrusted with public money, shall be eligible to the Legislature, or to any office of profit or trust under the State government, until he shall have obtained a discharge for the amount of such collections, and for all public moneys with which he may have been entrusted.

SEC. 25. Elections for Senators and Representatives shall be general throughout the State, and shall be regulated by law.

SEC. 26. The Legislature shall cause an enumeration to be made every ten years, commencing on the sixth day of February, 1875, of all the inhabitants (including Indians taxed) of the State, designating particularly the number of registered voters, and the age, sex and color of all, (herein following the classification of the United States census,) and the whole number of Representatives shall, at the next session after the several periods of making such enumeration, be fixed by the Legislature, and apportioned among the several counties, according to the number of population in each. The number of Representatives shall at present be fixed at twenty-six, and when the population of the State may exceed the number of two hundred and sixty thousand persons, then one additional Representative for each ten thousand of such excess of population shall be added; Provided, that the whole number of Representatives shall never exceed forty-two.

SEC. 27. Until changed by law, the apportionment of Senators and Representatives shall remain as fixed by the Ordinance attached to this Constitution.

SEC. 28. The number of Senators shall at present be fixed at thirteen; and when the population of the State may exceed the number of two hundred and sixty thousand persons then one additional Senator for each twenty thousand of such excess of population shall be added; Provided, that the whole number of Senators shall never exceed twenty-one.

SEC. 29. The first session of the Legislature, after the acceptance of this Constitution by the Congress of the United States, shall be held at the city of San Antonio, Bexar county, and thereafter until the year 1871, after which year the seat of government shall be permanently located by a vote of the people.

SEC. 30. The members of the Legislature shall receive from the Treasury of the State, as their compensation, (until changed by law,) the sum of five hundred dollars each, annually, and the members acting as President of the Senate or Speaker of the House of Representatives, shall receive double this compensation. The members shall also receive (until changed by law) the sum of eight dollars for each twenty-five miles traveled in going to and returning from the seat of government.

SEC. 31. In order to settle permanently the seat of government, an election shall be holden throughout the State at the usual places of holding elections, at the first general election after the year (1871) one thousand eight hundred and seventy-one, which shall be conducted according to law, at which time the people shall vote for such place as they may see proper for the seat of government; the returns of said election to be transmitted to the Governor with the other returns of that election. If either place voted for shall have a majority of the whole number of votes cast, then the same shall be the permanent seat of government. But in case neither place voted for shall have the majority of the whole number of votes given in, then the Governor shall issue his proclamation for an election to be holden in the same manner at the next following general election, between the two places having the highest number of votes at the first election. This election shall be conducted in the same manner as at the first, and the returns made to the Governor, and the place having the highest number of votes shall be the permanent seat of government.

# ARTICLE IV.

## JUDICIAL DEPARTMENT.

SECTION 1. The judicial power of this State shall be vested in one Supreme Court, in District Courts, and in such inferior courts as the Legislature may from time to time ordain and establish; and such jurisdiction may be vested in corporation courts as may be deemed necessary, and be directed by law.

SEC. 2. The Supreme Court shall consist of a Chief Justice and two Associates, any two of whom shall form a quorum.

SEC. 3. The Supreme Court shall have appellate jurisdiction only, which in civil causes shall be co-extensive with the limits of the State. In criminal causes no appeal shall be allowed to the Supreme Court, unless some Judge thereof shall, upon inspecting a transcript of the record sent up under such regulations as may be prescribed by law, believe that some error of law has been committed by the Judge before whom the cause was tried. Appeals from interlocutory judgments may be allowed, with such exceptions and under such regulations as the Legislature may prescribe. The Supreme Court and the Judges thereof shall have power to issue the writ of *habeas corpus*, and, under such regulations as may be prescribed by law, may issue the writ of *mandamus*, and such other writs as may be necessary to enforce its own jurisdiction. The Supreme Court shall also have power to ascertain such matters of fact as may be necessary to the proper exercise of its jurisdiction.

SEC. 4. The Supreme Court shall hold a session at the seat of government annually, between the months of October and June, and shall appoint its own Clerks, who shall hold their offices for four years, and be subject to removal by said court for neglect of duty, misdemeanor in office, and such other causes as may be prescribed by law.

SEC. 5. The Judges of the Supreme Court shall hold their offices for the term of twelve years, and the Judges of the District Court for eight years. The terms of the Supreme Judges shall be so arranged that the office of one shall become vacant at the end of every four years, and when, by death, resignation or other cause than expiration of term, a vacancy occurs, the appointment to the same shall be for the unexpired term. The Judges of the Supreme Court and District Courts, the Attorney General and District Attorneys, shall be appointed by the

Governor, by and with the advice and consent of the Senate; Provided, that at the first general election after the year one thousand eight hundred and eighty, (1880,) the question shall be submitted to vote, whether these officers shall thereafter be elected by the people.

SEC. 6. The State shall be divided into convenient judicial districts. For each district there shall be chosen a Judge who shall reside in the same, and hold the Courts at one place in each county, and at least three times in each year, in such manner as may be prescribed by law.

SEC. 7. The Judges of the Supreme Court shall receive a salary of four thousand dollars annually, and the Judges of the District Court a salary of three thousand dollars annually, and the salaries of the Judges shall not be diminished during their continuance in office.

SEC. 8. The Judges of the Supreme and District Courts shall be removed by the Governor, on the address of two-thirds of each House of the Legislature, for wilful neglect of duty or other reasonable cause; Provided, however, that the cause or causes for which such removal shall be required, shall be stated at length in such address, and entered on the journals of each House; and provided further, that the cause or causes shall be notified to the Judge so intended to be removed; and he shall be admitted to a hearing in his own defence before any vote for such address shall pass: And in all such cases, the vote shall be taken by yeas and nays, and entered on the journals of each House respectively.

SEC. 9. All Judges of the Supreme and District Courts shall, by virtue of their offices, be conservators of the peace throughout the State. The style of all writs and process shall be "The State of West Texas." All prosecutions shall be carried on in the name and by the authority of the "State of West Texas," and conclude, "Against the peace and dignity of the State."

SEC. 10. The District Court shall have original jurisdiction of all criminal cases; of all causes in behalf of the State to recover penalties, forfeitures and escheats; and of all suits and cases in which the State may be interested; of all cases of divorce; of all suits to recover damages for slander or defamation of character; of all suits for the trial of title to land; of all suits for the enforcement of liens; and of all suits, complaints, and pleas whatever, without regard to any distinction between law and equity, when the matter in controversy shall be valued at or amount to one hundred dollars, exclusive of interest; and the said Courts and the Judges thereof shall have power to issue all writs necessary to enforce their own jurisdiction, and to give them a general superintendence and control over inferior tribunals. The District Court shall also have appellate jurisdiction in cases originating in inferior Courts, with such exceptions and under such regulations as the Legislature may prescribe. And the District Court shall also have original and exclusive jurisdiction for the probate of wills, for the appointing of guardians, for the granting of letters testamentary and of administration; for settling the accounts of executors, administrators, and guardians, and for the transaction of all business appertaining to the estates of deceased persons, minors, idiots, lunatics, and persons of unsound mind; and for the settlement, partition, and distribution of such estates, under such rules and regulations as may be prescribed by law.

SECT. 11. There shall be a Clerk of the District Court for each County, who shall be elected by the qualified voters for members of the Legislature, and who shall hold his office for four years, subject to removal by information, or by presentment of a grand jury and conviction by a petit jury. In case of vacancy, the Judge of the district shall have the power to appoint a Clerk, until the next general election. The said clerk shall exercise such powers and perform such duties appertaining to the estates of deceased persons, lunatics, idiots, minors, and persons of unsound mind, in vacation, as may be prescribed by law. Provided that all contested issues of law or fact, shall be determined by the District Court.

By virtue of his office the District Clerk shall have control of all records, papers, and books of the District Court.

SEC. 12. There shall be chosen an Attorney General for the State, and a District Attorney for each Judicial District, who shall hold their offices for four years. The duties, salaries and perquisites of the Attorney General and District Attorneys shall be prescribed by law.

SEC. 13. There shall be elected in each county by the qualified voters of the different precincts thereof as may be directed by law, at least five Justices of the Peace, one of whom shall reside, after the election, at the county seat, and not more than one of said Justices shall be a resident of the same justice's precinct. They shall hold their offices for four years, and should a vacancy occur in either of said offices, an election shall be held for the unexpired term. They shall have such civil and criminal jurisdiction as shall be provided by law. And the Justices of the Peace in each county, or a majority of them, shall constitute a Court, to be called the "County Court," having such jurisdiction similar to that heretofore exercised by County Commissioners and Police Courts, as may be prescribed by law. And when sitting as such Court, they shall from among themselves choose their presiding officer. The times and manner of holding said Courts shall be prescribed by law. Justices of the Peace shall also be commissioned to act as Notaries Public. They shall also discharge all the duties of Coroner, and they shall have such fees and emoluments as may be fixed by law.

SEC. 14. The Justices of the Peace in each county, sitting as a County Court, shall appoint one Constable for each Justices' Precinct, who shall hold his office for four years, subject to removal by said Court for cause spread upon the minutes of the Court. And said Constables, or either of them, in addition to the ordinary duties of their office, shall discharge the duties of Sheriff in all cases where the Sheriff is disqualified or prevented from acting, or where the law may so provide.

SEC. 15. One Sheriff for each county shall be elected by the qualified voters thereof, who shall hold his office for four years, subject to removal on information, or presentment, and conviction by a petit jury. Process against the Sheriff, and all such writs as by reason of interest in the suit, or connection with the parties, or for other cause, the Sheriff is incompetent to execute, shall issue to and be executed by any Constable in the County. In case of vacancy in the office of Sheriff, the same may be filled by appointment of the Governor, until the next general election.

SEC. 16. There shall be a clerk elected by the voters of each county, who shall hold his office for four years. He shall attend upon and keep the records of the County Court, and shall act as recorder of instruments of writing for his county. He shall keep his office at the county seat, and shall perform such other duties and receive such fees and emoluments as may be fixed by law. He shall also be commissioned as a Notary Public. In case of vacancy in the office of County Clerk, the County Court may choose a person to fill the same until the regular election for this office.

SEC. 17. No Judge shall sit in any case wherein he may be interested, or where either of the parties may be connected with him by affinity or consanguinity, within such degrees as may be prescribed by law, or where he shall have been of counsel in the cause. When the Supreme Court or any two of its members shall be thus disqualified to hear and determine any cause or causes in said Court, or when no judgment can be rendered in any case or cases in said Court, by reason of the equal division of opinion of said Judges, the same shall be certified to the Governor of the State, who shall immediately commission the requisite number of persons learned in the law for the trial and determination of said case or cases. When the

Judges of the District Court are thus disqualified, the parties may, by consent, appoint a proper person to try the said case; and the Judges of the said courts may exchange districts, or hold courts for each other, when they may deem it expedient, and shall do so when directed by law, and the Governor may in such case appoint some person learned in the law, to try the case or cases whenever the Judge of the Court is disqualified, and the person so appointed shall receive such compensation as may be given by law.—The disqualification of Judges of inferior tribunals shall be remedied as may hereafter be by law prescribed.

SEC. 18. In the trial of all causes in the District Court, the plaintiff or defendant shall, upon application made in open court, have the right of trial by jury, to be governed by the rules and regulations prescribed in trials at law.

SEC. 19. In all cases arising out of a contract, before any inferior tribunal, when the amount in controversy shall exceed ten dollars, the plaintiff or defendant shall, upon application to the presiding officer, have the right of trial by jury.

SEC. 20. In all cases where Justices of the Peace, or other judicial officers of inferior tribunals shall have jurisdiction in the trial of causes, where the penalty for the violation of a law is fine or imprisonment, (except in cases of contempt,) the accused shall have the right of trial by jury.

SEC. 21. In case of incompetency or improper conduct on the part of a clerk of the District Court, or a Sheriff, such officer may be removed by the Governor, on recommendation of the District Judge, and in case this remedy is applied, the place of the officer removed shall be filled by appointment of the Governor, until the next general election.

SEC. 22. Capital offences shall be punished by imprisonment to hard labor for life, and every offense that may by law be punished by imprisonment in the State Penitentiary, shall be deemed a felony, but all offenses of a less grade than a felony, may be prosecuted upon complaint under oath, by any peace officer or citizen before any Justice of the Peace, or other inferior tribunal that may be established by law, and the party so prosecuted shall have the right of trial by a jury, to be summoned in such manner as may be prescribed by law.

Sec. 23. The Grand Jury system is hereby dispensed with in this State. The prosecution of offences in this State shall be by information or presentment of the District Attorney or Attorney General. The filing before any competent officer of an affidavit charging an offense, shall be sufficient to authorize and require an information or presentment before the proper tribunal. To the District Attorney or Attorney General is given the same authority heretofore exercised by Grand Juries, and these officers are required to institute examinations in regard to any offences that may be brought to their notice. For the institution of prosecutions for offences less than felony, the Legislature may authorize some more simple proceeding. The Legislature shall provide all needful regulations for carrying out the spirit and intent of this and the last preceding section: provided, that if the dispensing with the Grand Jury system shall be found inconvenient, the Legislature may, after five years from the acceptance of this Constitution by the United States Congress, re-establish that system.

Sec. 24. In all trials by Jury, the agreement of three-fourths of the Jurymen shall be sufficient to find a verdict.

Sec. 25. In all civil suits within this State, interest in the result of any suit, on the part of the person offering to testify therein, shall not be deemed a valid objection to his testimony, but the same shall go to the Court or Jury, and be weighed and considered.

## ARTICLE V.
### EXECUTIVE DEPARTMENT.

Sec. 1. The supreme executive power of this State shall be vested in the Chief Magistrate, who shall be styled the Governor of the State of West Texas.

SEC. 2. The Governor shall be elected by the qualified electors of the State, at the time and places of elections for members of the Legislature.

SEC. 3. The returns for every election of Governor shall be made out, sealed up, and transmitted by the returning officers to the seat of government, directed to the Speaker of the House of Representatives, who shall, during the first week of the session of the Legislature thereafter, open and publish them, in presence of both Houses of the Legislature. The person having the highest number of votes, and being constitutionally eligible, shall be declared by the Speaker, under the direction of the Legislature, to be Governor: but if two or more persons shall have the highest and an equal number of votes, one of them shall be forthwith chosen Governor, by a joint vote of both Houses of the Legislature. Whenever there shall be a contested election for the office of Governor, or any of the Executive officers to be elected by the qualified voters of the State, it shall be determined by the joint action of both Houses of the Legislature.

SEC. 4. The Governor shall hold his office for the term of four years from the regular time of installation, and until his successor shall be duly qualified, but shall not be eligible for more than eight years in any term of twelve years; he shall be at least twenty-five years of age, shall be a citizen of the United States, a qualified voter of the State of West Texas, and (after the first election) shall have resided in this State three years immediately preceding his election.

SEC. 5. He shall, at stated times, receive a compensation for his services, which shall not be increased or diminished during the term for which he shall have been elected. The first Governor shall receive an annual salary of four thousand dollars, and no more.

SEC. 6. He shall be Commander-in-Chief of the Militia of the State, except when they are called into the actual service of the United States; and shall have control and management of the police force of the State, for the purpose of suppressing disorder and maintaining the laws.

SEC. 7. He may require information in writing from the officers of the Executive Department, on any subject relating to the duties of their respective offices.

SEC. 8. He shall have power, by proclamation, on extraordinary occasions, to convene the Legislature at the seat of Government; but if the prevalence of dangerous disease, or the presence of the public enemy there shall render it necessary, then at any other place within the State he may deem expedient. In case of disagreement between the two Houses, with respect to adjournment, he may adjourn them to such time as he shall think proper, not beyond the day of the next regular meeting of the Legislature.

SEC. 9. He shall, from time to time, give to the Legislature information, in writing, of the state of the Government, and recommend to their consideration such measures as he may deem expedient.

SEC. 10. He shall take care that the laws be faithfully executed.

SEC. 11. In all criminal cases, except treason and impeachment, he shall have power, after conviction, to grant reprieves and pardons; and, under such rules as the Legislature may prescribe, he shall have power to remit fines and forfeitures. With the advice and consent of the Senate, he may grant pardons in cases of treason; and to this end, he may respite a sentence therefor until the close of the succeeding session of the Legislature; provided, that in all cases of remission of fines or forfeitures, or grants of reprieve or pardon, the Governor shall file in the office of the Secretary of State his reasons therefor.

SEC. 12. Nominations to fill vacancies occurring in the recess of the Legislature shall be made by the Governor during the first ten days of its session. And should any such nomination be rejected, the same person shall not again be nominated during the session, to fill the same office. Should the Governor fail to make nominations to fill any vacancy during the session of the Senate, such vacancy shall not be filled by the Governor, until the next meeting of the Senate.

SEC. 13. During the sessions of the Legislature, the Governor and heads of Departments shall be present where its sessions are held; and at all other times at the capital, except when, in the opinion of the Legislature, the public good may otherwise require.

SEC. 14. No person, holding the office of Governor, shall hold any other office or commission, civil or military.

SEC. 15. All commissions shall be in the name and by the authority of the State of West Texas, be sealed with the State seal, signed by the Governor, and attested by the Secretary of State.

SEC. 16. There shall be a Secretary of State, appointed by the Governor, by and with the advice and consent of the Senate, who shall continue in office during the term of service of the Governor elect. He shall keep a fair register of all official acts and proceedings of the Governor, and shall, when required, lay the same, with all papers, minutes and vouchers relative thereto, before the Legislature or either House thereof, and shall perform such other duties as may be required of him by law.

SEC. 17. Every bill, which shall have passed both Houses of the Legislature, shall be presented to the Governor for his approval. If he approve, he shall sign it; but if he disapprove, he shall return it, with his objections, to that House in which it originated; which House shall enter the objections at large upon the journals of the House, and proceed to reconsider it. If, after such reconsideration, two-thirds of the members present shall agree to pass the bill, it shall be sent with the objections to the other House, by which it shall likewise be reconsidered. If approved by two-thirds of the members present of that House, it shall become a law; but, in such cases, both

Houses shall determine the question by yeas and nays, with the names of the members respectively entered upon the journals of each House. If a bill shall not be returned by the Governor within five days (Sundays excepted) after it shall have been presented to him, it shall become a law in like manner as if he had signed it. Every bill presented to the Governor one day before the final adjournment of the two Houses, and not signed by him, shall become a law, and shall have the same force and effect as if signed by him. The Governor may approve any appropriation, and disapprove any other appropriation, in the same bill, by signing the bill, and designating the appropriation disapproved, and sending a copy of such appropriation, with his objection, to the House in which it originated; and the same proceedings shall be had on that part disapproved as on other bills disapproved by him; but if the Legislature shall have adjourned before it is returned, he shall return it, with his objections, to the Secretary of State, to be submitted to both Houses at the succeeding session of the Legislature.

SEC. 18. Every order, resolution, or vote, in which the concurrence of both Houses shall be required, except the question of adjournment, shall be presented to the Governor, and must be approved by him before it can take effect; or being disapproved, shall be repassed in the manner prescribed in the case of a bill.

SEC. 19. There shall be a Comptroller of Public Accounts, and a Treasurer of the State, who shall be elected by the qualified voters at the same time and in the same manner as the Governor is elected. These officers shall hold their offices for the term of four years, and shall perform such duties as may be prescribed by law. In case of vacancy in either of these offices it shall be filled by appointment by the Governor until the next general election.

SEC. 20. Until otherwise established by law, the salaries of the Comptroller and Treasurer of the State shall be twenty-five hundred dollars annually; the salary of Secretary of State shall be fifteen hundred dollars annually; the salary of Attorney General shall be two thousand dollars annually; the salaries of the District Attorneys shall be one thousand dollars annually. The Attorney General and District Attorneys shall have in addition such fees as may be fixed by law.

SEC. 21. In case of the death, resignation, removal from office, inability or refusal of the Governor to serve, or of his impeachment, or absence from the State, the President of the Senate shall exercise the powers and authority appertaining to the office of Governor, until another be chosen at the periodical election, and be duly qualified, or until the Governor impeached, absent, or disabled, shall be acquitted, return, or his disability be removed. Whenever the government shall be administered by the President of the Senate, or he shall be unable to attend as President of the Senate, the Senate shall elect one of their own members as President for the time being. And if, during the vacancy of the office of Governor, the President of the Senate shall die, resign, refuse to serve, or be removed from office, or be unable to serve, or if he shall be impeached, or absent from the State, the Speaker of the House of Representatives, for the time being, shall in like manner administer the government until he shall be superseded by a Governor elected by the people, or by the President of the Senate. The President of the Senate or the Speaker of the House, while he acts as such, shall receive for his services the compensation given by law to that office, and no more; and during the time he administers the government, as Governor, shall receive the same compensation which the Governor would have received had he been employed in the duties of his office, and no more. The Legislature shall provide who shall administer the government in case of vacancy, at the same time in the offices of Governor, President of the Senate and Speaker of the House of Representatives.

SEC. 22. There shall be a seal of the State, which shall be kept by the Governor, and used by him officially.

## ARTICLE VI.
### MILITIA.

SEC. 1. The Legislature shall provide by law for organizing and disciplining the Militia of this State, in such manner as they shall deem expedient, not incompatible with the Constitution and laws of the United States in relation thereto: Provided that no other than registered voters shall be enrolled as militia, and that the officers of the Militia shall be required in addition to the usual oath of office to take an oath that they have never aided or abetted any rebellion or insurrection against the United States.

SEC. 2. Any person who conscientiously scruples to bear arms, shall not be compelled to do so, but shall pay an equivalent for personal service.

SEC. 3. The Governor shall have power to call forth the militia to execute the laws of the State, to suppress insurrection and repel invasions.

## ARTICLE VII.
### GENERAL PROVISIONS.

SEC. 1. The boundaries of the State of West Texas are hereby defined as commencing at a point in the Gulf of Mexico, three miles from the shore opposite the middle of the main channel of Pass Caballo, thence up the middle of said channel and of Matagorda Bay to the mouth of Colorado River, thence up the middle of the main channel of said river, with its meanders to the point where said river is intersected by the thirty-second parallel of North latitude, thence along said parallel to a point        miles west from said river, thence in a straight line to the junction of the Pecos river and Rio Grande, thence down the main channel of the Rio Grande, with its meanders, to the Gulf of Mexico, thence along parallel to the shore of the Gulf of Mexico, three miles from the land to the place of beginning.

SEC. 2. The Constitution and laws of the United States of America, and the treaties and laws of the United States, made in pursuance of said Constitution, are the supreme law of this State. The laws enacted by the Legislature of the State of Texas, previous to the twenty-eighth day of January, eighteen hundred and sixty-one, where the same are not in conflict with the Constitution and laws of the United States, and are not changed by this Constitution, shall remain the law of this State until repealed or amended by the Legislature of the same: Provided that all laws or parts of laws which were enacted for the purpose of protecting or sustaining the institution of slavery, or which recognize any distinction among human beings in regard to their civil or political privileges, rights, and duties are to be considered as null and void, and of no binding force.

SEC. 3. Members of the Legislature, and all officers, before they enter upon the duties of their offices, shall take the following oath or affirmation:— "I, [A. B.] do solemnly swear (or affirm) that I will faithfully and impartially discharge and perform all duties incumbent on me as ———, according to the best of my skill and ability, and that I will support the Constitution and laws of the United States and of this State. And I do further swear (or affirm) that since the acceptance of this Constitution by the Congress of the United States, I, being a citizen of this State, have not fought a duel with deadly weapons, or committed an assault upon any person with deadly weapons, or sent or accepted a challenge to fight a duel with deadly weapons, or acted as second in fighting a duel, or knowingly aided or assisted any one thus offending, either within this State or out of it; that I am not disqualified from holding office under the 14th amendment to the Constitution of the United States, (or as the case may be, my disability to hold office under the 14th amendment to the Constitution of the United States, has been removed by act of Congress,) and further, that I am a qualified elector in this State.

SEC. 4. Every person shall be disqualified from holding any office of trust or profit in this State, who shall have been convicted of having given or offered a bribe to procure his election or appointment.

SEC. 5. Laws shall be made to exclude from office, serving on juries, and from the right of suffrage, those who shall hereafter be convicted of bribery, perjury, forgery, or other high crimes. The privilege of free suffrage shall be supported by laws regulating elections, and prohibiting, under adequate penalties, all undue influence thereon from power, bribery, tumult, or other improper practice.

SEC. 6. Any citizen of this State, who shall, after the adoption of this Constitution, fight a duel with deadly weapons, or commit an assault upon any person with deadly weapons, or send or accept a challenge to fight a duel with deadly weapons, either within this State or out of it, or who shall act as second, or knowingly aid and assist in any manner those thus offending, shall be deprived of the right of suffrage, or of holding any office of trust or profit under this State.

SEC. 7. In all elections by the people the vote shall be by ballot; and in all elections by the Senate and House of Representatives, jointly or separately, the vote shall be given *viva voce*, except in the election of their officers. In selecting all officers within this State, a plurality of votes shall elect.

SEC. 8. The Legislature shall provide by law for the compensation of all officers, servants, agents, and public contractors, not provided for by this Constitution, and shall not grant extra compensation to any officer, agent, servant, or public contractor, after such public service shall have been performed, or contract entered into for the performance of the same; nor grant by appropriation or otherwise, any amount of money out of the Treasury of the State, to any individual on a claim real or pretended, where the same shall not have been provided for by pre-existing law.

SEC. 9. No money shall be drawn from the Treasury but in pursuance of specific appropriations made by law; nor shall any appropriation of money be made for a longer term than two years, except for purposes of education; and no appropriation for private or individual purposes, or for purposes of internal improvement, shall be made without the concurrence of two-thirds of both Houses of the Legislature. A regular statement and account of the receipts and expenditures of all public money shall be published annually in such manner as shall be prescribed by law. And in no case shall the Legislature have the power to issue "Treasury Warrants," "Treasury Notes," or paper of any description intended to circulate as money.

SEC. 10. All civil officers shall reside within the State; and all district or county officers, within their districts or counties; and shall keep their offices at such places therein as may be required by law.

SEC. 11. The duration of all offices not fixed by this Constitution, shall never exceed four years.

SEC. 12. The Legislature shall have power to provide for deductions from the salaries of public officers, who may neglect the performance of any duty that may be assigned them by law.

SEC. 13. No member of Congress, nor person holding or exercising any office of profit or trust under the United States, or either of them, or under any foreign power, shall be eligible as a member of the Legislature, or hold or exercise any office of profit or trust under this State.

SEC. 14. The Legislature shall provide for a change of venue in civil and criminal cases; and for the erection of a Penitentiary at as early a day as practicable.

SEC. 15. It shall be the duty of the Legislature to pass such laws as may be necessary and proper to decide differences by arbitration, when the parties shall elect that method of trial.

SEC. 16. Within five years after the acceptance of this Constitution, the laws, civil and criminal, shall be revised, digested, arranged, and published, in such manner as the Legislature shall direct; and a like revision, digest, and publication, shall be made every ten years thereafter.

SEC. 17. No lottery shall be authorized by this State; and the buying or selling of lottery tickets within this State is prohibited.

SEC. 18. No divorce shall be granted by the Legislature.

SEC. 19. All property, both real and personal of the wife, owned or claimed by her before marriage, and that acquired afterwards by gift, devise, or descent, and the increase of such property, shall be her separate property; and laws shall be passed more clearly defining the rights of the wife, in relation as well to her separate property, as that held in common with her husband. Laws shall also be passed providing for the registration of the wife's separate property. And married women, infants and insane persons shall not be barred of their rights of property by adverse possession or law of limitation of less than seven years from and after the removal of each and all of their respective legal disabilities.

SEC. 20. The Legislature shall have power, and it shall be their duty to protect by law, from forced sale, a certain portion of the property of all heads of families. The homestead of a family, not to exceed two hundred acres of land (not included in a city, town or village,) or, any city, town or village, lot or lots, not to exceed in value in either case the sum of three thousand dollars at the time of their destination as a homestead, shall not be subject to forced sale for debts, except they be for the purchase money thereof, for the taxes assessed thereon, or for labor and materials expended thereon; nor shall the owner, if a married man, be at liberty to alienate the same, unless by the consent of the wife, and in such manner as may be prescribed by law. Provided that this exemption shall not take effect against debts in existence at the time of the destination of the homestead.

SEC. 21. The Legislature shall provide in what cases officers shall continue to perform the duties of their offices, until their successors shall be duly qualified.

SEC. 22. Every law enacted by the Legislature shall embrace but one object, and that shall be expressed in the title.

SEC. 23. No law shall be revised or amended by reference to its title; but in such case the act revised, or section amended, shall be re-enacted and published at length.

SEC. 24. Taxation shall be equal and uniform throughout the State — All property in this State shall be taxed in proportion to its value, to be ascertained as directed by law, except such property as two-thirds of both Houses of the Legislature may think proper to exempt from taxation. The Legislature shall have power to lay an income tax, and to tax all persons pursuing any occupation, trade or profession: Provided, that the term occupation shall not be construed to apply to pursuits, either agricultural or mechanical.

SEC. 25. The annual assessments made upon landed property shall be a lien upon the property, and interest shall run thereon upon each year's assessment.

SEC. 26. Landed property shall not be sold for the taxes due thereon, except under a decree of some court of competent jurisdiction.

SEC. 27. Provisions shall be made by the first Legislature for the condemnation and sale of all lands for taxes due thereon, and every five years thereafter, of all lands the taxes upon which have not been paid to that date.

SEC. 28. It shall be the duty of the Legislature to provide

by law, that in all cases where State or county debt is created, adequate means for the payment of the current interest, and two per cent, as a sinking fund for the redemption of the principal; and all such laws shall be irrepealable until principal and interest are fully paid.

SEC. 29. No corporate body shall hereafter be created, renewed, or extended, with banking or discounting privileges. The Legislature shall prohibit by law individuals from issuing bills, checks, promisory notes, or other paper to circulate as money.

SEC. 30. The Legislature shall have the power to enact general charters, or acts of incorporation only. Two thirds of the Legislature shall have power to revoke and repeal all private corporations by making compensation, if any in fact be due, for the franchise. The State shall not be part owner of the stock or property belonging to any corporation. No special charter shall hereafter be created, amended, renewed, or extended by the Legislature.

SEC. 31. The Legislature shall at the first session thereof, and may at any subsequent session, establish new counties for the convenience of the inhabitants of such new county or counties. Provided that no new county shall be established, which shall reduce the county or counties, or either of them, from which it shall be taken, to a less area than nine hundred square miles, unless by consent of two-thirds of the Legislature, nor shall any county be laid off of less contents. Every new county as to the right of suffrage and representation, shall be considered as part of the county or counties from which it was taken until entitled by numbers to the right of separate representation. No new county shall be laid off with less than one hundred and fifty qualified jurors, resident at the time therein, nor where the county (or counties) from which the new county is proposed to be taken, would thereby be reduced below that number of qualified jurors, and in all cases where from the want of qualified jurors, or other cause, the courts cannot properly be held in any county, it shall be the duty of the District Judge to certify such fact to the Governor, and the Governor shall, by proclamation, attach such county for judicial purposes to that county, the county seat of which is nearest the county seat of the county so to be attached.

SEC. 32. An Assessor and Collector of Taxes shall be elected by the people of each Senatorial District, under such regulations as the Legislature may direct. These officers shall be subject to the supervision and control of the Comptroller, and may be removed by him for incompetency, or improper conduct. They may assess and collect county taxes until otherwise ordered by the Legislature; and the Legislature may separate these two offices in any one or all of the Districts. They shall hold their offices for four years. In case of vacancy in this office, the same may be filled by appointment of the Governor, on recommendation of the Comptroller, until the next general election,

SEC. 33. No soldier shall, in time of peace, be quartered in the house or within the enclosure of any individual, without the consent of the owner, nor in time of war, but in a manner prescribed by law.

SEC. 34. All sales of landed property, made under decrees of Courts in this State, shall be offered to bidders in lots of not less than ten, not more than forty acres, except in towns and cities, including sales for taxes.

SEC. 35. The Legislature shall pass appropriate laws to compel the maintenance and education of illegitimate children.

SEC. 36. Each county in the State shall provide, in such manner as may be prescribed by law, a Manual Labor Poor House, for taking care of, managing, employing and supplying the wants of its indigent and poor inhabitants; and under such regulations as the Legislature may direct, all persons committing petty offences in the county, may be committed to such Manual Labor Poor House for correction and employment.

SEC. 37. All persons who, at anytime heretofore, lived together as husband and wife, and were precluded from the rites of matrimony, and continued to live together until the death of one of the parties, shall be considered as having been legally married; and the issue of such co-habitation shall be deemed legitimate. And all such persons as may be now living together in such relation, shall be considered as having been legally married, and the children heretofore, or hereafter, born of such co-habitation, shall be deemed legitimate.

SEC. 38. Provisions shall be made, under adequate penalties, for the complete registration of all births, deaths and marriages, in every organized county of this State.

SEC. 39. General laws, regulating the adoption of children, emancipation of minors, and the granting of divorces, shall be made; but no special law shall be enacted relating to particular or individual cases.

SEC. 40. The County Courts of the several counties in this State, shall have the power, upon a vote of two-thirds of the qualified voters of the respective counties, to assess and provide for the collection of a tax upon the taxable property, to aid in the construction of Internal Improvements, provided that said tax shall never exceed two per cent upon the value of such property.

SEC. 41. All civil officers of this State shall be removable by an address of two-thirds of the members elect to each House of the Legislature, except those whose removal is otherwise provided for by this Constitution.

SEC. 42. The Accounting Officers of this State shall neither draw nor pay a warrant upon the Treasury, in favor of any person, for salary or compensation, as agent, officer or appointee, who holds, at the same time, any other office or position of honor, trust or profit, under the State or the United States, except as permitted in this Constitution.

SEC. 43. Every person, corporation, or company, that may commit a homicide through wilful act, or omission, shall be responsible in exemplary damages to the surviving husband, widow, heirs of his or her body, or such of them as there may be, separately or jointly, without regard to any criminal proceeding that may or may not be had in relation to the homicide.

SEC. 44. The Legislature may prohibit the sale of all intoxicating or spiritous liquors in the immediate vicinity of any College or Seminary of learning: provided, said College or Seminary be located other than at a County seat or at the State Capital.

SEC. 45. The Legislature may pass protective laws, securing mechanics, artizans and laborers in the enjoyment of the fruits of their labor.

SEC. 46. Any loyal persons, or his heirs, or legal representatives, may, by proper legal proceedings, to be commenced within two years after the acceptance of this Constitution by the Congress of the United States, show proof in avoidance of any contract made, or revise, or annul any decree or judgment rendered since the 28th day of January, (1861,) eighteen hundred and sixty one, when, through fraud practiced, or threats of violence used toward such person, no adequate consideration for the contract has been received, or where, through absence from the State of such person, or through political prejudice against such person, the decision complained of was not fair or impartial.

SEC. 47. All persons offering themselves as security or bail for another, in any of the courts or offices of this State, shall append to their bond, or accompany their recognizance, with an affidavit, setting forth a description of their property, (or of sufficient of their property, to cover the amount for which they bind themselves,) and its value, and all encumbrances thereon, of every nature.

SEC. 48. The Legislature is authorized to provide reasonable laws of limitation, of civil and criminal actions, but these limitations in civil actions, must not be fixed at terms so short as to operate a deprivation of remedy, or encouragement of fraud.

SEC. 49. The Statutes of limitation of civil suits were suspended by the so-called act of Secession, of the 28th of January, 1861, and shall be considered as suspended within this State, until the acceptance of this Constitution by the United States Congress.

SEC. 50. All Usury laws are abolished in this State, and the Legislature is forbidden from making laws limiting the parties to contracts, in the amount of interest they may agree upon for loans of money, or other property: provided, this section is not intended to change the provisions of law, fixing rate of interest in contracts, where the rate of interest is not specified.

SEC. 51. The Legislature may pass suitable laws regulating mines and minerals, and securing to the discoverer and *bona fide* miner, the right to work mines on either private or public lands.

SEC. 52. The people of this State, being largely engaged in the business of grazing, the Legislature is directed to provide for the protection and development of the stock-raising interest. Provisions shall be made for the inspection of animals and hides sold within the State.

SEC. 53. The term "general election," as used in this Constitution, means any election for officers of the State, or of counties generally. The term "regular election," means the next election for the particular office, at the expiration of the proper term thereof. The term "legislature," when applied to a period of time, means the duration of the term of office of members of the House of Representatives.

SEC. 54. The separate ordinances accompanying this Constitution, apportioning Representatives and Senators, giving State aid to certain lines of Railroads, ordering elections, and defining the Judicial Districts, shall be considered as part of this Constitution, until changed by law.

## MODE OF AMENDING THE CONSTITUTION.

SEC. 55. The Legislature, whenever two-thirds of each House shall deem it necessary, may propose amendments to this Constitution: which proposed amendments shall be duly published in the public prints of the State, at least three months before the next general election of Representatives, for the consideration of the people, and it shall be the duty of the several returning officers, at the next general election which shall be thus holden, to open a poll for, and make a return to the Secretary of State, of the names of all those voting for Representatives, who have voted on such proposed amendments, and, if thereupon it shall appear that a majority of those voting upon the proposed amendments, have voted in favor of such proposed amendments, and two-thirds of each House of the next Legislature, shall, after such election, ratify the same amendments by yeas and nays, they shall be valid to all intents and purposes, as parts of this Constitution; Provided, that the said proposed amendments, shall, at each of the said sessions, have been read on three several days, in each House.

## ARTICLE VIII.

### REGISTRATION OF VOTERS.

SECTION 1. All male persons of the legal age, who have resided in this State for the length of time required by law, and who are citizens of the United States, or have declared their intention to become such, shall be entitled to register as voters, except those embraced under the following heads:

*Head* 1. All persons, who during the late rebellion against the United States Government, voluntarily aided or abetted the said rebellion in any manner, are prohibited from registry. Persons will not be considered as having voluntarily aided said rebellion, who throughout the rebellion disapproved of the same, but accepted office under the rebel government, or entered into the military force thereof, through compulsion, or for self-protection, or as a means of protecting their loyal friends. And all persons who abandoned the rebel service, and joined the United States forces at any time before the close of the rebellion, shall be authorized to register (if otherwise qualified) without regard to what may have been their motive in entering such rebel service.

*Head* 2. All persons who are disfranchised for crime or for rebellion, under the laws of the United States, or of any State thereof, are prohibited from registry.

*Head* 3. All editors of newspapers, or ministers of the Gospel, who approved of, or aided the said rebellion, by writing, preaching, speaking or publishing their views in favor thereof, are prohibited from registry.

*Head* 4. All persons who, during the late rebellion, voluntarily aided, abetted, or encouraged in any manner, unlawful violence against, or maltreatment of any citizen, soldier or seaman of, or resident within the United States, are prohibited from registry; Provided that it is not intended under this head to exclude those persons, who, (though serving in the rebel military force) carried on warfare according to the rules of civilized nations, unless such persons are excluded under some other head of this section.

*Head* 5. All persons who since the close of the said rebellion have continued as members of, or have become members of any secret organization designed in hostility to the United States, or the loyal people thereof, and known as "Sons of the South," or "Ku Klux Klan," or by any other name, are prohibited from registry; Provided, however, that all persons who are registered as voters under the reconstruction acts of Congress previous to voting on this Constitution, and who may vote for the adoption thereof, when the same is submitted to the people, shall be entitled to register (if otherwise qualified) though they may be excluded under the terms of any one of the foregoing heads.

SEC. 2. The following oath or affirmation shall be taken by all persons offering to register as voters: "I, [A. B.] do solemnly swear in the presence of Almighty God, (or affirm) that I am a citizen of the United States, (or that I have declared my intention in the manner prescribed by law, to become a citizen of the United States) that I have resided in this State and county the length of time previous to registry, required by the Constitution of this State. That I am not disfranchised, or excluded from the right to register as a voter, by reason of disqualification under the provisions of any of the heads of section 1st of this article, of the Constitution of this State, (or, that I, though excluded from registry under the terms of section 1st of this article of the Constitution of this State, did, at the election held on the question of the adoption of this Constitution, vote for the adoption of the same, I being at the time a registered voter under the reconstruction acts of Congress.) And I further swear (or affirm,) that I will faithfully support the Constitution and obey the laws of the United States and of this State, and will, to the best of my ability, encourage others so to do, and that I am in favor of equal civil and political rights for all human beings. So help me God."

SEC. 3. The County Court of each county shall be the Board of Registry of the county, and shall sit for this purpose at such times as the Legislature may direct. The County Clerk shall keep a public registry of the voters, setting forth briefly the grounds of admission or rejection of the applicant for registry; and shall also keep a record of the oath (or affirmation) made by each registered voter. The County Clerk and the County Court shall receive such compensation for their services in this respect as may be fixed by law.

SEC. 4. No person shall be authorized to vote at any election, unless he shall have registered as a voter at least thirty days previous to such election. All persons falsely taking the oath required under section 2nd of this article, shall be liable to prosecution for perjury, and the statute of limitations shall not be considered as interposing a bar to prosecutions under this section. The Boards of Registry are required to scrutinize closely the claims of persons offering to register, and no person shall be registered, who, after examination had, is, in the opinion of the Board disqualified, though such person may offer to take the required oath.

Sec. 5. The Legislature is required to pass all laws and regulations that may be found necessary to the carrying out of the spirit and intent of this article. The Legislature may also provide some mode and tribunal of appeal from the decisions of the Boards of Registry.

Sec. 6. The Legislature may by a vote of two-thirds of each house, relieve, by name, persons who are excluded from registry under the provisions of this article; Provided, however, that no person, who ever held any office under the United States, or any State thereof, and afterwards engaged voluntarily in insurrection or rebellion against the United States, or gave aid or comfort to the enemies thereof with intent to destroy the same, shall ever be permitted by the Legislature to register as voters, unless their disabilities have first been removed by Congress.

## ARTICLE IX.
### LAND OFFICE AND LANDS.

Sec. 1. There shall be one General Land Office in the State, which shall be at the Seat of Government, where all titles, which have heretofore emanated from the Government formerly exercising lawful jurisdiction over the territory of this State, or may hereafter emanate from this Government, shall be registered; and the Legislature may establish from time to time, such subordinate offices as they may deem requisite. Where original titles cannot be had, the Legislature may provide for the registry of copies proved, in such manner as the law may direct.

SEC. 2. The Legislature shall provide rules for ascertaining the genuineness of land certificates and titles to lands issued by the State of Texas, previous to the separation of this State, and owned or located within this State, and in relation thereto, the Legislature may enter into such arrangements with the other State, or States, within the limits of the former State of Texas, as may be just and proper. The Land Certificates, or Scrip, issued by the (so-called) authorities of the State of Texas during the late rebellion, are declared null and void; Provided, that where any of these Certificates, or Scrip, are now owned in quantities of six hundred and forty acres or less, by any actual settler on the public lands of this State, the same shall be considered valid.

SEC. 3. Immigrants to this State, from Europe and elsewhere, as well as residents of this State, who may settle on any part of the public lands of this State, shall be entitled to a portion of such land, as follows: Every head of a family, whether male or female, shall have one hundred and sixty acres; and every male person over the age of eighteen years, shall have eighty acres of the public lands. The only conditions attached to this donation, shall be, that each applicant for the same shall pay all expenses of survey thereof, and make such proof as the Legislature may require, that he or she has resided on the land to be donated, for three years preceding the issuance of the patent.

## ARTICLE X.

### IMMIGRATION.

SEC. 1. There shall be a Bureau, known as the "Bureau of Immigration," which shall have supervision and control of all matters connected with Immigration. The head of this Bureau shall be styled the "Superintendent of Immigration." He shall be appointed by the Governor, by and with the advice and consent of the Senate. He shall hold his office for four years, and (until otherwise fixed by law) shall receive an annual compensation of two thousand dollars. He shall have such further powers and duties connected with immigration, as may be given by law.

SEC. 2. The Legislature shall have power to appropriate part of the ordinary revenue of the State, for the purpose of promoting and protecting Immigration. Such appropriation shall be devoted to defraying the expenses of this Bureau, to the support of agencies in foreign seaports, or seaports of the United States, and to the payment, in part, or in toto, of the passage of immigrants from Europe to this State, and their transportation within this State.

## ARTICLE XI.
### IMPEACHMENT.

SEC. 1. The power of impeachment shall be vested in the House of Representatives.

SEC. 2. Impeachment of the Governor, Attorney-General, Secretary of State, Treasurer, Comptroller, and of the Judges of the District Courts, shall be tried by the Senate.

SEC. 3. Impeachment of Judges of the Supreme Court, shall be tried by the Senate. When sitting as a Court of Impeachment, the Senators shall be upon oath, or affirmation; and no person shall be convicted without the concurrence of two-thirds of the Senators present.

SEC. 4. Judgment, in cases of impeachment, shall extend only to removal from office, and disqualification from holding any office of honor, trust, or profit, under this State; but the parties convicted, shall nevertheless, be subject to indictment, trial, and punishment, according to law.

SEC. 5. All officers, against whom articles of impeachment may be preferred, shall be suspended from the exercise of the duties of their office, during the pendency of such impeachment.—The appointing power may make a provisional appointment to fill the vacancy occasioned by the suspension of an officer, until the decision on the impeachment.

SEC. 6. The Legislature shall provide for the trial, punishment, and removal from office, of all other officers of the State, by indictment or otherwise.

## ARTICLE XII.
### PUBLIC SCHOOLS.

SEC. 1. It shall be the duty of the Legislature of this State, to make suitable provisions for the support and maintenance of a system of Public Free Schools, for the gratuitous instruction of all the inhabitants of this State, between the ages of six and eighteen years.

SEC. 2. There shall be a Superintendent of Public Instruction, who, after the first term of office, shall be elected by the people; the first term of office shall be filled by appointment of the Governor, by and with the advice and consent of the Senate. The Superintendent shall hold his office for the term of four years.—He shall receive an annual salary of two thousand five hundred dollars, until otherwise provided by law. In case of vacancy in the office of the Superintendent, it shall be filled by appointment of the Governor, until the next general election.

SEC. 3. The Superintendent shall have the supervision of the Public Free Schools of the State, and shall perform such other duties concerning public instruction, as the Legislature may direct. The Legislature may lay off the State into convenient School Districts, and provide for the formation of a Board of School Directors in each district. It may give the District Boards such Legislative powers in regard to the Schools, School Houses, and School Fund of the District, as may be deemed necessary and proper. It shall be the duty of the Superintendent of Public Instruction, to recommend to the Legislature, such provisions of law as may be found necessary, in the progress of time, to the establishment and perfection of a complete system of education, adapted to the circumstances and wants of the people of this State. He shall, at each session of the Legislature, furnish that body with a complete report of all the Free Schools in the State, giving an account of the condition of the same, and the progress of education within the State. Whenever required by either House of the Legislature, it shall be his duty to furnish all information called for, in relation to Public Schools.

SEC. 4. The Superintendent shall establish a uniform system of Public Free Schools throughout the State.

SEC. 5. The Legislature, at its first session, (or as soon thereafter as may be possible,) shall pass such laws as will require the attendance on the Public Free Schools of the State, of all the Scholastic population thereof, for the period of at least four months of each and every year; Provided, that when any of the Scholastic inhabitants may be shown to have received regular instruction for said period of time in each and every year from any private teacher having a proper certificate of competency, this shall exempt them from the operation of the laws contemplated by this section.

SEC. 6. As a basis for the establishment and endowment of said Public Free Schools, all the funds, lands and other property heretofore set apart and appropriated, or that may hereafter be set apart and appropriated, for the support and maintenance of Public Schools, shall constitute the Public School Fund. And all sums of money that may come to this State, hereafter, from the sale of any portion of the public domain of the former State of Texas, shall also constitute a part of the Public School Fund. And the Legislature shall appropriate all the proceeds resulting from sales of public lands of this State, to such Public School Fund. And said Fund, and the income derived therefrom, shall be a perpetual fund, to be applied as needed, exclusively for the education of all the scholastic inhabitants of this State, and no law shall ever be made appropriating such fund, for any other use or purpose whatever.

SEC. 7. The Legislature, shall, if necessary, in addition to the income derived from the Public School Fund, provide for the raising of such amount, by taxation in the several School Districts in the State, as will be necessary to provide the necessary School houses in each District, and insure the education of all the scholastic inhabitants of the several districts.

SEC. 8. The Public Lands heretofore given to counties, shall be under the control of the Legislature, and may be sold under such regulations as the Legislature may prescribe, and in such case, the proceeds of the same shall be added to the Public School Fund.

SEC. 9. The Legislature shall, at its first session, (and from time to time thereafter, as may be found necessary,) provide all needful rules and regulations for the purpose of carrying into effect the provisions of this article. It is made the imperative duty of the Legislature to see to it that all the children in the State, within the scholastic age, are without delay, provided with ample means of education.


## ARTICLE XIII.

### SCHEDULE.

SEC. 1. That no inconvenience may arise from a change of Government, it is declared that all process, which shall be issued in the name of the State of Texas, prior to the organization of the State Government, under this Constitution, shall be as valid as if issued in the name of the State of West Texas.

SEC. 2. The validity of all bonds and recognizances, executed in conformity with the Constitution and laws of the State of Texas, shall not be impaired by the change of government, but may be sued for and recovered, in the name of the Governor of the State of West Texas, and all criminal prosecutions, or penal actions, which shall have arisen, prior to the organization of the State Government, under this Constitution, in any of the courts of the State of Texas, shall be prosecuted to judgment and execution in the name of this State. All suits which may be pending in any of the courts of the State of Texas, prior to the organization of this State Goverment, under this Constitution, shall be transferred to the proper court of this State, which shall have jurisdiction of the subject-matter thereof.

---

## ORDINANCE,

### GIVING STATE AID TO RAILROADS.

SECTION 1. The Legislature is authorized to provide for the guaranty, by the State, of the mortgage bonds, bearing seven per cent. interest, of the following Railroad lines:

1. From Columbus, via Gonzales to San Antonio, with branches to Seguin and Hallettsville.

2. From Lavaca via Texana to Wharton.

3. From Victoria to San Antonio, and thence via Fredericksburg and Fort Mason, in a northwesterly direction, to the northwest frontier of this State.

4. Railroad line diagonally across the State, from northeast to southwest, being intended as a link in the International Railroad through Mexico to the Pacific.

5. From Victoria to Goliad.

6. From Corpus Christi, to some point east of the Rio Grande, to tap the International Railroad.

7. From Brownsville to Point Isabelle.

8. From San Antonio, via New Braunfels, to the Colorado river, opposite Austin; Provided, that if the International Railroad takes this route, then this line is dispensed with.

SEC. 2. The Railroads contemplated under this ordinance, shall be constructed over the shortest feasible routes, between the termini herein provided for. They shall be constructed and supplied with rolling stock in the completest and best manner, and according to the requirements of the best railroads in the United States.

SEC. 3. The bonds to be guaranteed under this ordinance, shall (except as hereafter provided) be considered as second mortgage bonds on the Railroad lines to be guaranteed, and shall be for the sum of fifteen thousand dollars per mile in lawful currency of the United States. Where the bonds to be guaranteed are second mortgage bonds, the first mortgage bonds on the same lines, shall not exceed the sum of twelve thousand dollars per mile.

SEC. 4. In the event that the United States Government may propose to guarantee the mortgage bonds of the International Railroad, or other lines, or to issue their bonds for the purpose of aiding such line, or lines, then the mortgage bonds to be guaranteed by this State, shall operate as a first mortgage.

SEC. 5. Until the Railroad lines mentioned in the 1st section of this ordinance, are completed and finished, no other Railroads shall receive State aid; and further, no State aid beyond that herein provided for, shall be given by the Legislature, even after said Roads are finished, unless provision be made at the same time for the liquidation of the principal, and interest of the indebtedness thereby to be created, as required in the Constitution of this State.

SEC. 6. The Legislature shall provide all necessary rules

and regulations for carrying this ordinance into effect. The Legislature shall provide for such inspection of the roads built, under this ordinance, previous to the guarantee of the bonds, as will secure strict compliance with the requirements of section 2d thereof, and the building of the roads in conformity thereto.

SEC. 7. No bonds shall be guaranteed for any section of less than twenty-five miles of Railroad, built and equipped, unless the whole length of the Railroad to be built or finished, shall be less than this length.


## ERRATA.

In Article I, Sec. 2, the words, "but in consideration of public services," to be omitted.

In Article I, Sec. 9, the letter "a," in the word "habeas," is missing.

In Article I, Sec. 22, first line, the quotation marks should only embrace the word "Coolies."

In Article I, Sec. 23, next to last line, the word "attempts" should be "attempt."

To Section 3, Article V, add, "The Governor shall be installed on the 2nd Thursday after the organization of the Houses of the Legislature."

# BIBLIOGRAPHY

.

## ARCHIVAL COLLECTIONS

Bell, James H. Papers. Archives, Barker Texas History Center, University of Texas, Austin.

Graham, R. Niles–Pease, E. M. Collection. Austin–Travis County Collection, Austin Public Library, Austin.

Mills, W. W. Collection. Archives, Barker Texas History Center, University of Texas, Austin.

Newcomb, J. P. Collection. Archives, Barker Texas History Center, University of Texas, Austin. Includes correspondence, newspaper clippings, memoranda, and miscellaneous items.

Pease, E. M. Collection. Austin Public Library, Austin.

Smith, Ashbel. Papers, 1823–1926. Archives, Barker Texas History Center, University of Texas, Austin.

Texas. Executive Correspondence. Archives, Texas State Library, Austin.

————. Executive Records, Register Books 281, 283, 284. Archives, Texas State Library, Austin. Letters, messages, and proclamations of the governors.

————. Reconstruction Papers. Archives, Texas State Library, Austin.

U.S. Secretary of War. "Election Returns" (Texas), Fifth Military District, April 16, 1870, Letters Received, Record Group 393. National Archives, Washington, D.C.

## UNPUBLISHED MANUSCRIPTS

Andress, Elyse D. "The Gubernatorial Career of Andrew Jackson Hamilton." Master's thesis, Texas Tech University, 1955.

Armstrong, James Curtis. "The History of Harrison County, Texas, 1839–1880." Master's thesis, University of Colorado, 1930.

Gray, Ronald N. "The Abortive State of West Texas." Master's thesis, Texas Tech University, 1969.

————. "Edmund J. Davis: Radical Republican and Reconstruction Governor of Texas." Ph.D. dissertation, Texas Tech University, 1976.

McGraw, John C. "The Texas Constitution of 1866." Ph.D. dissertation, Texas Tech University, 1959.

Richter, William Lee. "The Army in Texas during Reconstruction." Ph.D. dissertation, Louisiana State University, 1970.

Rutherford, Phillip R. "The New England Emigrant Aid Company, Frederick Law Olmsted, and Texas Colonization." Unpublished manuscript in possession of Phillip R. Rutherford, Gorham, Maine.

Sandlin, Betty J. "The Texas Reconstruction Convention of 1868–1869." Ph.D. dissertation, Texas Tech University, 1970.

Shook, Robert W. "Federal Occupation and Administration of Texas, 1865–1870." Ph.D. dissertation, North Texas State University, 1970.

## NEWSPAPERS

*Austin American*, January–February, 1915; April, 1921; May, 1930.

*Austin Record*, October–December, 1869.

*Austin Republican*, November 13, 1867.

*Avalanche-Journal* (Lubbock, Texas), January, 1938; January–March, 1967; January–March, 1969; January–March, 1971.

*Cincinnati Commercial*, March 11, 1866.

*Daily Austin Republican*, June 1, 1868–March 9, 1871.

*Daily Herald* (San Antonio, Texas), June, 1868–May, 1869.

*Daily Morning Chronicle* (Washington, D.C.), February–April, 1869.

*Daily National Intelligencer* (Washington, D.C.), March–April, 1869.

*Daily Ranchero* (Brownsville, Texas), July 2, 1868; January 4 and January 12, 1870.

*Dallas Herald*, February 3, 1866; August, 1867–July, 1878.

*Dallas Morning News*, April–May, 1893; April, 1906; August 27, 1909; April–May, 1921; May, 1930; January, 1938; February 28–March 5, 1975.

*Flake's Daily Bulletin* (Galveston, Texas), June–August, 1868; January–September, 1869.

*Flake's Semi-Weekly Bulletin* (Galveston, Texas), May 12, 1869.

*Fort Worth Daily Democrat*, July–August, 1878.

*Frontier Echo* (Jacksboro, Texas), August 9 and August 16, 1878.

*Galveston Daily News*, July–August, 1878; April–May, 1893.

*Galveston News*, June–August, 1868; December, 1868; January–April, 1869; August 21, 1871.

*Harrison Flag, The* (Marshall, Texas), December, 1868–June, 1869.

*Houston Times*, February 17, 1869.

*Jefferson Jimplecute* (100th Anniversary Ed.), June 17, 1965.

*Lubbock Evening Journal*, January, 1938.

*New York Daily Tribune*, January, 1868–April, 1869.
*New York Herald*, March 21, 1869.
*New York Times*, February 14 and March 11, 1866; January–October, 1869; May, 1930; February–March, 1975.
*Niles' Weekly Register* 66 (1844).
*Northern Standard* (Clarksville, Texas), see *Standard*.
*Philadelphia Daily News*, October 19, 1955.
*San Antonio Express*, June, 1867–January 22, 1870; August 2–8, 1878; May 1, 1893. The title varies frequently (*San Antonio Daily Express*).
*Standard* (Clarksville, Texas), September–November, 1850; March, 1868– May, 1869. The title was *Northern Standard* until August, 1852.
*State Gazette* (Austin, Texas), December 5, 1849; October 30, 1852; August, 1867–December, 1869. The title varies frequently.
*Texas Republican* (Marshall, Texas), January, 1868–May, 1869.
*Texas State Gazette* (Austin, Texas), see *State Gazette*.
*Washington Globe*, February 28, 1845.

## GOVERNMENT PUBLICATIONS

Gammel, H. P. N., comp. *The Laws of Texas, 1822–1897.* 10 vols. Austin: Gammel Book Company, 1898.

Heitman, Francis B. *Historical Register and Dictionary of the United States Army, 1789–1903.* 2 vols. Washington, D.C.: Government Printing Office, 1903.

Richardson, James D., ed. *A Compilation of the Messages and Papers of the Presidents, 1789–1897.* 10 vols. Washington, D.C.: Government Printing Office, 1900.

Texas. *The Constitution As Amended, and Ordinances of the Convention of 1866, Together with the Proclamation of the Governor Declaring the Ratification of the Amendments to the Constitution, and the General Laws of the Regular Session of the Eleventh Legislature of the State of Texas.* Austin: Gazette Office, Jo. Walker, State Printer, 1866.

———. *Journal of the Reconstruction Convention, Which Met at Austin, Texas, June 1, A.D. 1868.* 1 Sess. Austin: Tracy, Siemering & Co., 1870.

———. *Journal of the Reconstruction Convention, Which Met at Austin, Texas, Dec. 7, A.D. 1868.* 2 Sess. Austin: Tracy, Siemering & Co., 1870.

———. *Journal of the Texas State Convention, Assembled at Austin, February 7, 1866.* Austin: Southern Intelligencer Office, 1866.

———. *Laws of the Republic of Texas.* 2 vols. Houston: Telegraph Office, 1838.

———. *Ordinances of the Constitutional Convention at Austin, Texas, June 1, 1868.* Austin, 1870.

————. *Rules of the Constitutional Convention, Convened June 1, 1868.* Austin: Austin Republican, 1868.

————. *Tabular Statement of Voters (White and Colored) Registered in Texas in 1867, and at Revision of the lists of 1867–1868–69; Showing also the Number (White and Colored) Striken off the Lists; and, Tabular Statement of Votes (White and Colored) Cast at Election Held in the State of Texas, under the Authority of the Reconstruction Acts of Congress.* Austin, 1870.

Texas Legislature, House. *Journals of the House of Representatives of the State of Texas.* 2 Leg., reg. sess., 1847–1848. Houston: Telegraph Office, 1848. The title of the House *Journal* varies frequently. For the convenience of the reader, journals are listed here in chronological order.

————. *Journal.* 3 Leg., extra sess., 1850. Austin: Texas State Gazette Office, 1850.

————. *Journal.* 4 Leg., reg. sess., 1851–1852. Austin: State Gazette Office, 1852.

————. *Journal.* 11 Leg., reg. sess., 1866. Austin: State Gazette Office, 1866.

————. *Journal.* 12 Leg., prov. sess., 1870. Austin: Tracy, Siemering & Co., 1870.

————. *Journal.* 12 Leg., 1 sess., 1870. Austin: Tracy, Siemering & Co., 1870.

————. *Journal.* 12 Leg., reg. sess., 1871. Austin: J. G. Tracy, State Printer, 1871.

————. *Journal.* 12 Leg., adj. sess., 1871. Austin: J. G. Tracy, State Printer, 1871.

————. *Journal.* 34 Leg., reg. sess., 1915. Austin: Von Boeckmann-Jones, Co., 1915.

Texas Legislature, Senate. *Journals of the Senate of the State of Texas.* 2 Leg., reg. sess., 1847–1848. Houston: Telegraph Office, 1848. The title of the Senate *Journal* varies frequently. For the convenience of the reader, journals are listed here in chronological order.

————. *Journal.* 11 Leg., reg. sess., 1866. Austin: State Gazette Office, 1866.

————. *Journal.* 12 Leg., prov. sess., 1870. Austin: Tracy, Siemering & Co., 1870.

————. *Journal.* 12 Leg., reg. sess., 1871. Austin: J. G. Tracy, State Printer, 1871.

————. *Journal.* 12 Leg., adj. sess., 1871. Austin: J. G. Tracy, State Printer, 1871.

————. *Journal.* 34 Leg., reg. sess., 1915. Austin: A. C. Baldwin & Sons, State Printers, 1915.

Texas Secretary of State. "Election Returns," 1868. Archives, Texas State Library, Austin.

U.S. *Statutes at Large*, vols. 5 (1856), 9 (1862), 14 (1868), and 15 (1869). Boston: Little Brown & Co., 1856–1869.

U.S. Congress. *Congressional Globe*. 28 Cong., 2 sess., December 16, 1844; January 10, 1845; January 23, 1845; January 28, 1845; February 6, 1845.

————. *Congressional Globe*. 31 Cong., 1 sess., January 16, 1850; February 28, 1850; May 8, 1850; August 5, 1850; August 9, 1850.

————. *Congressional Globe*. 40 Cong., 2 sess., December 3, 1867; June 9, 1868; June 15, 1868; July 2, 1868.

————. *Congressional Globe*. 41 Cong., 1 sess., March 16, 1869; March 19, 1869; March 22, 1869.

————. *Congressional Globe*. 41 Cong., 2 sess., February 25, 1870.

————. *Congressional Record*. 58 Cong., 3 sess., February 7, 1905.

————. *Congressional Record*. 59 Cong., 1 sess., April 10, 1906.

————. *Congressional Record*. 71 Cong., 2 sess., May 8, 1930; June 9, 1930.

————. *Congressional Record*. 94 Cong., 1 sess., February 27, 1975.

U.S. Congress, House. *Affairs in Texas. Letters from Governor Pease and Hon. C. Caldwell*. 40 Cong., 2 sess., 1868, House Misc. Doc. No. 57.

————. *Constitutional Convention of Texas. Letter from the Secretary of War*. 40 Cong., 3 sess., 1869, House Exec. Doc. No. 97.

————. *Interpretation of the Reconstruction Acts. Message from the President of the United States*. 40 Cong., 1 sess., 1868, House Exec. Doc. No. 34.

————. *Journal*. 41 Cong., 1 sess., 1869. Washington, D.C.: Government Printing Office, 1869.

————. *Memorial on Behalf of the Citizens of Western Texas*. 39 Cong., 2 sess., 1867, House Misc. Doc. No. 35.

————. *Message of the President of the United States. Report of the Secretary of War*. 40 Cong., 2 sess., 1868, House Exec. Doc. No. 1.

————. *Message of the President of the United States. Report of the Secretary of War*. 40 Cong., 3 sess., 1869, House Exec. Doc. No. 1.

————. *Reconstruction. Letter from the Secretary of War*. 40 Cong., 1 sess., 1868, House Exec. Doc. No. 20.

U.S. Congress, Senate. *Journal*. 31 Cong., 1 sess., 1849–1850. Washington, D.C.: Government Printing Office, 1850.

————. *Journal*. 41 Cong., 1 sess., 1869. Washington, D.C.: Government Printing Office, 1869.

————. *Proceedings of the Senate and Documents Relative to Texas. Mes-*

*sage from the President of the United States.* 28 Cong., 2 sess., 1844, Senate Doc. No. 341.

————. *Report on Registration of Voters by the General of the Army.* 40 Cong., 2 sess., 1868, Senate Doc. No. 53.

U.S. Department of the Interior. Census Office. *Ninth Census of the United States, Texas Population, 1870.*

Weeks, Wm. F., reporter. *Debates in the Texas Convention, 1845.* Houston: J. W. Cruger, 1846.


## BOOKS AND ARTICLES

Biesele, R. L. *The History of the German Settlements in Texas, 1831–1861.* Austin: Von Boeckmann-Jones Co., 1930.

Branda, Eldon Stephen, ed. *The Handbook of Texas: A Supplement.* Vol. III. Austin: Texas State Historical Association, 1976.

Bullard, Lucille B. *Marion County, Texas, 1860–1870.* Jefferson, Texas: Privately printed, 1965.

*Constitution of the State of West Texas.* N.p., [1869].

Crane, R. C. "The West Texas Agricultural and Mechanical College Movement and the Founding of Texas Technological College." *West Texas Historical Association Year Book* 7 (1931): 3–34.

Elliott, Claude. *Leathercoat: The Life History of a Texas Patriot.* San Antonio: Standard Printing Company, 1938.

Evans, L. D. *Speech of Hon. L. D. Evans on the Conditions of Texas, and the formation of new states.* Delivered in the Constitutional Convention of Texas, on the 6th of January, 1869. N.p., n.d.

Holden, W. C. *Alkali Trails: or Social and Economic Movements of the Texas Frontier, 1846–1900.* Dallas: The Southwest Press, 1930.

McConnell, W. J. *Social Cleavages in Texas.* New York: Columbia University, 1925.

McKay, S. S. *Seven Decades of the Texas Constitution of 1876.* Lubbock: Texas Tech Press, 1942.

Miller, Thomas L. *The Public Lands of Texas, 1519–1970.* Norman: University of Oklahoma Press, 1972.

Mills, W. W. *Forty Years at El Paso, 1858–1898.* El Paso: Carl Hertzog, 1962.

Norvell, James R. "The Reconstruction Courts of Texas, 1867–1873." *Southwestern Historical Quarterly* 62 (October, 1958): 141–163.

Nunn, William C. *Texas under the Carpetbaggers.* Austin: University of Texas Press, 1962.

Olmsted, Frederick. *A Journey through Texas: or a Saddle-Trip on the Southwestern Frontier.* New York: Mason Brothers, 1860.

Ramsdell, Charles W. *Reconstruction in Texas.* New York: Columbia University, 1910.

Richter, William L. " 'We Must Rubb Out and Begin Anew': The Army and the Republican Party in Texas Reconstruction, 1867–1870." *Civil War History* 19 (December, 1973): 334–352.

Roberts, O. M. "The Political, Legislative, and Judicial History of Texas, 1845–1895." In *A Comprehensive History of Texas, 1685–1897.* 2 vols., edited by Dudley G. Wooten. Dallas: W. G. Scarff, 1898.

Russell, Traylor. *Carpetbaggers, Scalawags, and Others.* Waco: Texian Press, 1973.

Smith, J. H. *The Annexation of Texas.* New York: Barnes and Noble, Inc., 1912.

Somers, Dale A. "James P. Newcomb: The Making of a Radical." *Southwestern Historical Quarterly* 72 (April, 1969):449–469.

*Texas Almanac for 1869.* Galveston: W. D. Richardson & Co., 1868.

Trelease, Allen W. *White Terror: The Ku Klux Klan Conspiracy and Southern Reconstruction.* New York: Harper and Row, 1971.

Wallace, Ernest. *Charles DeMorse: Pioneer Editor and Statesman.* Lubbock: Texas Tech Press, 1943.

———. *Texas in Turmoil, 1849–1876.* Austin: Steck-Vaughn Co., 1965.

Waller, John L. *Colossal Hamilton of Texas: A Biography of Andrew Jackson Hamilton.* El Paso: Texas Western Press, 1968.

Webb, Walter P., and H. B. Carroll, eds. *The Handbook of Texas.* 2 vols. Austin: Texas State Historical Association, 1952.

Winkler, E. W., ed. *Platforms of Political Parties in Texas.* Austin: University of Texas, 1916.

# INDEX

moderates (in Texas), 35, 36, 64, 72,
115, 131; and Constitutional Convention of 1866, 16; and Constitution of 1869, 66, 96 n. 19; and Reconstruction Convention, 49, 97,
108
Monroe, A. T., 42, 43, 47 and n. 4, 96
n. 19, 128; on cession of El Paso
County, 58; and Hamilton proposal, 56, 58; report of Committee
on the Division of the State by, 50,
54–55; on sale of public lands, 47;
on San Jacinto River as division
line, 47 n. 5; on Thomas resolution,
62, 63 n. 38
Montezuma Territory (proposed), 53
Montgomery, P. E., 146
Moore, W. B., 85, 86, 87, 132
Morgan Hamilton convention. See Radi-
cal Republican party
Morgan steamer, 126
"Morphis," 111 n. 6
Muckleroy, David, 74 n. 21
Mullins, Sheppard, 73
Mullins, W. H., 47 n. 4, 73, 99
Mundine, Titus H., 74 n. 21

National Hotel, 113
Navarro, Antonio, 110
Navarro County, 134
Neff, Pat M., 143, 144 and n. 17
Negroes, 18, 31, 42, 63 n. 38, 64, 72,
126; and A. J. Hamilton, 128; and
Democrats, 30, 64–65; in election
of 1868, 31, 32; in election of 1869,
130, 133–134; in Radical Republican party convention, 130; as radicals, 38, 134; in Reconstruction
Convention, 32, 33, 38, 73; registration of, 29, 133; and suffrage,
26, 39, 40, 42, 66; vote on division by, 92
Neighbors, Robert S., 9
New Braunfels Zeitung, 87
Newcomb, James P., 31, 39, 41–42, 99,
101, 102, 114; A. J. Hamilton on,

112, 128; and breakup of Reconstruction Convention, 75, 104–105,
106; with commissioners to Washington, 95, 109, 119; on conditions
in eastern Texas, 119; and Constitution of 1869, 71, 96 n. 19, 97 n. 21,
119; Daily Herald on, 89; and
Davis Memorial, 117; and division,
42, 56, 67, 76; and public meeting,
71; as radical, 30, 38; on suffrage,
42; and Thomas resolution, 62, 63
n. 38, 74, 76; western state advo-
cated by, 40, 79 n. 38; on West
Texas constitution, 78, 79–80, 85
New England, 145
New England Emigrant Aid Company,
15
New Jersey, 54
New Mexico: jurisdiction over, 5, 8
New Orleans, 112, 127
New York (city), 127
New York (state), 54, 55
New York Times: on Constitutional
Convention of 1866, 16; on Davis,
39; on divisionists, 90; on Garner
proposal, 145
Neyland, W. M., 22
Norris, James M., 19–20, 44
North (region): radical supporters of,
38. See also Unionists
North Atlantic region, 145
North Carolina, 52, 54
Northeast Texas, State of (proposed),
142
Northerners, 4; as carpetbaggers, 33
northern Texas: 1878 suggestion for
new state in, 140
North Texas, State of (proposed)
—1868, 56
—1871, 138 and n. 3
—1906, 141–142
—1915, 143
—1930, 145
northwestern Texas: and division, 141
Northwest Texas, State of (proposed),
142
Norton, A. B., 19, 20, 31

# Index

Wiley, A. P., 111 n. 6, 118 n. 27
Willacy County, 146
Williams, B. F., 63 n. 38, n. 40, 74
    n. 21
Williamson County, 138 n. 3, 143 n. 13
Wilmot, David, 8
Wilson, Erwin, 47 n. 4, 52, 74 n. 21,
    91
Wilson, Henry, 89

Wilson, L. H., 96 n. 16
Wise County, 21
Wood, Fernando, 119
Wood, George T., 9
Wright, Arvin, 75, 99
Wright Hotel, 144

Yarborough, Gilbert, 63 n. 38, 74 n. 21
Young County, 22